MORE CITY THAN WATER

More City Than Water

A HOUSTON FLOOD ATLAS

EDITED BY

Lacy M. Johnson
and Cheryl Beckett

UNIVERSITY OF TEXAS PRESS ⬥ AUSTIN

Support for this book comes from an endowment for environmental
studies made possible by generous contributions from
Richard C. Bartlett, Susan Aspinall Block, and the National
Endowment for the Humanities.

Requests for permission to reproduce material
from this work should be sent to:

> Permissions
> University of Texas Press
> P.O. Box 7819
> Austin, TX 78713-7819
> utpress.utexas.edu/rp-form

♾ The paper used in this book meets the minimum requirements
of ANSI/NISO Z39.48-1992 (R1997) (Permanence of Paper).

Library of Congress Cataloging-in-Publication Data

Names: Johnson, Lacy M., 1978– editor. | Beckett, Cheryl, editor.
Title: More city than water : a Houston flood atlas / edited by
    Lacy M. Johnson, Cheryl Beckett.
Description: First edition. | Austin : University of Texas Press, 2022.
Identifiers: LCCN 2021040781
    ISBN 978-1-4773-2500-1 (cloth)
    ISBN 978-1-4773-2566-7 (PDF)
    ISBN 978-1-4773-2567-4 (ePub)
Subjects: LCSH: Floods—Texas—Houston. | Floods—Social
aspects—Texas—Houston. | Floods—Environmental aspects—
Texas—Houston. | Floods—Political aspects—Texas—Houston. |
Floods—Texas—Houston—History. | Floods—Texas—Houston—
Maps. | LCGFT: Essays.
Classification: LCC GB1399.4.T4 M67 2022 | DDC 303.48/5—dc23/
    eng/20211020
LC record available at https://lccn.loc.gov/2021040781

doi:10.7560/325001

For Houston
with love

Contents

CONTENTS

MORE CITY THAN WATER

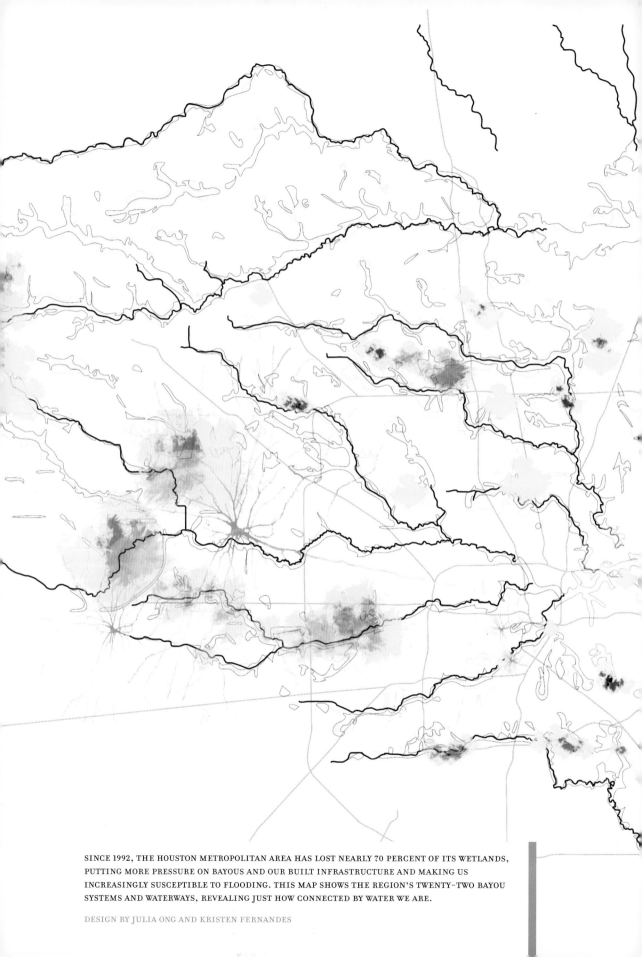

SINCE 1992, THE HOUSTON METROPOLITAN AREA HAS LOST NEARLY 70 PERCENT OF ITS WETLANDS,
PUTTING MORE PRESSURE ON BAYOUS AND OUR BUILT INFRASTRUCTURE AND MAKING US
INCREASINGLY SUSCEPTIBLE TO FLOODING. THIS MAP SHOWS THE REGION'S TWENTY-TWO BAYOU
SYSTEMS AND WATERWAYS, REVEALING JUST HOW CONNECTED BY WATER WE ARE.

DESIGN BY JULIA ONG AND KRISTEN FERNANDES

MORE CITY THAN WATER

More City Than Water

Lacy M. Johnson

There's a light pole on my street, a few houses down from mine, where one of my neighbors has painted a rainbow stripe, about as high as my chest, to mark the high-waterpoint reached during Hurricane Harvey in 2017. The paint has chipped a little in the several years since the storm. The houses in our neighborhood have been repaired; the dumpsters—filled with moldy sheetrock and furniture, carpet, and ruined family albums—have all been hauled away.

Hurricane Harvey made landfall on Friday, August 25, in Rockport, Texas, virtually destroying the entire town, before heading northeast along the Gulf Coast. The storm arrived in southwest Houston early Saturday and stalled over the city for five days, dropping as much as 61 inches of rain in some places—at that time it was the single greatest rainfall event in North America in recorded history.[1] Each of the eleven bayous in the city left its banks and entered the surrounding neighborhoods. But now, more than three years later, it is still unclear what percentage of people have lost or had damage to their homes. I've heard a third of the people. I've heard over 100,000 homes. Or 200,000 homes. In some places in the city, some people still haven't even begun the process of reconstruction. Their FEMA claims have been denied; their applications for a buyout have been denied. They called the disaster hotline for assistance and found no one who spoke their language.

In my neighborhood in west Houston, the worst of the flooding arrived when the Army Corps of Engineers decided to open the dams at Barker and Addicks Reservoirs to prevent what they were calling, somewhat euphemistically, "catastrophic failure" and "uncontrolled release." Downstream from the dams, a mile from Buffalo Bayou, my family and our neighbors had gone to bed grateful that the storm was finally beginning to move off to the east. But when we woke up in the morning, the bayou had become a river, over a mile wide, raging through the streets past our front door. At a press conference, men in official-looking uniforms told those of us who watched the livestream at home that the water would continue to rise, but that no one knew how much. Maybe one foot. Maybe three feet. Outside, the water bubbled up from storm drains, out of sewers, smelled of the rank contagion of human and industrial waste. One neighbor, a surveyor, got out his equipment to see how much more water the street could take before the flooding reached the houses. None of us could take much more.

Like thousands of others, my family chose to evacuate, carefully placing all our furniture on blocks before leaving our home. Helicopters circled overhead, and US Coast Guard members rode airboats along the rivers of our streets as we trudged through sewage to the end of the block, where we left the neighborhood and entered a militarized zone. Soldiers helped my elderly neighbors off high-water military vehicles while emergency medical responders administered oxygen and first aid under plastic tents. My family eventually found refuge at our friends' home across town, in a neighborhood where a few branches had fallen into yards here and there, but all the streets were dry. Buses were running. Pizza could be delivered to your door.

For weeks afterward, many people helped in the ways we knew how: by volunteering our time or labor; by organizing food for the thousands of evacuees; by collecting donations for families and schools in need. I heard dozens of stories of everyday heroism, and these stories—heard and repeated, over and over—have become the official stories of the storm: a story of sacrifice and resilience, of working together for the common good. We repeat these stories because we like what they say about us as a community, as people—but these stories aren't complete, and they are only partially true.

I also heard the story of a man whose house, built up on a raised foundation above the street level, did not flood at the end of a street where every other house went underwater. The day after the flood receded, when his neighbors were allowed back to their homes, he sat on his porch with a gun over his knee and aimed it at anyone who tried to park in front of his driveway—flaunting his dry privilege, as well as the coldness of his heart. I heard, too, the story of a single mother in the predominantly African American neighborhood of Houston Gardens in northeast Houston, who was living in a tent in her yard because she had been denied assistance by FEMA. She was trying to muck out the house herself, to make it livable again, before volunteers finally arrived to help. But when a friend's home flooded on the other side of town, in Meyerland, which is predominantly affluent and white, her family received help from FEMA and insurance adjusters, and within days, a team of contract laborers were swinging hammers and putting her house, and life, back into place. These stories, and the inequality they represent, also tell us who we are as a community, as people.

My proximity to flooding during Harvey has made me think a lot about flooding over the past several years, though for a long time I almost never thought about flooding at all. When I moved to Houston in 2004 with my then boyfriend, we rented a tiny apartment on the second floor of a duplex in Montrose and shared only one car between us. We didn't have a television at that time and had little access to the news. A few times each June through November, during Houston's annual hurricane and heavy rain season, my mom would call from Missouri to ask whether our house was flooded. "Houston is all over the news," she would say, watching footage of flooded underpasses and high-water rescues. Our neighborhood was on high ground, I explained; our street was dry except for a few puddles. I knew that a few blocks from our home, Buffalo Bayou had probably left its banks to fill Eleanor Tinsley Park. Soon it would drain, and the flooding would disappear, and I would forget the city had ever flooded at all.

This all changed in 2005 when all the televisions in restaurants and waiting rooms showed footage of people waving white towels from the roofs of their submerged houses. Hurricane Katrina had struck New Orleans, and the storm surge, which had broken the levees, flooded 80 percent of the city, killing over eighteen hundred people and displacing over one million from their homes. A quarter of these people found their way to Houston, migrating in buses, in cars, on boats, leaving behind communities, histories, memories, and generations of making a place a home. For the first time, I began to realize that though rain might fall without regard for social or economic disparities, flooding reinforces the inequalities that surround us every day.

Two weeks later, before many of the evacuees had found permanent shelter, Hurricane Rita took aim at Houston, and then Governor Rick Perry ordered an evacuation of the entire metropolitan area. Traffic was gridlocked in some places for twenty-four hours as the temperature rose to over one hundred degrees. Hurricane Rita weakened before turning and making landfall in Louisiana, but not before 118 people had died in their cars on the interstate, casualties of the storm that never came.

Suddenly, it seemed, flooding was everywhere. The following year, in 2006, when I was pregnant with my first child, one especially heavy June storm dropped over six inches of rain in just under seventy-five minutes. Berry and Sims Bayous left their banks and rushed into 3,370 homes, 561 apartments, and one nursing home, where over one hundred elders had to be evacuated. In 2008, when my child was nearly two, Hurricane Ike made landfall at Galveston Island, recording a storm surge of twenty-two feet at Sabine Pass, dropping twenty inches of rain in two days; an estimated 100,000 structures flooded, Galveston Island was declared uninhabitable, and power outages left millions in the dark for more than ten days. The following year, in 2009, spring storms flooded over 2,000 structures; highways closed; five children drowned in a car. In 2012, after our second child was born, overflowing creeks flooded dozens of structures; in 2014, the year we bought our home, Greens Bayou left its banks and entered over 100 homes; in 2015, over Memorial Day weekend, entire watersheds filled, damaging more than 6,000 structures and killing seven people. The following year, in April, seven more died and nearly 10,000 structures were flooded during the Tax Day Flood; and in 2017, creek and river flooding damaged over 1,000 additional homes at the end of May. Eight major floods in eleven years—not even counting all of the unnamed minor flooding that occurs each time we have a good rain.

By the time Harvey hit in late 2017, my young family had moved to the far west part of the city. We were excited to find a place only a mile from Buffalo Bayou and to find that the bayou had a park where I could run. We lived there uneventfully for several years, long enough for us to befriend neighbors, to learn that one of them was willing to run in the park with me several times a week, and to understand how the Bayou changes throughout the year. The sun comes up behind the bayou's southern bank in winter, and over the northern bank in the height of summer. The flowers that grow in May and June are different from the ones that grow in January. I had learned I couldn't run in the park after even a few hours of heavy rain because in the park's lowest places, the bayou leaves its banks and muddies the path. I learned that after an entire day of heavy rain, the bayou fills the low basins of the park, though usually only briefly. I began to see how the hills and valleys that make this park so beautiful and a challenge to run had been carved by flooding during all the bayou's seasons, beginning long before I moved to Houston, when my neighborhood had been undeveloped coastal prairie, and well before that, when the Bidai and Akokisa people came to fish and trade along the water's edge. The bayou had a memory of all the time before, of journeying beyond its banks to shape and reshape the place that nearly seven million people now call home.

"All water has a perfect memory," Toni Morrison writes, but people tend to forget.[2] Or, perhaps we remember quite well, but the memory of water is longer than our own. Two years after Hurricane Harvey, in 2019, Houston flooded again—this time from Tropical Storm Imelda, which dropped forty-three inches of rain in two days. This flood was the fifth five-hundred-year flood Houston had suffered in five years. For the fifth year in a row, we pulled one another from submerged vehicles and flooded homes. This time, a man drowned in his van, another in a pickup, one in a car, another trying to rescue his horse. One man drowned in a ditch. For a short time, the entire town of Winnie, Texas, was underwater. Port Arthur was destroyed—again. Barges containing toxic chemicals crashed into one another along the Houston Ship Channel, again, but the second-largest petrochemical complex in the world continued to supply the only nation to have withdrawn from the Paris Climate Accord with enough petroleum and natural gas to cause ice in the Arctic to melt, to cause sea levels to rise, and to cause natural disasters to become more catastrophic here and around the world every single year. Our growing numbness to these events makes us more susceptible to disaster in the future, not less.

Houston is designed to flood, I have heard people say again and again, as they replace more and more of the coastal prairie with streets and interstates and apartment buildings and enormous multimillion-dollar estates. But I do not hear anyone saying what this means when we see that catastrophic flooding does not touch people's lives equally. In the greater Greenspoint area—a low-income community situated along Greens Bayou—some homes have flooded more than ten times since Tropical Storm Allison in 2001. In Independence Heights—the first Black municipality in Texas—homes never flooded until TxDOT built the I-610 interchange. On the east side, near the ship channel, residents deal not only with chronic catastrophic flooding from rain and storm surges but also with a flooding of toxins, and not only when it rains. In contrast, the wealthiest neighborhoods, especially those located in the city center—River Oaks, Montrose, and West University—almost never flood at all.

This is a story that needs telling, even if the official one resists change. In this city, buildings go up, buildings come down. One hundred thousand people move here every year, cramming into tiny apartments, or three-bedroom homes in suburbs, or tents along the bayous, or vast sprawling estates. Refineries churn thousands of tons of toxic chemicals into the air every year, and gardens bloom here every day. An ideal map of the city should include, marked in different inks, this history and all its implications: articulated and silent, evident and hidden.

JUST AFTER HURRICANE HARVEY—at least partially in response to our city's persistent collective numbness about catastrophic flooding—I began working to bring together a massive team of people to launch the Houston Flood Museum: a project that is meant to discover and collect these histories, as many as we can, about this storm and all the others, about the flooding to which this city is exceptionally prone, and to think in a critical way about the city and its heroes and its flaws. For me, this is the broad purpose of telling any story: to make sense of that which is nonsense, to make order from chaos, to make meaning from the messiness and joy and occasional disaster that is life.

This atlas is the second-year project of the Houston Flood Museum. With generous funding from the Houston Endowment and the Humanities Research Center at Rice University, I began working on this project in 2018, just after the launch of the museum in August. In response to the essays—some of which have been previously published; some were commissioned specifically for this project—a group of twenty-five senior graphic design students at the University of Houston created maps under the supervision of Professor Cheryl Beckett. A smaller group of six designers has continued working on this project after their graduation: Manuel Vázquez, Kristen Fernandes, Ilse Harrison, Jesse Reyes, Julia Ong, and Clarisse Pinto. I am grateful to Kristen, Julia, and Clarisse in particular for their vision, patience, and continued dedication to this project.

The title for this atlas comes from a photograph of a sign I saw in the days after the storm: "More Love Than Water" it read, meant to signify that however much water surrounded us, we were surrounded by even more love. I drew strength from that idea, and I want to carry that sentiment forward in this atlas, with the idea that whatever it is that holds us together in this city is more powerful than the destruction that is trying to tear it apart.

The maps you will find in these pages will not help you navigate a commute to the Woodlands, or learn the fastest route to the beach in Friday afternoon traffic, because what we hope to navigate here is not traffic or congestion, but rather our relationship to the land, to the future, to flooding, and to one another. In this regard, Houston does seem a bit lost. Less than a year after Hurricane Harvey, the Houston City Council unanimously backed a developer's plan to build hundreds of homes in a west Houston floodplain. Development continues more or less unchecked today. Some people seem to think more infrastructure will save us from future storms: more channelizing the bayous, larger drain pipes, and possibly a third reservoir. Meanwhile, on the other side of town, a handful of corporations continue to expand their investment in fossil fuels, lobbying local, state, and federal government agencies to ease environmental restrictions and regulations without regard for the harm they are doing to the people those laws and regulations are designed to protect.

This atlas isn't comprehensive; it doesn't include every perspective on flooding, but it does bring together, in eighteen essays, three interviews, and accompanying maps, some of what I consider the best thinking about it. In "From Ice to Inundation," Rice anthropology professor Cymene Howe considers what new satellite modeling reveals about the relationship of melting ice in the Arctic to sea level rise in the Gulf of Mexico. In "Higher Ground," Bryan Washington describes the chaos and confusion of the early days after the storm, and the many obstacles people faced while trying to attend to the needs of their communities. In "Community Power," Ben Hirsch writes about the birth of West Street Recovery, an organization dedicated to providing recovery assistance to people who have been excluded from the broader recovery effort. In "Gusher," Houston native Sonia Hamer writes about the history of oil discovery and its relationship to enduring wealth inequality and environmental racism. And, in "Ombrophobia," my coeditor Cheryl Beckett offers a visual essay about her uneasy intimacy with hurricanes.

For this atlas, I've asked writers to share their thoughts about what is revealed or obscured by catastrophic flooding. Their responses are grouped into three sections: "History," "Memory," and "Community," and move along a spectrum from intimate and personal forms of reckoning to more public and analytical forms. My hope is that, taken together, these writings and maps may offer a vision, critical as it may be, of who and where we are to make space for more voices within broader conversations about policy, infrastructure, and climate change. I hope that more honesty and candor about our collective history might help us learn from it, mourn what we have lost, and, with any luck, find inspiration about how we might move together into the future.

HISTORY

GUSHER

HOUSTON, TX

BAYTOWN

MAGNOLIA PARK

GOOSE CREEK OIL FIELD

PASADENA

HAZARDOUS LIQUID PIPELINES

EXXONMOBIL BAYTOWN COMPLEX

SPINDLETOP OIL FIELD

BEAUMONT, TX

THIS MAP EXAMINES THE RELATIONSHIP BETWEEN THE GUSHER DISCOVERY IN BEAUMONT IN THE PAST AND ITS EFFECTS ON BAYTOWN DURING HURRICANE HARVEY.

DESIGN BY TAMILA AMANZHOLOVA

Gusher

Sonia Hamer

John I. Gaillard first noticed the bubbles while fishing in the shallow warmth of Tabbs Bay. Each time he rowed between his own marshy land, located at the mouth of Goose Creek and nearby Hog Island—so named for the pigs its owner kept there—he found his boat pursued by a series of soft, erratic pops. Wet kisses from the coquettish Earth. Like much of the surrounding area, the creek's mouth made for a hazy sort of shoreline—no shifting sands or rocky beaches here, just the pungent mud and grass of the tidal marsh. At first, John mistook the bubbles for the foraging of buffalo fish, pushed out into the salty muck from their freshwater hunting grounds upstream. But these splashes did not seem like the flick and twist of scaly bodies. They came too loudly, too suddenly, too often. They came both in the brackish shallows and in the deeper water, where no buffalo fish would be. They came, unlike animals that preferred the cool of dawn or dusk, without regard for night or day.

And then there was the smell: like someone had spilled a can of kerosene, its sickly sweet scent rising from the silt and the twirling strands of swamp grass. John knew what that smell meant. One day he rowed out into the bay with his beat-up dinghy, intent on performing a certain experiment. He searched until he heard the familiar pops. Dropping his oar, he fumbled in his pockets as his heart pulsed with excitement. Hand shaking, he pulled his tin match safe from his vest. The match sparked and sputtered when he struck it, falling from his fingertips and opening upward into a great bloom of flame as it met the rising gas. John jumped backward at the flare unfurling toward him from the water. He looked down once at his empty hands, and then he smiled.

Oil.

Within weeks the land had been leased. The would-be oilmen had arrived with their big dreams and their mule teams, their mineral rights and their hastily constructed derricks. All along the eastern edge of Tabbs Bay, they surveyed, drilled, and dredged. They tramped through wetlands and exploded bedrock and produced pile after pile of pulverized sand—all to no avail. Dry wells and a few sluggish barrels were all their hopeful hustle brought them. Gaillard discovered the promise of surface methane bubbles in 1903, but it would be another thirteen years before Goose Creek got its "first honest-to-goodness gusher."[1] An American Petroleum contractor named Charles Mitchell brought in the well on August 23, 1916. His team drilled for two thousand feet before they hit the pocket, boring down through an existing well known as Gaillard No. 1. When the team struck the pocket, oil erupted from the end of the pipe. It spewed out in black, viscous sheets and blanketed the men, the machines, the rolling water, and the marsh. From the ground, it boiled up and came rushing, rushing into the world. The men cheered. The oil poured. There would be no putting it back.

I mention the story of Goose Creek's first gusher for a reason. The spirit of that strike presses forward into the present day, spilling over into the complicated aftermath of contemporary disasters. Because, just over a hundred years after that scene around Gaillard No. 1, on August 26, 2017, Hurricane Harvey made landfall in Rockport, Texas. From Rockport the storm swept east, flooding the coast from Corpus Christi to Port Arthur, inundating the flaring heart of the petroleum industry that had grown up along the Gulf. Though the days of the gusher had long faded, the oil strikes of old had left their mark on the region. After the strike at Goose Creek, a new wave of hopeful wildcatters poured into the area. The rule of first capture governed their frenzy: whoever scooped up the oil first, kept it. Consequently, productive oil fields became battle grounds, the sites of dramatic races to "pump as much oil as rapidly as possible," efficiency and safety be damned.[2] Local newspapers covered the chaos at Goose Creek, describing tent cities, bustling streets, bar fights, and legal disputes. In Pelly, one of the towns closest to the field, a makeshift restaurant sprang up, built in a burned-down cottage with tables set up under the open sky. And everywhere, blankets of oil draped across the plants, the animals, the water. "Trees drip with petroleum," the *Houston Post* proclaimed, "and their leaves glisten in greasy splendor." When all that oil finally dried up, a ready infrastructure of refineries, ports, and pipelines was left behind.

Harvey tore through that spreading industrial web. Its waters breached containers and shut down security measures. In the storm's wake, contaminated water washed across parks, schools, neighborhoods. Most of these areas are poor, and many of them are populated largely by people of color. Oil refineries don't loom over luxury urban lofts or master-planned communities. Above the water, volatile organic chemicals billowed into the atmosphere, released by downed air scrubbers and burst pipelines. Watersheds and airsheds picked up these contaminants and sent them percolating out into the world.

And, not far from the spot where Mitchell and his men had stood watching oil spew into the air, another gusher appeared. Water damage to ExxonMobil's Baytown complex, the largest integrated refinery and petrochemical plant in the United States, released a torrent of almost half a billion gallons of industrial wastewater. Elsewhere in the complex, floating roof tanks used for the storage of various products failed, releasing toxic benzene, butadiene, and vinyl chloride into the air. The story that began at the confluence of Tabbs Bay and Goose Creek with oil blanketing a marshy field came to its fruition as petroleum byproducts poured into the boiling waters of an unprecedented storm.

THE SUN HAD YET TO RISE when it came time to take the boats out, to carry them from the shipping container where we stored them down toward the unkempt bayou and the undergrowth-choked protrusions of industry. Most mornings, the squelching, waterlogged ground would rise up to encase our feet as we picked our way toward the makeshift dock, causing us to stumble and sway beneath the unwieldy shells. The mud usually stank of rich decay, a smell that mingled, depending on the way the wind was blowing, with the fumes of the nearby refineries. And each time we lowered our boats into the water a parade of soggy trash—diapers, plastic bags, a deflated soccer ball—saluted our struggle as they floated past.

That was years ago, before the storm. I don't remember why I joined the rowing team now. Not really. Whatever it was, I couldn't have been very committed; I quit after just one semester of early-morning practices and predawn drives across the city. We practiced on a bendy bit of Buffalo Bayou, past downtown but before the Houston Ship Channel, where the water flows between Denver Harbor and the Second Ward.

Nineteen years I'd lived in Houston, and the first time I'd seen that portion of it was at five in the morning, gearing up to steer a $10,000 piece of aluminum past the dormant warehouses and steel mills. There were other people from Houston on the team, too, including our coach. None of them knew much about the neighborhood we were practicing in, either, let alone the people who lived in it. If we'd thought about it, we likely would have called ourselves visitors. Get in, get out. By seven each morning, we'd be gone.

I try not to make a secret of the fact that I grew up in the suburbs; that I lived behind the hedges at Rice for four years; that I continue to benefit from things I didn't earn. When I say I'm from Houston, what I should really say is that there are a lot of Houstons. I come from one of them. And, at nineteen, coasting along that bayou, I still thought of my Houston as separate, somehow, from the other ones. Walled off, protected. *Elevated*. I could feel guilt about the difference, sure. But it wasn't like that guilt drove me to *do* anything. I just wanted off the hook. Those people weren't me, after all. Those problems weren't mine.

And then we met Harvey. It came through, and our city wound up underwater, on the news. Eventually, the water receded, replaced by a rising tide of information. Breaking reports and exposés chronicled the inequity and insufficient accountability witnessed during the flood and its aftermath.[3] These findings confirmed a reality I'd slowly been learning about on my own. As I worked on cleanup and distribution of recovery funds in the wake of the storm, it wasn't difficult to see in what direction the aid flowed. As more data emerged regarding the exposure to toxic materials during and after the storm, it also became apparent who bore the brunt of Houston's flooded industrial core.

But there's another element in this equation, the part I refused to think about at nineteen, floating down the bayou. Inequality isn't random. It's part of a system, one that relies on extracting profits meant for some and pawning off the costs on others. The illusion of separation disguises that relationship, to the benefit of those reaping the advantages. It encourages them to believe in their own fictions: that they are safe, that they are protected. That they themselves are not implicated in the hardship of others.[4] Harvey swept away those fictions. The storm illuminated the city's interconnectedness, shined a spotlight on the way we all link together in a diffuse, delicate web. What happens in one part of the city has repercussions elsewhere.[5] When rain falls in the west, it flows downstream, out of the bayous and the drainage ditches, into the streets, rushing and rushing until, eventually, it reaches the sea.

The bayou my teammates and I rowed on unites the two sides of the city, flowing from west to east. A slow, silty ribbon, Buffalo Bayou begins as spring water and surface runoff in the prairies and subdivisions surrounding Katy (this includes rainfall collected in the infamous Addicks and Barker Reservoirs). Then it winds its way toward downtown Houston, meeting up with several tributaries along the way.[6] After joining with White Oak east of downtown, the bayou starts to swell. But water isn't the only thing that accumulates in the east. As the river widens and deepens, various industrial enterprises start to crowd along its banks. The Port of Houston begins where Brays disappears into Buffalo Bayou, just inside the East Loop. Technically speaking, the port is twenty-five miles of ship berths, cargo terminals, and assorted private enterprises—refineries, chemical plants, and shipping companies—that stretch along the Houston Ship Channel and into Galveston Bay.

If water and industrial development flow east, then money flows in the opposite direction. It's no secret that energy built the city; in Houston, most pipelines lead to oil. Every sector of our economy owes something to its thick, viscous lifeblood. People flocked to the city for decades after the oil strikes of the early twentieth century, fueling almost eighty years of explosive growth. Even today, thirty years after the economic diversification spurred by the oil bust of the 1980s, "175,000 Houston-based employees [are] working directly in production, oil services and machinery and fabricated metals, and tens of thousands more serve as suppliers or contractors."[7] In 2016, Houston alone provided about 40 percent of the country's base petrochemical capacity.[8] Housing boomed because of oil, as did everything from commercial construction to banking to retail. The LBJ Space Center came to Houston in part because of a deal negotiated between the then vice president and Ross S. Sterling, Humble Oil's founder. The Texas Medical Center was built with money donated by industry leaders. Universities, museums, and nonprofits across the city all benefit enormously from the energy sector's philanthropy.

But all of this wealth has not been shared equally. The people who live the closest to Houston's industries—the people who provided the labor power for all of this profit—bear the most and benefit the least. The vast majority of Houston's oil wealth does not go to those working in the refineries. Rather, it goes to the executives living on the western side of the city. Oil's profit flows uphill, with just a minute fraction left behind to maintain the human labor force supporting the city's industrial base. And as automation increases, fewer and fewer of the city's oil jobs are industrial. With the cost of labor thus reduced and wages depressed, the gap stands to widen even further.

Disproportionate paychecks don't constitute the only disparity of risk and reward, though. In a recent study published in the *Proceedings of the National Academy of Science (PNAS)*, for instance, researchers specializing in civil engineering established that "on average, black and Hispanic minorities bear a disproportionate burden from the air pollution caused mainly by non-Hispanic whites." According to the study's metrics, majority white populations experience approximately 17 percent less air pollution exposure than is caused by their consumption,[9] whereas majority Black and Latino populations experience 56 to 63 percent *more*.

The roots of that disparity reach deep into our shared history. When I slipped down Buffalo Bayou with my teammates, we might as well have been rowing through the pulsing arteries of Houston's checkered past. After oil began to flow along the coast, refineries bloomed beside the deep clearances of the ship channel, just inland enough to shelter them from the capricious storms of the Gulf. Consequently, the East Side's population began to swell. Mexican immigrants fleeing the turmoil of the Mexican Revolution and Tejanos drawn from rural parts of the state to the west and south began moving to the Second Ward and Magnolia Park. Whites from East Texas and Louisiana began settling in Deer Park, Pasadena, and Baytown, while their Black counterparts came to the Fifth Ward. Creoles of color from southeastern Louisiana settled there as well, forming their own enclave in the area still known as Frenchtown. Regardless of their race, most of these new migrants were drawn to the east side by its proximity to work. But the tidy divisions of the final arrangement didn't happen by accident. The Houston they settled in was a Houston divided by de jure and de facto color lines. Legally speaking, the city was divided into Black and white, which contributed to the development of nearly autonomous Black enclaves in each section of the city, including the East Side. Meanwhile, Anglo discrimination against ethnic Mexicans—considered white in the eyes of the law, though the communities themselves had identities rooted in histories of acknowledged racial admixture—ensured that yet another spatial separation emerged.

Both private and government-sanctioned forces maintained these divisions; violence committed by both officers of the law and private individuals was backed by the systemic denial of resources to certain parts of the city. White-dominated local government starved non-white areas of funds for education, development, and infrastructure. White-controlled industries ensured that young white employees had greater economic mobility than their nonwhite counterparts.[10] While many individuals flourished despite such rampant and pervasive discrimination, on the systemic scale, the violence did its work: inequality calcified.[11] Today, in addition to living on less than half of the income of their fellow Houstonians, the residents of many communities on the east side face ambient concentrations of seven separate pollutants at levels that pose a definite health risk. None of the East Houston census tracts have fewer than three pollutants in the highest risk category. Almost 90 percent of the census tracts located here have four or more pollutants present. "Definite risk pollutants" include diesel particulate matter; carcinogenic 1,3 butadiene; chromium IV; benzene; chlorine; and formaldehyde.[12] With a few exceptions (Deer Park, as well as portions of La Porte and Baytown), much of the population in these communities self-identified as Latino or African American in the 2010 census.[13]

So, while the mass migrations of the twentieth century ensured a steady supply of cheap labor to keep profits on the rise, systemic discrimination meant that oil would lose only a fraction of this growing work force to brighter economic horizons. It's no coincidence, then, that in the local politics of the early twentieth century, supporters of segregation joined forces with industry under the banner of states' rights.[14] Free from federal intervention, de jure segregation could continue, and industry could thrive under a system of self-regulation. For sixty years, refineries and other industrial enterprises polluted the communities around them virtually unchecked by anything except their own profit margins. From the original oil strikes, to the post–World War II petroleum boom, to the uphill civil rights battles of the 1960s, local policies ensured a system of profitable inequality that persists into the present day. Time has passed, regulation has been strengthened, and industry technology has improved, but the overall dynamics of injustice have changed little. Local enforcement of regulation has often been lackluster. Over the years, the city has allowed industry to build leak-prone storage vats, animal-feed factories, and metal shredding facilities with little regard for the comfort or safety of the surrounding community. Often, even when regulations are enforced, businesses find that penalties are cheaper than the cost of compliance. We've witnessed the truth of that calculation countless times over the years. Harvey isn't the first example; it's not even the most recent. But no matter how many times we learn something (or no matter how many times we ignore it), there always remains a choice.[15] Do we allow the injustice to continue? Or do we take measures, however small, to confront it? Do we let the knowledge crush us? Or do we stand up and try our best to make our world a better place?[16]

Most days, our coach would have us row until just past sunrise. The swell of the approaching light provided a longer rhythm, one long beat to encase the frantic chopping of our oars. When dawn broke over the bayou, the smog-laden air would scatter the orange embers of daybreak deep into the fading violet of the night. Sometimes we'd cheer to see it; if we could witness that chemically enhanced sunrise from the boat, it meant we were rowing west, against the current. It meant practice would soon be over, that we'd dock and make our way home. That soon enough, we'd turn our backs on the people and the places once again illuminated by daybreak's spreading light.

I DOUBT, when John Gaillard dropped his match, that his thoughts were of destruction. Just opportunity. Likewise, I don't think Mitchell wanted to unleash anything more than oil, wealth, progress. Those who raced to Baytown, the ship channel, the east side, west Houston—none of them were, individually, supremely good or supremely evil. Accretion has no individual culprit. We're all a part of something larger.

But none of that changes the unequal reality of our most recent hurricane, or the inequality that has persisted and widened in its wake. Because as oily water poured into the Channel beside Baytown, more damage was erupting upstream. Waves of runaway oil spilled across Galena Park. A chemical plant in Crosby exploded. Valero's major refinery, located between Harrisburg/Manchester and the southern bank of Buffalo Bayou, released clouds of carcinogenic benzene. Entanglement Technologies, monitoring on behalf of the Environmental Defense Fund and Air Alliance Houston, recorded benzene levels of about 324 parts per million in nearby neighborhoods.[17] The wrath of nature aside, we cannot ignore the reasons that certain communities are exposed to these risks in the first place; that some of their members watch chemical vats steam from their porches and refineries flare from their backyards. None of this is an accident; rather, our nation has been built so that certain groups of people succeed while the price is paid by others.[18] The hardships faced by these communities have arisen and ossified so that elsewhere others can have their oil and drink it, too; so that they can dance in the gusher without worrying about the acid in the rain.

RECENTLY, I PAID A VISIT TO Hog Island. ExxonMobil owns it now— Gaillard bought the land from its original owner for $2,000, then turned around and sold it to Humble Oil for $300,000. Over the years, the island has hosted a boardinghouse, a ferry landing, and a landfill. It has served as a hideaway and a lover's lane. Now, though, without a link to the mainland, the island stands abandoned. Subsidence has caused a portion of the island to sink beneath sea level, allowing the surrounding water to rush in and split the island in two.[19] Despite the numerous "No Trespassing" signs, intrepid boaters and kayakers still venture out to the island from the nearby shore, carrying on the spirit of John Gaillard. Slathered in sunscreen and wearing floppy hats, they paddle down Goose Creek—beneath the abandoned railroad bridge painted with the words "Live to Inspire"—and make their way across Tabbs Bay to beach their bright plastic boats on the island's eastern shore. Sometimes, too, local historians lead tours out to a cluster of ruins on the northern tip of the island, remnants of a nineteenth-century ferry crossing. After Harvey, I'm told, the island was just a mass of muddy, debris-laden scar tissue. The ground was so moist that one feared it might merge with the surrounding water, get swept down the Channel and out into the Gulf. But the island has been cleaned up since then. Much of the grass has grown back, although bare spots remain where stunted trees once grew. Depending on which side of the island you stand on, you can see the spires of the Fred Hartman Bridge, the suspended bit of Highway 146 that allows motorists to cross between La Porte and Baytown. It's a big, yellow, cable-stayed bridge that rocks when the wind picks up. If you squint, perhaps you can see ExxonMobil's complex beyond it, off to the north beside Mitchell Bay. Beyond the bridge, the vats and silos of industry spread out on both sides of the ship channel: a shining, distant network of humming pipes, scaffolded spires, and dancing flares that shine through the daylight and into the night. When the sun sets here, the refineries spread out like a city of stars, their lights and little fires reflecting on the water as if in compensation for the occluded sky.

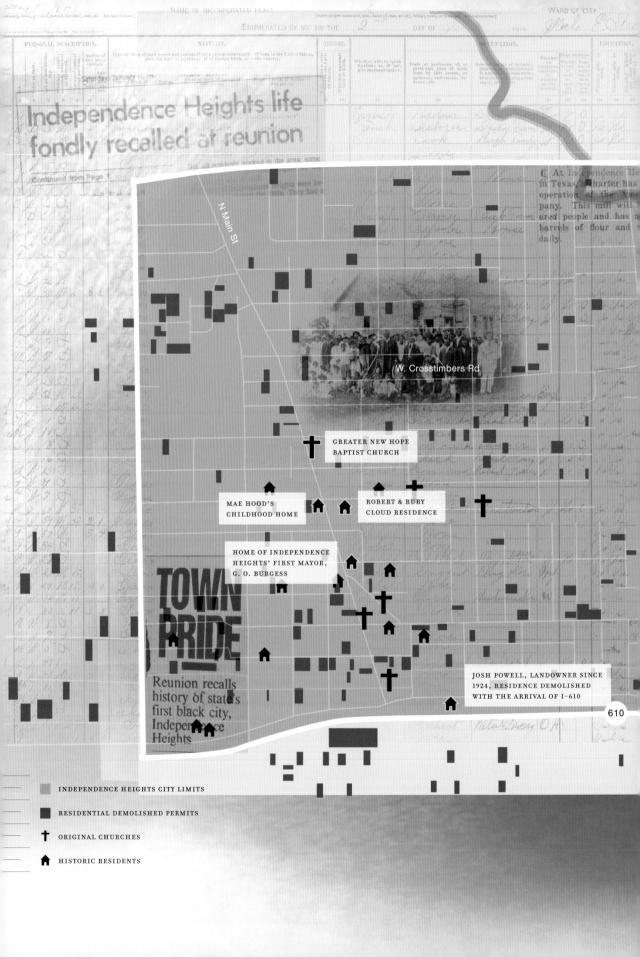

Independence Heights life
fondly recalled at reunion

Continued from Page 1

N Main St

W. Crosstimbers Rd

GREATER NEW HOPE
BAPTIST CHURCH

MAE HOOD'S
CHILDHOOD HOME

ROBERT & RUBY
CLOUD RESIDENCE

HOME OF INDEPENDENCE
HEIGHTS' FIRST MAYOR,
G. O. BURGESS

TOWN
PRIDE

Reunion recalls
history of state's
first black city,
Independence
Heights

JOSH POWELL, LANDOWNER SINCE
1924, RESIDENCE DEMOLISHED
WITH THE ARRIVAL OF I-610

610

INDEPENDENCE HEIGHTS CITY LIMITS

RESIDENTIAL DEMOLISHED PERMITS

ORIGINAL CHURCHES

HISTORIC RESIDENTS

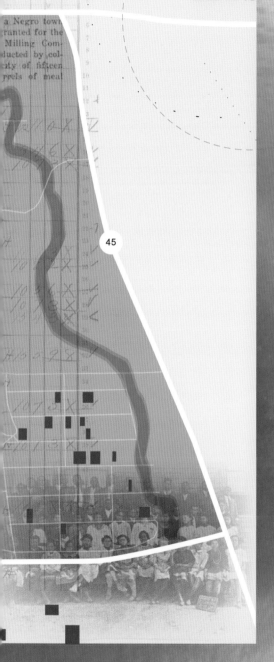

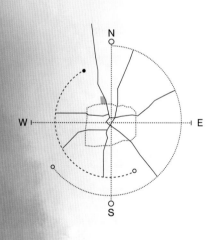

HISTORY DISPLACED

a Negro tow
granted for the
Milling Com
ducted by col
ity of fifteen
rrels of meal

45

AUSTIN, SATUR

ss. WEEKLY FREE MAN'S PRESS

AUSTIN, TEXAS,
SATURDAY MORNING, AUGUST 1, 1868

Get A Home.

IN THE WAKE OF HURRICANE HARVEY, INDEPENDENCE HEIGHTS HAS BEEN WORKING TO PRESERVE
ITS HISTORY. THIS MAP INDICATES THE FIRST RESIDENTS AND PUBLIC PLACES IN INDEPENDENCE
HEIGHTS, AND HOW THE LACK OF CITY DEVELOPMENT OF THESE AREAS HAS SHAPED THE
NEIGHBORHOOD'S INFRASTRUCTURE TODAY.

DESIGN BY ALEXA ABAD

History Displaced

FLOODING THE FIRST BLACK
MUNICIPALITY IN TEXAS

Aimee VonBokel with Tanya Debose
Alexandria Parson, Research Assistant

"Black people owned everything in this town," Tanya Debose told me. We were sitting in the car on North Main Street next to Ebenezer United Methodist Church in Houston, Texas. She had wanted to save the old town hall, she said. I turned my head to follow her gesture and saw an empty lot.

Independence Heights was the first Black municipality in Texas—incorporated in 1915 by a few dozen families who had migrated from small towns and farms in eastern Texas and southern Louisiana. In 1924, when Tanya's great-grandfather arrived with his wife, Georgia, and his son, McKinley, he settled on what was then East 31st Street. That's where McKinley met Tanya's grandmother, who lived on the other side of 31st Street with her mother. Both families attended True Light Missionary Baptist Church, where Tanya's family still attends services on Sundays. Tanya learned her history at church, and under the guidance and mentorship of Pastor James Bowie Sr., she grew into the community leader she is today.[1]

Houston was still a small town in the early twentieth century, surrounded by a bunch of smaller towns—not just Independence Heights, but ship-channel towns like Harrisburg and Magnolia Park—and middle-class developments like Houston Heights. Independence Heights was different, however. Unlike the others, it was an all-Black town with a Black mayor in Jim Crow–era Texas, "an exclusive colored community of Texas," W. E. B. Du Bois's New York–based *Crisis Magazine* reported in 1918. Only about eight hundred residents lived in Independence Heights, according to the 1920 census records, but nearly every family owned their home.

By most accounts, the earliest Black settlers arrived in this area around 1908. Then came their brothers, sisters, parents, cousins, in-laws, and grandparents. Within months of the first subdivision, platted in 1910, another subdivision appeared on the map: Independence Heights Annex, and the next year, another subdivision—for a school.

Oliphant L. Hubbard led the movement to create the Independence Heights school in 1911; he also became its first teacher. A lawyer and a graduate of Prairie View A&M, he worked with his neighbors, local landowners, and Harris County officials to secure a two-room house and funding for a teacher. Residents moved a wooden schoolhouse from the white community of Sunset Heights up to 39th Street. With each year, the settlement expanded eastward toward the Little White Oak Bayou, and after the seventh platted subdivision, residents voted to incorporate, electing thirty-eight-year-old lawyer George O. Burgess as their mayor in 1915.

With land ownership came freedom. A piece of land "will be your castle," the Austin *Free Man's Press* proclaimed. "No man has a right to tear you from it, or to molest it. You have a right to defend it against every intruder."[2]

The year 1924, when Josh Powell arrived in Houston, was the "high-water mark" for the Klan in Texas, according to the Texas State Historical Association. Whether Mr. Powell set out for the Houston area with the explicit aim of escaping the Klan, no one knows. But in contrast to rural Wharton County, where Mr. Powell was raised, in Independence Heights, the sheriff, deputies, and even the tax assessor were Black. And when the Ku Klux Klan "paid a visit" to the town's second mayor, O. L. Hubbard, "Hubbard greeted them with a .30-30 rifle," his daughter Vivian recalled, and they left.

The threat of racial violence in the rural South certainly pushed migrants out of the country and into cities like Houston. But there was a pull factor, too: the promise of jobs. The Houston Ship Channel, which opened in 1914, "internationalized the city almost overnight," as one writer put it. The channel "provided jobs and elevated the economy of the whole region."[3] Oil refineries sprang up along the coast. Companies like Sinclair, Texaco, and Crown built campuses along the ship channel and workers came. As the population of the region swelled, Houston began annexing those little towns at its perimeter: Houston Heights in 1919,

Magnolia Park and Harrisburg (both in 1926), and later, Independence Heights in 1929. In many cases, annexation was a win-win: the annexed areas got sewer systems, electricity, and paved roads, and Houston benefited from the increased property-tax revenue. But in Independence Heights, the infrastructure was slow to arrive. Long after annexation the streetcars still stopped well south of the town's southern border—leaving residents to walk the rest of the way home along dirt roads.

Following annexation, the neighborhood continued to operate much as it had before. Churches formed the core of the community, and the duties that once fell to elected officials now fell to the ministers. By 1940, the Studewood Streetcar Line connected Independence Heights with downtown Houston. Many residents traveled to work in white people's homes and yards by day—then returned to their tight-knit community at night. Though they no longer elected their own local mayor, residents continued to guard their hard-won right to vote. Two different men created voting precincts in Independence Heights in the 1950s. One was the proprietor of the funeral home; the other, a migrant from Boing-Iago, in Wharton County. It was still a small town in spirit (if not legally defined as an independent municipality) until the freeway came through in the late 1950s.

Independence Heights changed radically when the Texas Department of Transportation (TxDOT) took 30th and 31st Streets via eminent domain to build Interstate 610. Tanya's great-grandfather, then in his late seventies, moved from his family's social pocket on the south side of Independence Heights, on what was East 31st Street, to an address on the north side, at East 38th Street. In total, TxDOT claimed 330 parcels from Independence Heights to build, first, I-610, and eventually its intersection with I-45, but as construction of the freeway traveled west, it avoided the homes in the affluent white neighborhood of Garden Oaks. The swerve of the I-610 loop at Yale is the physical manifestation—the residue—of the power imbalance between the two neighborhoods in the 1950s.

One of the worst legacies of I-610 is not just the road itself—which formed a fourteen-lane concrete divide between the Black neighborhood of Independence Heights and the surrounding white neighborhoods— or the pollution caused by traffic or the loss of property or the deterioration of the social fabric or the loss of businesses, but rather the culvert

TxDOT built at the edge of the first Black municipality in Texas to channel Little White Oak Bayou underneath the road. The culvert is too small,
and the water backs up into Independence Heights. The neighborhood
has struggled with flooding ever since.

Flooding may seem like an engineering problem—or a challenge we
should hand over to the water experts. But in this case, it's a problem
with social, political, and racial dimensions. In 1962, when the interchange went in, the culvert created flooding in the established Black
residential neighborhood in the northwest quadrant of the intersection,
but not in the white neighborhoods to the south or east of the intersection. For nearly sixty years, the residents and property owners of
Independence Heights have endured flooding because, in contrast to
wealthier neighborhoods, residents haven't had the political power to
demand a corrective measure.

When people say racism doesn't exist, and that slavery was a long
time ago and why doesn't everyone get over it, they're not thinking
about the cascading impact of past policies as they manifest in the present. Many of Independence Heights's original landowners deeded their
properties to their children, who, in turn, deeded them to their children.
But unlike white-owned land, which has generally increased in value,
historically, Black-owned properties have lost value.[4] The cycle goes like
this: Black families buy land and build a community. Their community
is surrounded by incinerators or polluting industrial sites (as happened
in Pleasantville and Houston's Fifth Ward, where a cancer cluster has
been identified). Or their community is flooded (as in Independence
Heights). Or a highway comes through and rips apart the social and
economic fabric (which is what happened to Freedman's Town, also
known as Houston's Fourth Ward). Banks refuse to approve lending in
Black neighborhoods, a trend well documented since the Community
Reinvestment Act of 1977. Under such conditions, homes fall into disrepair. People who've sunk their life savings into their homes don't move
because they can't. But the next generation leaves. The land is abandoned or put to other uses until speculators arrive. With the backing of
powerful investors, they fix the flooding or draft restrictive covenants
to keep out polluting neighbors—because they have money and power
and connections. They develop the land for non-Black newcomers. The
newcomers buy land, and it increases in value again.

Houston has grown a lot since 1908. Once located at the outer edge of the city with muddy dirt roads and limited access to public transportation, Independence Heights is now near the center of a sprawling, congested, automobile-dependent metropolis. The land is valuable for its proximity to the urban core. "Minutes from downtown!" the real estate ads proclaim. But after half a century of recurring flooding, the old homes are in disrepair—or they've been demolished. Families have held on a long time, but they can't borrow against devalued land to repair the cumulative damages they've endured. And the land will only regain its value if TxDOT fixes the flooding by redesigning the culvert. The repairs are part of the revaluation process. The value accrues for newcomers—not for Black legacy residents.

Today, in 2020, Tanya continues to work in the neighborhood. She's fighting to keep legacy families here—fighting against the for-profit tax-collecting entities that target poor and elderly people of color, against encroaching gentrification from Garden Oaks and Houston Heights, and against flooding from the Little White Oak Bayou. For those who don't know the history of Independence Heights (which was almost everyone, until Tanya spoke up), it might be tempting to treat the flooding in particular as a natural disaster or an engineering problem: one that should be handed over to the "technical experts" to solve. But when Tanya tells the story from her perspective, we can see how the politics and infrastructure of a racist era destroyed the social fabric of the first Black municipality in Texas, and continue to erode Black family wealth.

"We can't continue on this path," Tanya says. "We need to do something different. We need to do something better."

ANTHROPOCENE CITY

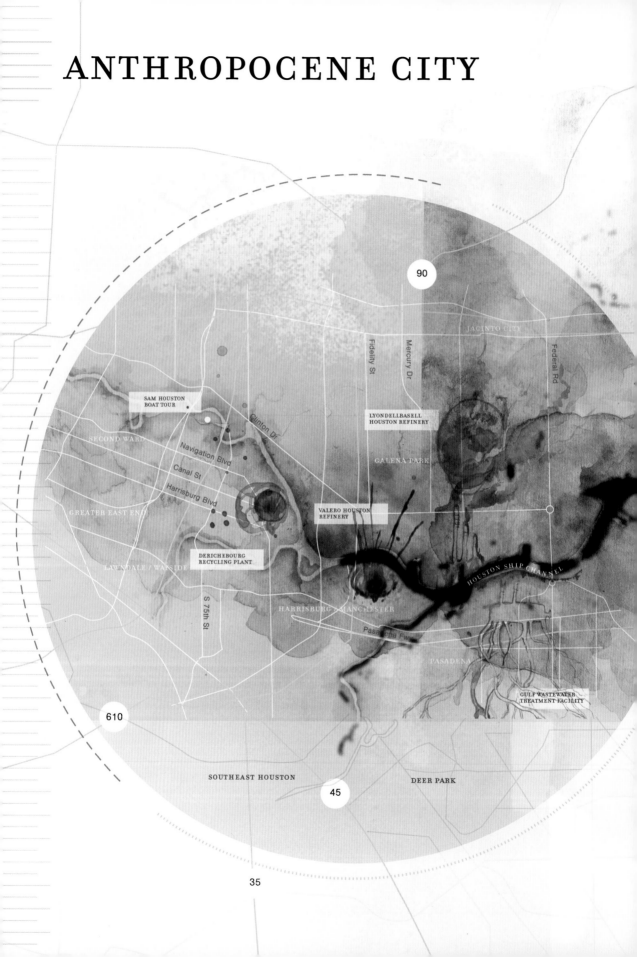

CHANNELVIEW

BUFFALO BAYOU

10

8

225

225

N

W — E

S

ALONG THE HOUSTON SHIP CHANNEL, WILD REFINERIES, WASTE TREATMENT PLANTS, AND RECYCLING
FACILITIES ARE ILLUSTRATED AS DESTRUCTIVE HYBRID MECHANICAL BEASTS AND BLACK HOLES,
EMPHASIZING THE IDEA OF THE HYPEROBJECT—A THING SO LARGE, WITHOUT ORIGIN OR END,
REMAINING AS COLOSSAL, MYSTERIOUS AND FRIGHTENING AS THE UNIVERSE.

DESIGN BY GRANT FLOWERS AND ILSE HARRISON

Anthropocene City

HOUSTON AS HYPEROBJECT

Roy Scranton

Imagine an oyster. Imagine waves of rain lashing concrete, a crawdad boil, a fallen highway, and a muddy bay. Imagine a complex system of gates and levees, the Johnson Space Center, a broken record on a broken player. Imagine the baroque intricacy of the Valero Houston oil refinery, the Petrobras Pasadena oil refinery, the LyondellBasell oil refinery, the Shell Deer Park oil refinery, the ExxonMobil Baytown oil refinery, a bottle of Ravishing Red nail polish, a glacier falling into the sea. Imagine gray-black clouds piling over the horizon, a chaos spiral hundreds of miles wide. Imagine a hurricane.

Isaiah whirls through the sky, gathering strength from the Gulf of Mexico's warm waters. City, state, and federal officials do the sensible thing, evacuating beach towns and warning citizens and companies in Texas's petro-industrial enclaves from Bayou Vista to Morgan's Point to prepare for the worst.

The massive cyclone slows and intensifies as it nears the barrier islands off the coast, with wind speeds reaching over 150 mph. By sunset, several hours before landfall, the storm's counterclockwise arm is pushing water over the Galveston Seawall; by the time the eye finally crosses the beaches east of San Luis Pass, the historic city of Galveston has been flattened by a twenty-foot wave.

As Isaiah crosses into Galveston Bay, it only grows in strength, adding water to water, and when it hits the ExxonMobil Baytown refinery, some fifty miles inland, the storm surge is over twenty-five feet high. It crashes through refineries, chemical storage facilities, wharves, and production plants all along the Houston Ship Channel, cleaving pipelines from their moorings, lifting and breaking storage tanks, and strewing toxic waste across east Houston.

The iridescent, gray-brown flood rises, carrying jet fuel, sour crude, and natural gas liquids into strip malls, schools, and offices. By the time Isaiah passes inland, leaving the ruined coast behind, more than two hundred petrochemical storage tanks have been wrecked, more than a hundred million gallons of gas, oil, and other chemicals have been spilled, total economic damages for the region are estimated at over a hundred billion dollars, and 3,682 people have been killed. By most measures, it is one of the worst disasters in US history: worse than the 1906 San Francisco earthquake, worse than Hurricane Katrina, worse than the terrorist attacks of September 11.

The effects ripple across the globe. The Gulf Coast is home to roughly 30 percent of the United States' proven oil reserves; the Gulf Coast and Texas hold 35 percent of its natural gas reserves. The refineries and plants circling Galveston Bay are responsible for roughly 25 percent of the United States' petroleum refining, more than 44 percent of its ethylene production, 40 percent of its specialty chemical feed stock, and more than half of its jet fuel. Houston is the second-busiest port in the United States in terms of pure tonnage and one of the most important storage and shipping points in the country for natural gas liquids. Isaiah shuts all that down. Within days of the hurricane's landfall, the NYSE and NASDAQ plummet as the price of oil skyrockets. Fuel shortages ground flights across the country, airline ticket prices soar, the price of beef and pork shoots up, and gas prices at the pump leap to seven or eight dollars a gallon. The American economy slips into freefall.

Meanwhile, as the oil-poisoned water in east Houston flows back toward the sea, it leaves behind it the worst environmental catastrophe since the BP Deepwater Horizon spill. Rather than diffusing into open water, though, all the sludge is cradled within the protective arms of Galveston Bay.

The good news is that Isaiah hasn't happened. It's an imaginary calamity based on models and research. The bad news is that it's only a matter of time before it does. Any fifty-mile stretch of the Texas coast can expect a hurricane once every six years on average, according to the National Weather Service. Only a few American cities are more vulnerable to hurricanes than Houston and Galveston, and not one of those is as crucial to the economy.

The worse news is that future hurricanes will actually be more severe than Isaiah. The models Isaiah is based on, developed by Rice University's Severe Storm Prediction, Education and Evacuation from Disasters (SSPEED) Center, don't account for climate change. According to Jim Blackburn, SSPEED's co-director, other models have shown much more alarming surges. "The City of Houston and FEMA did a climate change future," he told me, "and the surge in that scenario was 34 feet. Hurricanes are going to get bigger. No question. They are fueled by the heat of the ocean, and the ocean's warming. Our models are nowhere close."

Imagine Cobalt Yellow Lake. Imagine Cy Twombly's Say Goodbye, Catullus, to the Shores of Asia Minor. *Imagine colony collapse. Imagine refugees drowning off the shores of Asia Minor. Imagine causality, a bicycle tire, a million lost golf balls, a Styrofoam cooler, a bucket of crab claws, polyurethane, polypropylene, three copitas of mezcal, polyester, polyacrylic acid, polybutylene terephthalate, barbecue sauce, polycarbonate, polyether ether ketone, polyethylene, a Waffle House, polyoxymethylene, polyphenyl ether, polystyrene, the* Wizard of Oz, *polysulfone, polytetrafluoroethylene, polyvinyl chloride, a pair of pink crocs.*

I made a reservation aboard the M/V *Sam Houston* to take a boat tour of the Houston Ship Channel, the fifty-mile artery connecting Houston to the Gulf of Mexico, and the densest energy infrastructure nexus in North America. It seemed the perfect place to ask Timothy Morton about hyperobjects, dark ecology, and strange loops—some of the concepts they've been developing, as one of the leading thinkers of "speculative realism," in the effort to make philosophical sense of climate change.

In person, Morton is gentle, funny, and self-effacing, equal parts Oxbridge and cybergoth. We drove out to the ship channel in their white Mazda. As we rose and fell through the soaring grandeur of Houston's swooping highway exchanges, we talked about writing practice and work-life balance: Morton had two books coming out in 2016 and was writing two more, and when they're not busy writing, spending time with their kids, giving lectures, blogging, or collaborating with the Icelandic singer/songwriter Björk, they teach courses on literary theory and "Arts in the Anthropocene" at Rice University, where they hold the Rita Shea Guffey Chair in English.

Turning off the highway, we descended into the petro-industrial gray zone that sprawls from Houston to the sea. A Port of Houston security guard checked our IDs and we drove past hundred-foot-long turbine blades, massive shafts, and what looked like pieces of giant disassembled robots. I asked Tim how they liked living in Houston.

"This is the dirty coast," they said. "Dirty in the sense that something's wrong. We're holding this horrible, necessary energy substance, and it's like working in an emergency room or a graveyard or a charnel ground. You're basically working with corpses, with fossils from millions of years ago, you're working with deadly toxic stuff all the time, stuff that has very intense emotion connected to it. If I was going to find a word that described Texan-ness, I'd use the word 'wild'— phenomenologically, emotionally, experientially wild."

We parked and boarded the M/V *Sam Houston*. As the boat spun away from the pier and headed east, Tim and I went out on deck. Across the brown-black water enormous claws and magnets shifted scrap metal from one heap to another, throwing up clouds of metal dust, while the engine thrummed through my feet and the wind whipped across the mic of my voice recorder.

"The thing is," Tim said, "being aware of ecological facts is the very opposite of thinking about or looking at or talking about nature. *Nature* is always conceptualized as an entity that's different or distinct from me somehow. It's in my DNA, it's under my clothes, it's under the floorboards, it's in the wilderness. It's everywhere except for right here. But ecology means it's in your face. It *is* your face. It's part of you and you're part of it."

Several industrial recycling companies line the upper reaches of the Houston Ship Channel, including Derichebourg Recycling USA, Texas Port Recycling, and Cronimet USA, all recognized emitters of one of the most potent carcinogens known to science, hexavalent chromium. Behind the giant cranes and heaps of scrap lies the predominantly Hispanic neighborhood of Magnolia Park, whose residents have long complained of unexplained smoke and gas emissions, persistent pollution, and strange, multicolored explosions.

"The simplest way of describing that is *ecology without nature*," Tim continued. "That doesn't mean I don't believe in things like coral. I believe in coral much more than someone who thinks that coral is this 'natural' thing. Coral is a life form that's connected to other forms.

Everything's connected. And how we think about stuff is connected to the stuff. How you think about stuff, how you perceive stuff, is entangled with what you're perceiving."

In among the recycling yards sat Brady's Landing, a steak-and-shrimp restaurant. Through its plate-glass windows dozens of empty white tables shone like pearls in black velvet. I imagined diners eating crab-stuffed trout, watching the water rise up over the Ceres wharfs across the channel, rise up over the pilings at the edge of Brady's Island, rise up over the restaurant's foundations and up the windows—one foot, two feet, six feet—and the glass would crack, creak, and burst open, and the tide would rush in over fine leather shoes and French cuffs and napkin-covered laps and lift them, the diners, their tables, plates, pinot noir, and crab-stuffed trout, lift them and spin them in a rich and strange ballet.

"It's like when you realize you're actually a life form," Tim said. "I'm Tim but I'm also a human. That sounds obvious but it isn't. I'm Tim but I've also got these bits of fish and viral material inside me that *are* me. That's not a nice, cozy experience; it's an uncanny, weird experience. But there's a kind of smile from that experience, because ecological reality is like that. Ecological phenomena are all about loops, feedback loops, and this very tragic loop we're on where we're destroying Earth as we know it."

Interstate 610 loomed above, eighteen-wheelers and SUVs rolling through the sky. In the distance, gas flares flashed against the cloud cover. Pipes fed into pipes that wrapped back into pipes circling pipes, Escher machines in aluminum and steel.

"Ecological thinking is about never being able to be completely in the center of your world. It's about everything seeming out of place and unreal. That's the feel of dark ecology. But it isn't just about human awareness: it's about how *everything* has this uncanny, looped quality to it. It's actually part of how things are. So it's about being horrified and upset and traumatized and shocked by what we've been up to as human beings, and it's about realizing that this basic feeling of twistedness isn't going away."

A voice boomed out from the bowels of the boat as we broke from the highway's shadow: "First refinery to the right is Valero. This refinery began operations in 1942. It will handle 145,000 barrels of oil per day." Directly behind Valero lay Hartman Park, with its green lawns and baseball diamonds—the jewel of Manchester, one of the most polluted neighborhoods in the United States. Manchester is blocked in on the north by Valero, and on the east, south, and west by a chemical plant, a car-crushing yard, a water treatment plant, a train yard, I-610, and a Goodyear synthetic rubber plant. In 2010, the EPA found toxic levels of seven different carcinogens in the neighborhood. The area is 88 percent Hispanic.

"At some point," Tim said, "instead of trying to delete the twisty darkness, you have to make friends with it. And when you make friends with it, it becomes strangely sweet."

Imagine Greenland. Imagine Kellogg Brown & Root. Imagine Uber, the Svalbard Seed Vault, a roadkill raccoon, six months in juvie, Green Revolution, amnesia. Imagine ZZ Top. Imagine White Oak Bayou flooding its banks. Imagine Mexican gardeners swinging weed-eaters. Imagine boom and bust, the murmur of Diane Rehm, sizzurp, a sick coot, Juneteenth, coral bleaching, amnesia. Imagine losing Shanghai, New York, and Mumbai. Imagine "In the Mood." Imagine amnesia.

From Houston, the ship channel goes south through Galveston Bay, cutting a trench approximately 530 feet wide and 45 feet deep through the estuary bottom to where it passes into the Gulf of Mexico. As you follow the channel south along I-45, strip clubs and fast-food franchises give way to bayou resorts and refineries, until the highway finally leaps into the air, soaring over the water with the pelicans. It comes down again in downtown Galveston, once known as the "Wall Street of the South": a mix of historic homes, drydocked oil rigs, beach bars, and the University of Texas Medical Branch. The gulf spreads sullen and muddy to the south, its placid skin broken by distant blisters of flaming steel.

Galveston Bay is a Texas paradox. One of the most productive estuaries in the United States, it offers up huge catches of shrimp, blue crab, oysters, croaker, flounder, and catfish, and supports dozens of other kinds of fish, turtles, dolphins, salamanders, sharks, and snakes, as well as hundreds of species of birds. Yet the bay is heavily polluted, so full of PCBs, pesticides, dioxin, and petrochemicals that fishing is widely restricted. The bay is Houston's shield, protecting it from the worst of the Gulf Coast's weather by absorbing storm surges and soaking up rainfall, but hydrologists at Rice University are worried it might also be Houston's doom: the wide, shallow basin could, under the right conditions, supercharge a storm surge right up the ship channel.

The fight to protect Houston and Galveston from storms has been going on for more than a century, ever since Galveston built a seventeen-foot seawall after the Great Storm of 1900, a Category 4 hurricane that killed an estimated 10,000 to 12,000 people. The fight has been mainly reactive, always planning for the last big storm, rarely for the next. The levees around Texas City, for instance, were built after Hurricane Carla submerged the chemical plants there in ten feet of water in 1961. Today, Hurricane Ike, which hit Texas in 2008, offers the object lesson.

Hurricane Ike was a lucky hit with unlucky timing. Forecasts had the hurricane landing at the southern end of Galveston Island, and if they'd been right, Ike would have looked a lot like Isaiah. Instead, in the early morning hours of September 13, 2008, Ike bent north and hit Galveston dead on, which shifted the most damaging winds east. The sparsely populated Bolivar Peninsula was flattened, but Houston came out okay.

Still, Ike killed nearly fifty people in Texas alone, left thousands homeless, and was the third-costliest hurricane in American history. It would have been the ideal moment for Texas to ask Congress to fund a comprehensive coastal protection system. But on that Monday, September 15, Lehman Brothers filed the largest bankruptcy in US history, and the next day the Federal Reserve stepped in to save the failing insurance behemoth American International Group (AIG) with an $85 billion bailout. Nature's fury took a back seat to the crisis of capital.

Since then, two main research teams have led the way in preparing for the next big storm: Bill Merrell's "Ike Dike" team at Texas A&M Galveston (TAMUG), and the SSPEED Center at Rice University, led by Phil Bedient and Jim Blackburn. Despite shared goals, though, the relationship between the two teams hasn't always been easy. Bill Merrell's cantankerous personality and obsessive drive to protect Galveston have clashed with SSPEED's complex, interdisciplinary, Houston-centric approach.

Merrell's Ike Dike has the blessing of simplicity, which softens the sticker shock: it is estimated to cost between $6 billion and $13 billion. The plan is to build a fifty-five-mile-long "coastal spine" along the gulf. The plan's main disadvantage is that a strong enough hurricane could still flood the Houston Ship Channel, because of what Bedient calls the "Lake Okeechobee effect."

"The Okeechobee hurricane came into Florida in 1928 and sloshed water to a twenty-foot surge," Bedient explained. "Killed 2,000 people.

But Lake Okeechobee is unconnected to the coast. It was just wind. Galveston Bay has the same dimensions and depth as Lake Okeechobee in Florida. So imagine we block off Galveston Bay with a coastal spine, and we have a Lake Okeechobee."

Bedient worked on the Murphy's Oil spill in St. Bernard Parish, Louisiana, where flooding from Hurricane Katrina ruptured a storage tank, releasing more than a million gallons of oil, and ruined approximately eighteen hundred homes. One of Bedient's biggest worries is what a storm might do to the estimated forty-five hundred similar tanks surrounding Houston, many of them along the ship channel. If even 2 percent of those tanks were to fail because of storm surge, the results would be catastrophic.

The SSPEED Center advocates a layered defense, including a midbay gate that could be closed during a storm to protect the channel. On its face, the plan seems unwieldy, but SSPEED's models show it could stop most of the surge from going up the ship channel, with or without the Ike Dike, at an estimated cost of only a few billion dollars.

On the government side, various entities are at work in the ponderous and opaque way of American bureaucracy. The US Army Corps of Engineers (USACE) has its own research and development process, and it is working on a study of the Galveston-Houston area as part of its more comprehensive Gulf Coast research agenda, which could, eventually, lead to a recommendation for further studies, feasibility and cost-benefit analyses, environmental impact reports, and perhaps someday a project, which, were it funded by Congress, might even get built. One must be patient. It took the Army Corps of Engineers twenty-six years to build the Texas City Levee. When Katrina hit New Orleans and breached the levee system there, the Corps had been working on it since 1965, and it was still under construction.

Meanwhile, the Gulf Coast Community Protection and Recovery District (GCCPRD) is working to synthesize SSPEED and TAMUG's work into its own proposal. The GCCPRD was established by Texas governor Rick Perry in 2009, in the wake of Ike, but wasn't funded until 2013, when the Texas General Land Office (GLO) stepped in with a federal grant from the Department of Housing and Urban Development. The GCCPRD board comprises county judges from Brazoria, Chambers, Galveston, Harris, Jefferson, and Orange Counties, three additional members, and a president, currently former Harris County judge Robert Eckels, and has hired Dannenbaum Engineering, a local company with a strong track record in public infrastructure, to put the report together. The GCCPRD takes its lead from the GLO, headed today by Commissioner George P. Bush, and the specific language of the HUD grant restricts their work to analysis and general-level planning. Any more specific plans will have to come later, pending additional funding.

If there's one thing Houston can teach us about the Anthropocene, it's that all global warming is local. I went down myself to see representatives from all of these organizations—the USACE, SSPEED, TAMUG, the GLO, and the GCCPRD, plus the Texas Chemical Council and the Bay Area Houston Economic Partnership—testify before the State of Texas Joint Interim Committee on Coastal Barrier Systems (JICCBS), a special committee of the Texas state legislature, held at the TAMUG campus in Galveston.

Over five hours of presentations, talking points, and questions, a rough sense of the future began to take shape. As I sat in the back row listening to politicians ask about how various projects might affect insurance rates, how long different projects might take to build, and how the pitch could be put to the US Congress asking for the billions of dollars needed, I imagined a single white feather, numinous in the golden light of the PowerPoint, drift across the conference room, float over the heads of the senators, administrators, and scientists, and rise, rise, rise on an ever-expanding wave of confidence.

What obstacles might have remained between this roomful of committed public servants and the building of one of the largest coastal infrastructure projects in the world seemed for a moment insubstantial. The fact that environmental impact studies taking years to complete had yet to be started, that any of the land in question would have to be bought or seized under eminent domain, that all the planning at this stage was merely notional and actual designs would have to be bid on, contracted out, and approved, that there was no governmental agency in place to take responsibility for a coastal barrier system and maintain it, much less build it, and that somebody still had to come up with the money, somewhere, perhaps somehow convincing divided Republicans and embattled Democrats in the US Congress to send a bunch of Texas pols and their cronies a check for $13 billion—these were all mere details, nothing to worry about. I felt sure the political will manifest in that conference room would find a way.

And I had total confidence that those same feelings of goodwill, pragmatism, and accomplishment would be found, more or less, at the next Joint Interim Committee on Coastal Barrier Systems meeting, and the next academic conference on "Avoiding Disaster," and the next policy symposium on energy transition, and the next global conference on sea level rise, and the next plenary on carbon trading, and the next colloquium on the Anthropocene, and the next Conference of Parties to the United Nations Framework Convention on Climate Change, and the next, and the next, and the next, and the next, and journalists would report on it, and philosophers would ponder it, and activists would tweet about it, and concerned people like you would read about it. The problem is, it's not enough.

Imagine Earth. Imagine "Pretty Hurts." Imagine Lakewood Church, wind-lashed magnolias, a bottle of Topo Chico, the Astrodome. Imagine surface and depth, weather drones, the Geto Boys, thermodynamic disequilibrium, a body in a hole. Imagine the economy slowing, snowy egrets nesting in a live oak, becoming one with the Ocean of Soul, a Colt Expanse carbine. Imagine purple drank and a bowl of queso. Imagine the movie Terms of Endearment. *Imagine stocks and flows, a pearl, a rhizome. Imagine the end of the world as we know it.*

The *Sam Houston*'s ninety-minute tour of the Houston Ship Channel only goes a few miles out before turning around at the LyondellBasell refinery, one of the largest heavy-sulfur-crude refineries in the United States, processing around 268,000 barrels a day. The loudspeaker voice offered us complimentary soft drinks. I asked Tim Morton whether dark ecology had a politics.

"Obviously," they said, "it's not just that unequal distribution is connected to ecological stuff. It *is* ecological. It's not like we need to condescend to include fighting racism and these other issues under the banner of ecological thinking. It's the other way around. These problems were *already* ecological because the class system is a Mesopotamian construct and we're basically living in Mesopotamia 9.0. We're looking at these oil refineries and it's basically an upgrade of an upgrade of an upgrade of an agricultural logistics that began around 10,000 BC and is directly responsible, right now, for a huge amount of carbon emissions but also absolutely necessitated industry and therefore global warming and mass extinction."

We passed the CEMEX Houston Cement Company East Plant, the Gulf Coast Waste Disposal Authority's Washburn Tunnel Wastewater Treatment Facility, the Kinder Morgan Terminal, and Calpine's Channel Energy Center, a natural gas steam plant.

"This is where I have to say something English, which is 'Give us a chance, mate.' Because we can't do everything all at once, and we come to the conversation with the limitations and the skill sets that we have, and we're getting round to stuff. But maybe the first thing to do is to notice: We. Are. In. A. Shit. Situation. Maybe the first thing to do is go, okay, we're causing a mass extinction the likes of which hasn't been seen since the end-Permian extinction that wiped out 95 percent of life on Earth. Dark ecology has a politics but it's a very different kind of politics because it means that the idea that humans get to decide what reality is needs to be dismantled. It's an ontological war."

Off our starboard, Public Grain Elevator #2 poured wheat into the hold of a Chinese freighter, a hundred yards from a giant mound of yellow Mexican gypsum. The Valero refinery rose again to port, flare stacks burning against the sky, just beyond where Sims Bayou broke off from the channel and meandered in toward South Park and Sunnyside, poverty-stricken African American neighborhoods largely abandoned by Houston's government. One area of Sunnyside was recently rated the second most dangerous neighborhood in America. Seventy-six percent of the children there live in poverty. Residents have a 1 in 11 chance of becoming a victim of violent crime.

"Take hyperobjects," Tim said, staring fixedly at the Valero refinery. "Hyperobjects are things that are so huge and so long-lasting that you can't point to them directly; you can only point to symptoms or parts of them. You can only point to little slivers of how they appear in your world. Imagine all the oil on earth, forever, and the consequences of extracting and burning it for the next 100,000 years. That would be a hyperobject. We're going through this ship channel and these huge gigantic entities are all symptoms of this even larger, much more disturbing thing that we can't point to directly. You're in it and you *are* it, and you can't say where it starts and where it stops. Nevertheless, it's this thing here, it's on Earth, we know where it is."

We passed Brady's Landing and Derichebourg Recycling and Brays Bayou. The boat motored back much faster than it had gone out, and I had to strain to catch Tim's voice against the noise of the wind and water.

"My whole body's full of oil products," they said. "I'm wearing them and I'm driving them and I'm talking about them and I'm ignoring them and I'm pouring them into my gas tank—all these things I'm doing with them, precisely *that* is why I can't grasp them. It's not an abstraction. It's actually so real that I can't point to it. The human species is like that: instead of being this thing underneath appearance that you can point to, it's this incredibly distributed thing that you *can't* point to. The one thing that we need to be thinking right now, which is that *as a human being* I'm responsible for global warming, is actually quite tricky to fully conceptualize."

The *Sam Houston* throttled down and bumped against the wharf, the crew laid out the gangplank, and we disembarked. Tim and I got back in their white Mazda and they punched directions into their phone.

"We're in shock, and that's on a good day," Tim said, changing lanes. "Most days it's just grief work because we're in a state of total denial. I am too. I can only allow myself to feel really upset about what's going on for maybe one second a day; otherwise I'd be in a heap on the floor all the time crying."

We took Alt-90 to I-10, passing a Chevron and a Shell and a Subway and Tires R Us and Mucho Mexico, then rose into the flow of traffic cruising the interstate west.

"We're constantly trying to get on top of whatever we're worrying about, but if you look at it from an Earth magnitude, that's magical thinking. We've given ourselves an impossible-to-solve problem. The way in which we think about the problem, the way in which we give it to ourselves, is part of the problem. How do you talk to people in a deep state of grief when you're also in that deep state of grief?"

The lanes split and we wove from I-10 to 59 and then, just past Fiesta Mart's enormous neon parrot, slid down the ramp to Fannin Street.

Imagine black. Imagine black, black, black, blue-black, red-black, purple-black, gray-black, black on black. Imagine methane. Imagine education. Imagine wetlands. Imagine a brown-skinned woman in white circling the Rothko Chapel chanting "Zong. Zong. Zong." Imagine a regional, comprehensive approach to storm surge risk management, lemonade, the Slab Parade, increased capacity, complexity, attribution studies, progress, a wine and cheese reception, TACC's Stampede Supercomputer, an integrative, place-based research program, Venice's Piazza San Marco, sea level rise, Destiny's Child. Imagine a red line. Imagine two degrees. Imagine flare stacks. Imagine death.

Maybe it was the eleventh straight month of record-breaking warming. Maybe it was when the Earth's temperature hit 1.5 degrees Celsius over preindustrial levels. Maybe it was new reports that Antarctica and the Arctic were melting faster than anyone expected. Maybe it was when Greenland started melting two months early, and then so quickly that scientists didn't believe their data. Maybe it was watching our world start to come apart, and knowing that nothing would be done until it was too late.

WE'VE KNOWN THAT CLIMATE change was a threat since at least 1988, and the United States has done almost nothing to stop it. Today it might be too late. The feedback mechanisms that scientists have warned us about are happening. Our world is changing.

Imagine we've got twenty or thirty years before things really get bad. Imagine how that happens. Imagine soldiers putting you on a bus, imagine nine months in a FEMA trailer, imagine nine years in a temporary camp. Imagine watching the rich on the other side of the fence, the ones who can afford beef and gasoline, the ones who can afford clean water. Imagine your child growing up never knowing satiety, never knowing comfort, never knowing snow. Imagine politics in a world on fire.

Climate change is hard to think about not only because it's complex and politically contentious, not only because it's cognitively almost impossible to keep in mind the intricate relationships that tie together an oil well in Venezuela, Siberian permafrost, Saudi F-15s bombing a Yemeni wedding, subsidence along the Jersey Shore, albedo effect near Kangerlussuaq, the Pacific Decadal Oscillation, the polar vortex, shampoo, California cattle, the Great Pacific Garbage Patch, leukemia, plastic, paper, the Sixth Extinction, Zika, and the basic decisions we make every day, are forced to make every day, in a world we didn't choose but were thrown into. No, it's not just because it's mind-bendingly difficult to connect the dots. Climate change is hard to think about because it's depressing and scary.

Thinking seriously about climate change forces us to face the fact that nobody's driving the car, nobody's in charge, nobody knows how to "fix it." And even if we had a driver, there's a bigger problem: no car. There's no mechanism for uniting the entire human species to move together in one direction. There are more than seven billion of us, and we divide into almost two hundred nations, thousands of smaller subnational states, territories, counties, and municipalities, and an unimaginable multitude of corporations, community organizations, neighborhoods, religious sects, ethnic identities, clans, tribes, gangs, clubs, and families, each of which faces its own internal conflicts, disunion, and strife, all the way down to the individual human soul in conflict with itself, torn between fear and desire, hard sacrifice and easy cruelty, all of us improvising day by day, moment by moment, making decisions based on best guesses, gut hunches, comforting illusions, and too little data.

But that's the human way: reactive, ad hoc, improvised. Our ability to reconfigure our collective existence in response to changing environmental conditions has been our greatest adaptive trait. Unfortunately for us, we're still not very good at controlling the future. What we're good at is telling ourselves the stories we want to hear, the stories that help us cope with existence in a wild, unpredictable world.

Imagine life. Imagine a hurricane. Imagine a brown-skinned woman in white circling the Rothko Chapel chanting "Zong." Imagine grief. Imagine the Greenland ice sheet collapsing and black-crowned night herons nesting in the live oaks. Imagine Cy Twombly's *Say Goodbye, Catullus, to the Shores of Asia Minor*, amnesia, a broken record on a broken player, a tar-stained bird, the baroque complexity of a flooded oil refinery, glaciers sliding into the sea. Imagine an oyster. Imagine gray-black clouds piling over the horizon, a sublime spiral hundreds of miles wide. Imagine climate change. Imagine a happy ending.

A different version of this essay appeared in the New York Times *(as "When the Next Hurricane Hits Texas," on October 7, 2016) and was also published in* Mustarinda *(on December 31, 2016). This piece was written before Hurricane Harvey hit Houston in 2017, causing massive flooding across Houston and billions of dollars in damage.*

IF YOU DIDN'T
KNOW YOUR HOUSE
WAS SINKING

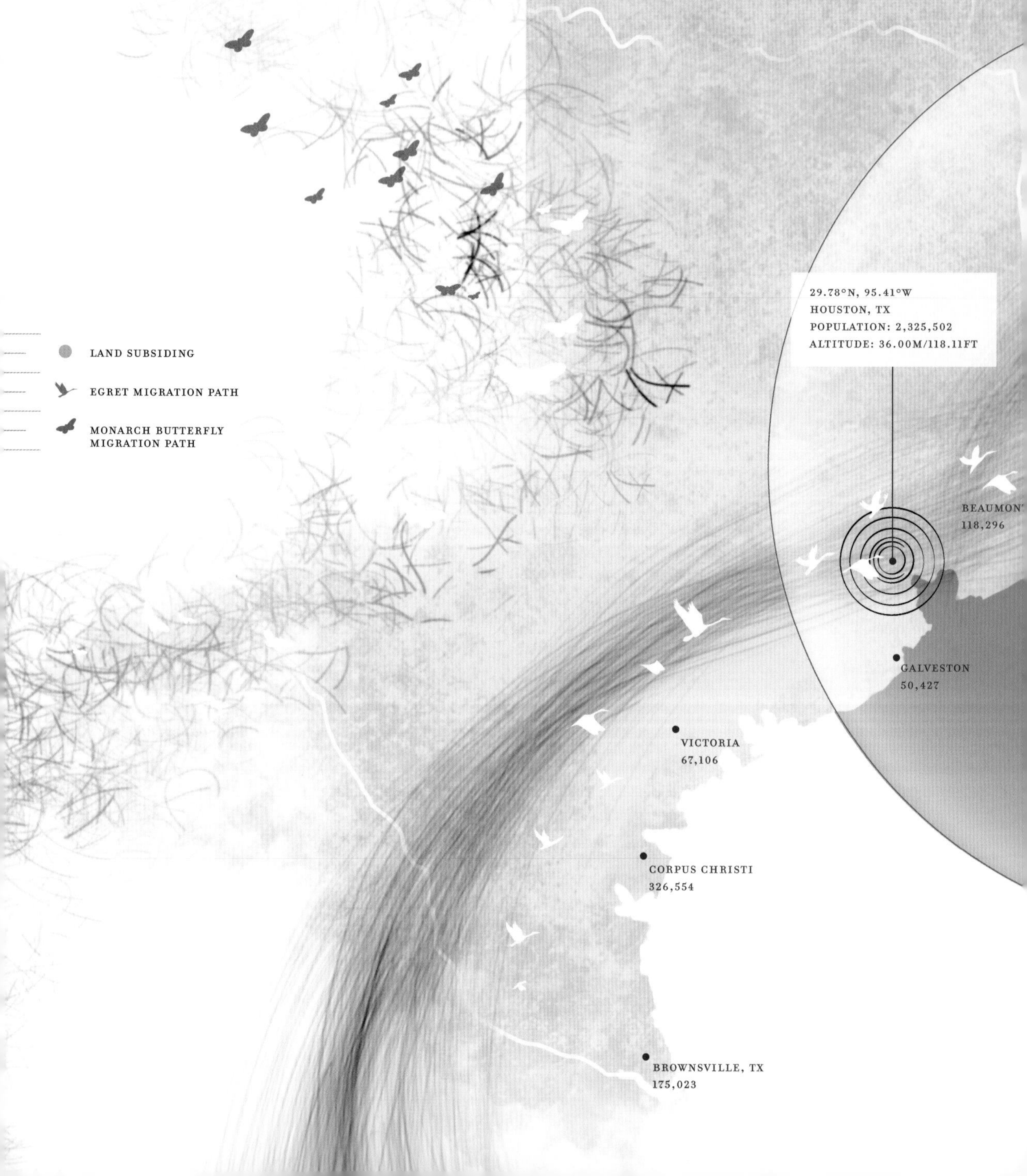

LAND SUBSIDING

EGRET MIGRATION PATH

MONARCH BUTTERFLY
MIGRATION PATH

29.78°N, 95.41°W
HOUSTON, TX
POPULATION: 2,325,502
ALTITUDE: 36.00M/118.11FT

BEAUMONT
118,296

GALVESTON
50,427

VICTORIA
67,106

CORPUS CHRISTI
326,554

BROWNSVILLE, TX
175,023

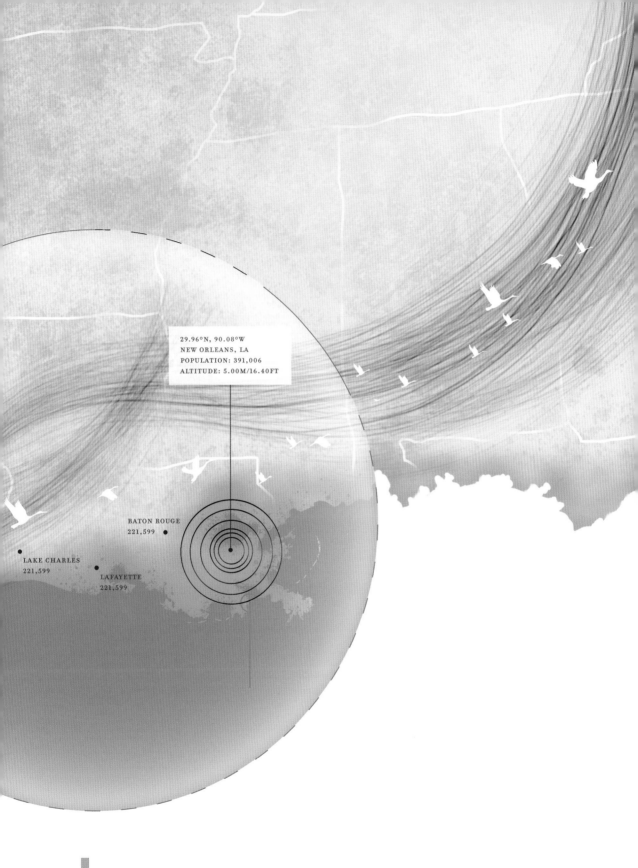

29.96°N, 90.08°W
NEW ORLEANS, LA
POPULATION: 391,006
ALTITUDE: 5.00M/16.40FT

BATON ROUGE
221,599

LAKE CHARLES
221,599

LAFAYETTE
221,599

CITIES ALONG THE GULF COAST ARE HOME TO MANY PEOPLE WHO ARE AT RISK OF FLOODING AT ALL TIMES. WITH THE LOUISIANA COAST DWINDLING FAST, HUMANS WILL HAVE TO LEARN TO BE AS NIMBLE AND FLUID AS THE NOBLE EGRET OR THE MONARCH BUTTERFLY TO SURVIVE.

DESIGN BY CAMILO MONROY, JULIA ONG, AND JAALON PRATT

If You Didn't Know Your House Was Sinking

Martha Serpas

If you didn't know your house was sinking, it's not the fault of the egrets, which have come every time it rains hard to peck insects around the pools of standing water in your yard. "This is marsh," their plumes say, half their black legs missing under the water. "This was marsh when you built, it is marsh now, and someday it will be open water, at which point we will stop coming to tell you that your house is sinking."

This particular conversation is taking place out my window, on Grand Isle, the last human-inhabited barrier island in Louisiana and setting of *The Awakening*. Even without the visiting egrets, I think everyone's clear on what's happening, even without the National Flood Insurance Program demanding higher and higher piers, without the oft-repeated long elegiac o's of "coastal erosion." When I drive south, sometimes my phone says, "Your current location is less than half a mile away." The accompanying graphic is an even-colored light blue indicating open water. There's a tiny arrow in the middle, a directive that represents me and my orientation, a little pirogue spinning in a borderless canal.

In Houston, where I now live and teach, my GPS always depicts solid land. The streets all have names, which seem to give them permanence. There's always land down there somewhere, even under the floodwaters of Hurricane Harvey. The egrets mostly stick to the bayous, whether cement-sloped or not, and black top and pavement don't collect much water until they suddenly, often quite suddenly, do. Then the water elicits a response the way some guests do at a parade-route Mardi Gras party: A few you don't expect show up, and then more and then more, and soon your bathroom looks like the Fairgrounds. You tape a

"Turn around, don't drown" sign on the keg, but within minutes the black Marks-A-Lot is streaking from the masking tape and is trampled on the ground.

It's not always as clear in Houston how much we depend on water. In Galveston and all along the Gulf Coast, trawlers dump nets of seafood that feed many. The Houston Ship Channel, hidden to most of us, launches and docks ocean-going vessels vital to the commerce of the region and to the entire country. Houstonians depend on the faucet, it sometimes seems, disconnected from the water it delivers. In the big city, even images of a burning house focus on the firefighters, but seldom the water. Then a drought descends (as began in 2010): tens of thousands of trees die; even the old oaks brown. Where's the rain?, we ask. Where's that rain that ruined my engine, that fell through the New Year's bullet holes in my roof? Water washes in the green and the nutrients, and then it rushes in toxins and filth. Water is indifferent. Water shares the good and the bad of the strata it flows through. It does not discriminate, but we do.

As the Tao says, water does not disdain the low places. It really doesn't. It seeks them out like some seek out the front row. We would be well served to be like the Tao: live close to the ground, keep to the simple, which is the true meaning of humility. We all know the problem: water is humble, and too few of us are. Too many people have been nudged off ridges and pushed to live on floodplains or in channels that run near levees and dams. Levees will eventually be breached. Sometimes they will be blown open like the fragile walls of the heart. Sometimes some hubristic surgeon will open the valves.

Really, there are just too many of us, but first we think, "There's too much water." Ice that melts becomes water, and eventually that water becomes steam. Humans don't really become anything. We lack the dynamic. What we prefer is irrelevant, though. Nature will restore a balance, in its own time and its own way, without discrimination.

The Hebrew Bible tells us God sent a flood as punishment for human bad behavior. Most cultures have retained a similar story. The Great Flood reveals our human will to survive and the need to share our lifeboat even with brown recluse spiders, water moccasins, and roaches. (I doubt we'd have a choice about the tree roaches.) The flood obscures the *why*'s for the necessary solidarity: regardless of our hierarchical preferences, the fire ants still float on top.

We call the east side of the hurricane "the dirty side" because it shoves up the greatest tidal surge. It's often destructive beyond what's ripped apart by the eye wall. It's dirty, unlike a Bombay Sapphire martini, though. We call that dirty, and then we drink it.

My East End neighborhood did not flood during Hurricane Harvey. It was built on mud dredged during the ship channel's construction, creating a human-made ridge. It was a short walk downtown to the Convention Center when my friend and I finally ventured out. I mostly sat with people who live outside, frustrated with FEMA because they were told they hadn't lost anything they owned and therefore were not eligible for assistance. If you sleep under an overpass, that is your home; and your home was flooded. Did no one suffer the loss of our Texas turnarounds because they belong to all of us, so they belong to none of us?

I sometimes wonder whether Mary Shelley intended us to heed her warning in *Frankenstein* or just hoped to reveal our true essence. Literary historians tell us Mary Shelley wrote a horror story. Perhaps it was meant only to scare us with a reflection of our grotesque insatiability, not as a cautionary lesson with hope of our conversion. We may delude ourselves for a while trying to control nature. Ancient thinking may encourage us to adopt a creed of toxic Prometheanism, but in the end we will fail and die. We can believe this agon is fated and serves some purpose, that wild, unrealistic aspiration is part of human nature. After all, we got thrown out of the Garden; but rather than learn from our mistakes, we have enshrined them.

Shouldn't we try to restore harmony as Phyllis Trible argues in *God and the Rhetoric of Sexuality*, an ecofeminist reading of Genesis and the Song of Songs?[1] The woman and creation are rib-level partners to *adom* (not Adam, but a sex-unspecified "earth creature." "Man" is a different word in Hebrew; Adam is a poor translation of a word that appears nowhere else in the Biblical text. [I could go on]). The woman is a helper to *adom*, but not subservient. (God also is called a "helper" elsewhere is Genesis.) Song of Songs restores the power balance between man, woman, and creation lost in the Fall.

Maybe keeping to the low place is meant to be purely metaphoric, literal only if you are water. Simone Weil writes, "The evil lying in at the handle of the sword is transmitted to the point."[2] Fighting for the highlands doesn't sound compassionate or productive. Sharing the land with all life, even water moccasins and sage grouses, will require sharing the ridges. We will need help relocating and having our needs met while grieving our ancestral homes. Some places *will* go back to swamps, marshes, and open water whether people drown there or not.

Given our habit of planning without establishing trust, the map of harmony will be a difficult one to draw. It will require a committee that meets often and in person. (Nature will be the final cartographer and on its own schedule.) There will need to be Noahs and Mary Shelleys, residents of every topography, and a recognition that Houstonians, Staten Islanders, Floridians, Louisianans, and Californians face the same challenges. We would do well to share our mistakes and ideas. After generations suffering loss in the lowlands, some will have a hard time accepting Simone Weil's warning; but hers may be the most important message. Shifting us around high to low, low to high, privilege turned to preference, preference to privilege is like bailing water with a colander, from the long point of view. Even if the servants get moved to the staterooms, the crew to the promenade, the elites to the watertight compartments, the ship is still going down.

Out my window now are the egrets. I see them clearly, chasing each other and ruffling their plumage. I choose to be here, telling myself I am keeping my little parcel free from any further development until it falls into the Gulf. For those without good choices, I owe much empathy. I have enjoyed much because others have had little, and some have profited from my lacks as well. We need to fill our lowest places with more mercy and generosity, or we will repeat a past that has never stopped being our present.

MEANDER BELT

⬤ FLOODPLAIN

⬤ 100-YEAR FLOODPLAIN

⬤ PARKS

☐ WASTEWATER TREATMENT FACILITY

HOUSTON'S THIRTY-NINE WASTEWATER TREATMENT PLANTS ARE LOCATED SO CLOSE TO ITS BAYOUS AND PARKS THAT SPILLAGE FROM THESE PLANTS AS A RESULT OF FLOODING CAN HAVE ADVERSE EFFECTS ON THE HEALTH OF PEOPLE AND BIOMES ON A BACTERIAL LEVEL, AS SEEN IN WATER TESTS AFTER HARVEY.

DESIGN BY PARICHAT KITTIKORNMETA, CLARISSE PINTO, AND ANNETTE WONG

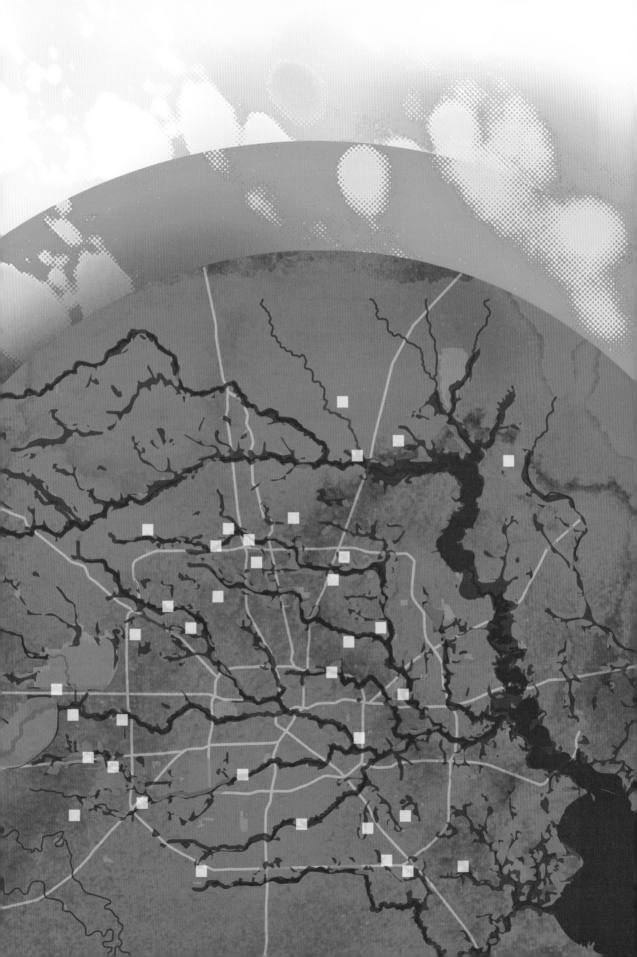

Meander Belt

A NATIVE HOUSTONIAN
REFLECTS ON WATER

Elaine Shen

My aspiration to become a marine biologist is a paradox. My first conceptions of the ocean were formed through weekly fishing trips with my father on rocky jetties along the Gulf of Mexico, oftentimes with offshore oil platforms and commercial ships in sight. The industrialization of Houston's waterways—starting from the bayous running through the center of downtown and flowing into the Houston Ship Channel that connects us to the rest of the world—was commonplace and normal to me. As a kid, I focused mainly on the excitement of feeling a bite on the other end of my fishing line, pulses of underwater life that I couldn't directly access otherwise. On our car rides home, I didn't question whether the Oz-like smokestacks rising above the illuminated Energy Corridor belonged on the landscape—it was just a secondary skyline that I accepted as part of the view. These trips fueled my family with a fresh source of seafood, cooked with passed-down Chinese recipes, as well as my fascination with the ocean, manifested in many school projects in elementary school.

My familiarity with the Gulf Coast never coupled with awe as I grew older. The more I studied marine biology, the more contrast I saw between the murky brown waters of Galveston and the breathtaking images of tropical coral reefs elsewhere in the world. As a result, I rarely thought of the Gulf Coast in the context of marine biodiversity and conservation; the two ideas seemed incompatible, given that I never saw them discussed together. I daydreamed about the time when I could finally start seriously pursuing my interest in marine biology . . . somewhere *else*, a picturesque marine ecosystem deemed worthy of investigation, attention, and admiration from scientists and nature television shows alike.

Fishing is just one example of how my relationship to Houston is an awkward contradiction. Until this past year, I have lived the majority of my life within a five-mile radius of the Texas Medical Center. Even when I felt the most claustrophobic in Houston (senior year of high school, at the cusp of freedom from my parents), I still chose to attend Rice University, just fifteen minutes from my parents' house. I thought I'd have a home-court advantage: I was a local Museum District/Chinatown expert and eager to give restaurant and coffee shop recommendations to my non-Houstonian friends. Very quickly, however, I realized that sharing these personally meaningful places opened them up to external evaluation. I attributed a lot of my sense of self to Houston and was quick to defend the city against its critics, who cited more exciting, more progressive, more indescribably cool venues in their own hometowns and travels.

I felt less equipped to justify my love for my hometown in my classes at Rice University, where professors from all over the world gazed upon Houston as an academic subject. In the classroom, I couldn't fight facts with my personal experience. My environmental science courses all focused on Houston's prolific petroleum industries and their undeniable impact on local and global issues, especially those related to environmental justice and climate change.[1] For the first time, I was asked to critically evaluate my hometown rather than simply live in it. In one of my introductory environmental science classes, for example, we were asked to write a review of the Wiess Energy Hall in the Houston Museum of Natural Science (HMNS). This should have been simple for me, as I could've navigated the museum's halls blindfolded after the countless visits with my parents and on various school field trips. But the tone of the assignment wasn't to re-create the sense of wonder I had had in grade school—it was to notice that the most well-funded exhibit in the museum was sponsored by big oil and, unsurprisingly, left out any mention of human-mediated climate change. In another class, I visited the town of Manchester, a low-income, largely Latino neighborhood surrounded by industrial petrochemical complexes and the Houston Ship Channel. These residents live their daily lives across the street from a Valero refinery plant that regularly emits toxic pollutants into the air, resulting in elevated rates of cancer, leukemia, and other fatal health conditions.[2] This same class took me on an excruciatingly boring tour of ExxonMobil's refinery, in which our tour guide skillfully avoided answering any questions about climate change and redirected our attention to recent advancements in petroleum engineering. These field trips were both eye-opening and emotionally exhausting: on each ride back to campus, an overwhelming guilt came over me for being a proud Houstonian. My upper-middle-class privilege and, more importantly, the consequences of it were on full display. I felt both ignorant and complicit in these injustices as I saw how entangled with big oil (my) daily life in Houston had become.

During one semester at Rice, as I was shopping around for study abroad programs in the tropics (where the *real* nature was), I half-heartedly accepted a research project that involved analyzing underwater images of a decommissioned oil platform located one hundred nautical miles from Galveston. This platform, HI-A-389A, was installed by ExxonMobil in 1981, acquired by W&T Offshore, Inc. in 2002, and continued to extract petroleum from the seafloor until 2012. It is within the boundaries of the Flower Garden Banks National Marine Sanctuary, one of the National Oceanic and Atmospheric Administration's fourteen federally designated marine protected areas and the only one in the Gulf.[3] Just a mile away from the platform is the East Flower Garden Bank, one of the two major reefs in the sanctuary that sit above a unique salt dome system found nowhere else on the Gulf Coast. These reefs were discovered only in the 1960s, when marine biologists were still debating whether or not Texas reefs even existed. My project was to add to a different debate: whether or not the defunct oil platform should stay as an artificial reef with Texas Parks and Wildlife's Rigs-to-Reefs program despite its proximity (and potential threat) to a nearby natural reef ecosystem.

The steel beams, a rare source of hard substrate in an otherwise muddy seafloor, were unrecognizable—over the past forty-plus years, layers of algae and invertebrates had encrusted them, competing for shallow-water real estate. The colorful but invasive Indo-Pacific cup coral dominated in some areas, likely carried from the ballast water of commercial ships on their way to the Houston Ship Channel. Even though I knew from my own experiences fishing in the Gulf that life did in fact thrive there, I didn't realize the extent to which it was teeming with biodiversity. This conundrum of life successfully living on in spite of the human-made intrusions made the debate of removing the platform convoluted. Because of the marine life it has been accumulating, including large schools of fish and sharks, this platform served an important role for the local community as a unique recreational dive site and fishing ground. On the other hand, there was a threat of oil leaks and the spread of invasive species, not to mention the permanent damage the platform would inflict if a natural disaster were to dislodge it from its place. Since my project was an indirect contribution, I found out later that the platform was approved for Texas Parks and Wildlife's Rigs-to-Reefs program, which required the removal of the top sixty-five feet of the platform so that the structure sat safely below the water's surface.[4] This policy, like living in Houston, was about making the best of the local physical realities of big oil despite the obvious contradiction it represents.

A more conspicuous example of this contradiction is Houston's bayou system. When Houston was established at the confluence of Buffalo Bayou and White Oak Bayou in 1836, Buffalo Bayou was designated as a commercial trading route, but White Oak Bayou was left untouched to be enjoyed for its natural beauty and lushness. While Buffalo Bayou was getting dredged in preparation for its large role in making Houston a major port city, early descriptions of White Oak are hardly recognizable now: there used to be a saloon and hotel next to its banks near today's Stude Park, and residents would visit and drink from its various springs and enjoy its swimming holes as a reprieve from early industrial life. Eventually, industrialization (especially after the 1901 oil boom) caught up with White Oak and reached its peak when intense flooding in 1929 and 1935 prompted the district and the Army Corps of Engineers to channelize Houston's bayous and streams. By 1960, almost all flowing waterways in the city had had some form of human intervention, be it widening, deepening, straightening, or paving over existing waterways with concrete.[5]

The exceptions were a choice few that were saved by the conservationist Terry Hershey in 1966 when she created what is now known as the Bayou Preservation Association. Very few natural riparian ecosystems remain, but Terry's initial fight against the channelization of the bayous started an environmental consciousness in Houston that has led to renovation and habitat restoration projects all along the bayous.[6]

Now, these bayous are reconceptualized as "greenways" that we eas-ily recognize all over the city as recreational running trails and picnic spots. These great turnovers and changes to the bayous' landscape don't happen in favor of industrialization anymore—development projects hardly reach the scale that they did before, and instead focus on intro-ducing more green spaces for the public to enjoy. Large oil execs are now making philanthropic donations in public-private initiatives that have the goal of creating more accessible green spaces in Houston's most forward-facing areas, which undoubtedly benefits the local com-munities that live there. However, these same powerful figures are the ones responsible for environmental injustice elsewhere in the city, where no amount of landscaping can adequately greenwash decades of corruption, toxic pollution, and fatal health problems.[7]

But on a typical run along Buffalo Bayou in my neighborhood, none of these injustices are apparent. It's hard to remember to see something so commonplace in my life as having a complicated history filled with generations of exploitation of people and the natural world. After seeing concrete rivers my whole life, I was immune to this feature that makes my upbringing in Houston different from everywhere else. Like most people, I did not spend that much time dwelling on the built environ-ment around me; it hardly changed on a daily basis, and my thoughts were spent reflecting on the constantly changing other worlds. That is, until a disturbance finally brought the Houston I knew out of equilib-rium and into the national news cycle.

To say the least, Hurricane Harvey reinforced my belief in the power of water. It is still difficult to describe how jarring it was to watch the endless rain, rising waterline of the bayous, and news reports of sub-merged neighborhoods. Like many others around Houston, my par-ents' home was very close to flooding, but it was ultimately spared. I will never forget the images of downtown Houston underwater; the build-ings that once seemed like the most defining and permanent fixtures of Houston were surrendering control to the rising tide. All I could do was watch, grieving the loss of stability in the human-made infrastructure I once thought of as invincible.

Even our water infrastructure, the third largest in the United States, wasn't enough to handle the one-thousand-year storm. Houston's bay-ous are another familiar backdrop to the daily human functions that occur around them, nothing to gawk at on their own anymore. These once naturally lush slow-moving streams had their fate determined by rapid urbanization, which channelized, widened, deepened, and paved over them in the name of flood control—but all of this engineering was no match for an extreme storm like Hurricane Harvey. During Harvey, seven out of thirty-nine wastewater treatment plants flooded and spilled raw sewage into the bayous, making their way into the streets and homes of thousands of Houstonians.[8] When Harvey floodwaters were sampled from the bayous, streets, and inside homes, fecal indicator bacteria (like *E. coli*) and genetic sources of antibacterial resistance were well beyond the concentration that is considered safe for direct human contact by the EPA.[9] Heavy rainfall and flooding events like these in urban areas are the main cause of waterborne disease outbreaks, which we know from the presence of pathogenic microbes that begin to proliferate. These floodwaters eventually emptied into the Gulf, bringing along with them 149 million gallons of raw sewage, industrial discharge, and chemical spills from over one hundred companies.[10] Some of that toxic waste reached as far as the Flower Garden Banks, flooding the sponges with microbes and human pathogens.[11] Though the long-term impacts of this storm runoff on the reef are uncertain, it is clear that water carries the effects of onshore activities out to offshore ecosystems. For me, if I were to go out fishing in the Gulf now like I did as a girl, I'd think twice about eating anything I caught.

As Houstonians raced to their neighbors' aid during the days that followed the storm, I could not help but feel a sense of pride. The many local volunteering efforts showed the true resilience and spirit of Houston and reminded me, after a long period of disenchantment with it, why I loved the city so much. But once life returned mostly back to normal, an eviler undertone revealed itself. Eventually, as I reflected on the aftermath of Harvey, I couldn't help but think that we should have seen this kind of a storm brewing, given the disproportionate and obvious impact Houston's businesses play in climate change. We live uniquely at the visible intersection of climate cause and effect—how will we grapple with that? It seems only appropriate that our entanglement with big oil has to be accepted as a major part of Houston's fabric as well.

At the same time, we are not the only ones to blame. Everyone is entangled with big oil, even the most passionate advocates for the environment, even if our landscapes don't always remind us of that fact. I wanted to outright reject the parts of my upbringing that did not fit into a typical ecologists' coming-of-age experience with nature, but I could not bring myself to ignore the joy I had felt being a sprightly young fisherwoman or inquisitive museum guest. Though I still feel an inner turmoil about the institutional powers that made my childhood possible, I am happy to accept the fact that I am, and will always be, a walking hypocrite of an environmentalist. To me, being a hypocrite is what's normal in this rapidly changing and petroleum-filled world—not the "wild" landscapes that are sold to us as devoid of human influence. It means that we are able to mull over what came before us and shapes us, an act of caring for the places that initially gave us our sense of being. Even though I thought I knew Houston so well by the simple fact of being a Houstonian, I've recognized that it is impossible for me to fully comprehend the essence of any place. Rather, I should be open to renegotiating my relationship with my home rather than stubbornly grasping onto a false sense of homegrown expertise. How we relate to the environment is perhaps more explicit here than in other places. It gives us an opportunity to see our realities, and we shouldn't take that for granted.

ALLISON

OMBRO*phobia* (FEAR OF RAIN)

Cheryl Beckett

HARVEY

harvey

Over sixty hurricanes have made landfall on the Texas Gulf Coast since 1850. I moved to Houston in the late 1980s, at the beginning of a period when hurricanes spared the city for an entire decade. Hurricanes were not a big concern in my early years in Texas; the big concerns were the lack of zoning, the oil bust, congested roadways, and the fight over the proposed MetroRail. **The Great Storm** of 1900 in Galveston seemed a long-ago tragedy of little relevance [Category 4 hurricane caused more than 6,000 fatalities, most due to a fifteen-foot storm surge].[1] **Alicia (1983)** [Category 3 hurricane sent a ten-foot surge of water inland, killed twenty-one people, and caused about $5 billion in damages][2] was before my time. In 1994, my husband and I purchased a "bungalow on blocks" in Woodland Heights. Although its elevation played no part in our decision to buy this house, it saved us when Tropical Storm **Allison (2001)** hit Houston. The storm dumped over thirty-five inches of rain in a six-day period; some areas received twenty-eight inches in one day. [Twenty-two fatalities, 95,000 damaged vehicles, 73,000 damaged residences, 30,000 residents moved to shelters, more than $5 billion in property damage][3] We waded through the streets in torrential rain to check White Oak Bayou as it inched its way, block by block, closer to our house. At daybreak, I-10 and the bayou were one giant waterway whose depth was suggested by totally submerged semis. Weeks of news coverage reported losses—people, property, and infrastructure. The high water created a real possibility of drowning while commuting to work. I began carrying a ball peen hammer in my car, before buying a Seatbelt Cutter/Window Breaker/ Emergency Escape Tool. [The "Turn Around, Don't Drown" campaign was launched on May 22, 2003.][4]

New Orleans bore the brunt of **Katrina (2005)**. [Eighty percent of New Orleans underwater, 1,833 fatalities, and $108 billion in damages][5] Houston took in about 250,000 residents in the aftermath, and Houstonians believed officials when they concluded that what stranded tens of thousands in New Orleans's Superdome for over a week was residents' "failure to evacuate." [Fifty levees failed and 400,000 people were permanently displaced.][6] When **Rita (2005)** took aim at Houston two weeks later, residents evacuated, a mass migration that caused its own disasters. [Approximately 2.7 million Houston-area residents evacuated, and more than one hundred evacuation-related fatalities][7] Some families and pets were stuck on freeways for thirty-six hours in 100° heat. At 3:00 a.m. at a gas station off of I-10, I learned that the line between civility

KATRINA

·IKE
ike

NEW ORLEANS

HOUSTON

FAY

ALLISON 2001

ALICIA

HUMBERTO

GRACE

HARVEY 2017

CLAUDETTE

66

AUDREY

and anarchy is very thin. Although it took four hours to go five miles, we did not run out of gas and did not have to join the people forced to camp in Walmart parking lots. Stay or go, go or stay. Rita turned at the last minute and hit Louisiana instead. Three years later, **Ike** (2008) didn't turn, and the coast took a direct hit. [Highest storm surge recorded on Galveston Island since 1915, 110 mph sustained wind, $27 billion in damages][8] The storm surge scattered tanker trucks full of gas and oil onto highways and sent families to their rooftops through holes punched through attics. Our friend's bay area house imploded from that surge, while our 100-year-old garage apartment swayed but stayed. The storm inspired "Ike Dike" proposals, a seventy-mile coastal barrier to protect our port and petrochemical industry. The "Ike Dike" received a $31 billion go-ahead from the Army Corps of Engineers in 2018. Like the seventeen-foot seawall built after the 1900 Galveston hurricane, each big storm inspires infrastructural solutions.

Though we enjoyed another quiet stretch after Ike, we remained fearful; "Storm Season" carried an ominous tone. Just when we let our guard down, storms returned in quick succession. Flood maps were revised, the 100-year floodplain erased as 500-year storm levels were reached by the **Tax Day Flood** (2016). [Over fifteen inches of rain fell in twelve hours, making it a 500- to 1,000-year rainfall.][9] Just over a month later the **Memorial Day Flood** (2016) hit. [Eleven inches over twelve hours, 531 water rescues][10] Then came **Harvey** (2017), and Harvey was catastrophic. [One trillion gallons of rainwater fell across Harris County in four days, covering the county's 1,800 square miles with an average of thirty-three inches of water; 120,000 structures flooded, $125 billion in damages and 106 fatalities][11] Yet even as some homeowners felt they had escaped, the literal floodgates were opened when water was released from reservoirs that were unfortunately surrounded by houses built too close by developers that did not care about future ramifications.

BERTHA

EDOUARD

DEAN

BONNIE

ANDREW

FELICE

IVAN

KATRINA 2005

RITA 2005

THE GREAT STORM

IKE 2008

GUSTAV

CINDY

IVAN

CAMILLE

HILDA

CARLA

HOUSTON

500-YEAR-FLOOD MAP

100-YEAR-FLOOD MAP

BAYOUS OUT-OF-BANK

CATEGORY 1

CATEGORY 2

CATEGORY 3

CATEGORY 4

CATEGORY 5

DIRTY SIDE OF THE STORM

DETENTION POND

EYE

EVACUATION MAP BY ZIP CODE

FLOOD GAUGES

FLOOD MITIGATION

FLOODPLAIN

FLASH FLOOD WARNINGS

HIGH WATER LOCATIONS

HURRICANE SEASON

We witnessed the futility of miles of bayou projects meant to mitigate flooding. So in addition to detention basins and making the bayous wider and deeper, homes will be moved. [Project Brays expects to remove 15,000 houses; remaining homes should take on less water after the project is completed; homes that took on four feet during a 100-year storm may now expect two feet.][12]

In 2019, on the two-year anniversary of Harvey, local media discussed whether Houston was more prepared. The answer was "no." Shortly after, we took our students to Rockport, Texas, to study coastal wetland bird migrations and see the effects of Harvey. Leaving town, we barely escaped **Imelda (2019)**, which crept up almost unannounced. [National Weather Service predicted tropical storm status only two days before landfall; forty inches of rain in fourty-eight hours in some areas; four major floods in five years.][13] We raced out of the city with Imelda following close behind.

Our reference points to named storms shift too quickly. "What happened to you during Allison?" That once-in-a-lifetime storm was replaced by Ike, then Harvey. It's a disaster roll call, or maybe an honor roll for those of us who have the dubious distinction of having survived storms whose names are retired from the six-year rotation due to their disastrous impact. [In the 1950s, meteorologists replaced the system of latitude-longitude numbers with peoples' name because they were easier to remember.][14] We remember the names of the storms, and all the loss that's too big to name.

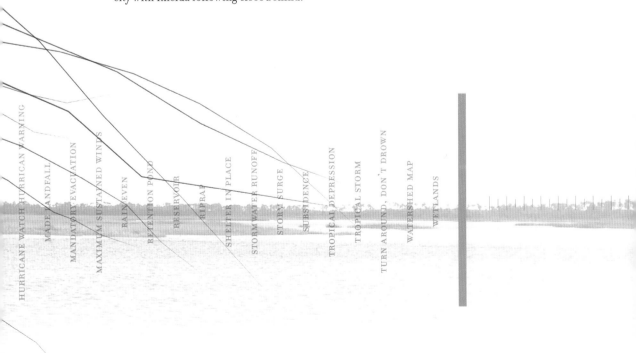

MEMORIAL DRIVE

BUFFALO BAYOU

ALLEN PARKWAY

FREEDMEN'S TOWN
4TH WARD YOUTH CENTER

FREEDMEN'S TOWN
ASSOCIATION

THE RUTHERFORD B. H. YATES MUSEUM,
FOUNDED IN THE COMMUNITY IN 1996,
CONTINUES TO WORK TODAY TO SAVE THE
HOUSES AND BRICK-PAVED STREETS LAID OUT
BY FREEDMEN IN THE 1860S FROM FURTHER
DESTRUCTION AND REDEVELOPMENT.

45

THE AFRICAN
AMERICAN LIBRARY

TAFT STREET

BAGBY STREET

REGULATORY FLOODWAY

SPECIAL FLOOD HAZARD AREA

0.2% ANNUAL CHANCE
FLOOD HAZARD

FREEDMEN'S TOWN HOLDS HISTORICAL AND CULTURAL RELEVANCE FOR THE
HOUSTON AFRICAN AMERICAN COMMUNITY. HOWEVER, ITS PROXIMITY TO THE
BAYOU'S FLOODWAY ZONES, AS WELL AS DOWNTOWN HOUSTON'S EVERGROWING
DEVELOPMENT, PUTS THIS AREA'S RESIDENTS AND HISTORY AT RISK OF BEING
OVERTAKEN BY EITHER UNPREDICTABLE WEATHER OR BY CITY EXPANSION.

DESIGN BY JULIA ONG

The Task in Front of Us

A CONVERSATION WITH RAJ MANKAD

Lacy M. Johnson

I first met Raj Mankad when he and I were both graduate students in the University of Houston's Creative Writing Program. I became a quick and early fan of his essays and his range, writing as passionately about the experience of finding grubs in his backyard compost pile as about the then decaying Astrodome. Since that time, Raj has gone on to work as the managing editor for the journal *Feminist Economics*, and then from 2008 to 2019, he served as editor of *Cite: The Architecture + Design Review of Houston*, where he frequently contributed articles about flooding, public housing, and transportation. His insistence on writing from the perspective of someone walking or taking a bus often reveals the injustice inherent in seemingly neutral infrastructure and a joy in resisting it. In 2013, he launched a petition for a Sunday Streets program and led volunteers to support its successful launch by the city. He is currently the op-ed editor for the *Houston Chronicle*, a Next City Vanguard Fellow, and a Senior Fellow of the American Leadership Forum. He has taught at the University of Houston Gerald D. Hines College of Architecture and Design and has served on the jury for Preservation Houston's Good Brick Awards. I spoke with Raj over Zoom in early 2021 about Houston's troublesome history, the relationship of flooding to suburban development, and the kind of bold vision our city needs for the future. Our conversation has been edited for length and clarity.

LMJ: Before you started at *Cite*, you had already been thinking quite a lot about the built environment. Will you tell us about how your background informed your work at *Cite* and your thinking about Houston?

RM: I grew up in Mobile, Alabama, which is in a really similar geographic position to Houston. It's also on a bay, and it frequently gets hit by hurricanes. Mobile is older than Houston, and it has a longer pre–civil war history, and that history is more visible in the built environment than in Houston. The legacy of enslavement is thick in the air. It is a historical present.

My parents, both physicians, moved there in the 1970s when I was two. People like my parents got steered into this new postwar west side section of Mobile with these little cul-de-sac houses. The realtors didn't take my parents to see the antebellum homes with the live oaks in the old part of Mobile. My father was a sickle cell physician, so he specialized in serving the Black community. The hospital was in a Black neighborhood, and it was just a couple of blocks from where a young man, Michael Donald, was lynched in 1981 and hung from a tree.

The way I experience the world, it's very much defined by that experience in Alabama, where the whole world was divided by this Black-and-white binary and the tremendous amount of racism and oppression, and by my not really fitting into that binary and moving back and forth across it, and the way you could feel that in the physical environment.

LMJ: You also spent some time volunteering in India with women's cooperatives in rural villages, and I imagine that time also shaped your thinking about the built environment, but in a different way. Can you speak to that?

RM: Yes. I always think about that because the area where my family is from is a salt desert.

I took a short leave from graduate school at the University of Houston and went back to live where my grandfather was born in this town called Dhrangadhra, where the water only ran in the pipes for about thirty minutes a day. Every house has this tank and it fills up for the thirty minutes—hopefully. Then you have to go outside and you have to get this pump working and pump the water up onto the roof. You have to be really conservative about how much water you use the rest of the day. For me, having lived there and having come from that tradition, water is sacred. Rain is a gift. It doesn't matter how much suffering and how many floods I see here in Houston, I still see water as a resource, as something to revere and to value. I can't shake that. Even in the middle of Harvey I still felt that way. I think I moved to Houston because I wanted to be here. I wanted to be with the rain.

LMJ: When did you move to Houston?

RM: In 2001. I moved here the week or so after Tropical Storm Allison hit. I missed the storm itself, but there were huge piles of sheetrock everywhere. At UH, the Roy Cullen Building had flooded. People were teaching out of trailers.

LMJ: One of the reasons for this project is that I think Houston is in denial about its history of flooding, and maybe that's partly because so many people are moving to Houston every year—some years as many as 100,000 people have moved to Houston. The laws here are such that landlords are not required to disclose to tenants if a property has flooded in the past, and so there's constant learning that happens. I wonder, then, if you can speak a little bit to what you have learned about flooding in this region as a result of your work at *Cite*?

RM: Yes. There's so much to say. On the one hand, this region has always flooded. Even to talk about it as flooding is a little bit disingenuous. It becomes flooding when we decide to settle it in a certain way. The very earliest accounts of Houston involve epic amounts of water and just miles and miles of inundated land.

And yet, a lot of the decisions made now around federal recovery funding are based on cost-benefit analysis, and that cost-benefit analysis isn't based on the history of the land, but on the value of the property. You can have two identical houses, but if one house is in a high-value neighborhood, then the cost-benefit analysis will steer money to benefiting that neighborhood even if the houses are completely identical.[1]

The thing that makes one house less valuable than an identical house in another neighborhood often comes back to racism. It's built into mathematical equations. If you just print out the piece of paper and you read it, you won't see the inequality, you won't see the human side of it. That is the defining issue with flooding and hurricanes: its disparate impact, the way that the disasters accelerate and amplify the processes that are already unequal, that already produce unequal outcomes for low-income people, especially Black and Brown folks.

LMJ: You can look at the numbers and pretend that numbers are neutral, but of course, how those numbers are generated is informed by all the things that we carry with us.

RM: Yes. There was one time I went to the Harris County Flood Control District, and they had these wall-sized computer screens. They showed me the actual maps of whose houses had flooded—the maps the public is not allowed to see. It was so bad. It was so much worse than I thought. It was all over the whole region. I was like, "Wait, what? That house, that house, that entire neighborhood?" It was so bad. When they were showing us the Mid-Brays area, we were like, "That should all be bought out. Nobody should live there." Every single house was red. He said something along the lines of "That's a no-go." We can't even touch that. There's no discussion of buying those people out because of a whole range of reasons, but partly the money and the political clout.

On the one hand, the Army Corps of Engineers is more likely to invest hundreds of millions of dollars to widen bayous and raise bridges to reduce flooding for a wealthier, whiter neighborhood. FEMA and insurers are more likely to pay homeowners in those neighborhoods enough to repair their homes. On the other hand, in the low-income neighborhoods, the government is more likely to buy out homes.

After Harvey hit, or while Harvey was hitting—because it was unfolding over weeks and weeks, as you know—we put together a special issue of *Cite*. For the piece I contributed I just tried to bring together all the recommendations about flooding, all the smart proposals that had been put on the table, and just make a one-page list and try to make sense of them and group them. When I went through that exercise, the glaring omission from the list was a comprehensive approach to the shape of our built and natural environment.

There were all these specific proposals like, "Okay, we should require that all new houses or rebuilt houses be a certain number of feet above such and such base flood elevation." It's definitely a good idea. There was a proposal to widen or deepen bayous or build a new reservoir. But what nobody was really putting on the table was a plan for the region as a whole, for making decisions about where people could live, and what areas not to develop.

In the next year, a lot of the proposals on that list were actually put into practice. The city and the county passed new regulations that had been proposed before Harvey but were at that time considered infeasible, like treating the 500-year floodplain as the standard instead of the 100-year floodplain, which is a really big deal. It has massive financial consequences for thousands of people. It changes the math for developers.

It's a really amazing thing that those regulations got changed, and it will have a meaningful impact decades from now. With those higher standards in place, the next time a Harvey hits, a lot of those houses will be amphibious. They'll be surrounded by water for a few hours or maybe for a few days or weeks, but the drywall and the couch and the carpets will be dry, the people inside will be safe if they can stay inside without getting hurt. That's all good. But our inability and unwillingness to make a comprehensive plan and carry out actual urban design mean we'll go on having this disparate impact. The people who have the resources to make a plan for where they live, they'll do that. They'll hire an architect or an urban planner, and their hopes and dreams will get incorporated into policy, often in ways that aren't explicit or transparent to normal people. The people who don't have the resources to hire a professional to lobby the Texas Department of Transportation or Harris County Flood Control District, they are left in the gaps.

You have other cities and other regions where Black and low-income people were much more explicitly zoned into hazardous conditions. But we end up having many of the same or worse outcomes because lack of planning, weak regulation, and cost of property all work in concert with the history of white supremacy in this region.

LMJ: Will you say more about that?

RM: Well, like right now I'm reading *Seeds of Empire* by Andrew J. Torget. It's a history of the way the cotton economy created the conditions for the colonization of Texas by English-speaking Anglo people who brought enslaved people with them, and the degree to which the Stephen Austin settlement and then the Texas Revolution were all profoundly wrapped up in the cotton economy and the enslavement that made the cotton economy possible. That is something that Texans just haven't reckoned with. In Alabama, there was no illusion.

Like I was saying earlier, you don't really feel the presence of that history here, not the same way that you do in Mobile. I don't really want that psychic burden on me all the time, but not having that constant visual reminder has the drawback of people behaving and living and voting and making decisions as if it never happened, as if this part of Texas wasn't settled through enslavement.

LMJ: I think we see that history in Houston's geography as well. I'm sure you've seen those maps of Houston's diameter over the years, how at one time "Houston" was just basically what we now understand as downtown. Freedmen's Town was on land that tended to flood and that whites did not want to settle. Later, Independence Heights, a city established and governed by African Americans, was annexed by Houston and sliced and diced by the Texas Department of Transportation's highways that blocked the outflow of water. Part of the neighborhood was turned into a flood pool by the highway. It's really hard to tease all of this apart, the way that racism is so integral to how we relate to the actual land on which we live. That what we're seeing with flooding is the consequence of white supremacy, the idea that we can build wherever and extract whatever we want.

RM: Yes. I think of all cities, you could argue that Houston is an expression of neoliberal capitalism, where everything is monetized and there's no other narrative to the city. It was established by real estate speculators. It's not like Philadelphia; there's no other story to it. It's not like Salt Lake City or any of these cities that were established by religious idealists. No, Houston doesn't have a soul to lose unless you consider the soul to be speculative real estate development. The logic of it is given so much force, and there are so few limits that it feels as if the city is capitalism's greatest expression.

But it's also disempowering to think about it that way. Let's go back for a second to *Seeds of Empire*. When [Stephen F.] Austin came and he got his land grant from the Spanish government and then from Mexico, he sent out his advertisements to potential colonists saying the settlers would get extra land if they brought enslaved people with them.

At that time, there was a major anti-slavery movement all around the world that was picking up steam. The Mexican Revolution had these ideals of freedom and liberty, and there was a big push within Mexico for abolition. But Stephen Austin, and the Tejanos that were his allies, spent years lobbying the Mexican government to allow slavery in Texas so that they could keep encouraging these plantation developments.

I'll get back to the contemporary connection in a moment, but the political argument they were making was, "Okay, just let Texas establish for itself whether it's going to have its slavery or not. Then if people in Central Mexico don't want slavery, people could abolish it there." Basically, that became the logic behind the American Civil War. The argument for local control was, to a large extent, about enslavement.

What we see now is the decentralization and weakening of government and pushing regulation down to its most local parts, that same distrust for central planning and urban design and collective thinking about the built environment, and that attitude is part of that history, the history of enslavement and then Jim Crow. It is a pattern of putting profit over people, especially people of color.

LMJ: That makes me wonder, do you think there is a way to incorporate justice into how a city is built and planned? Can the ideals of justice and equality be retrofitted onto a city that's already been built?

RM: That's the question. That's a great question. Yes, there is. After Harvey, the Rice Design Alliance brought this guy, Henk Ovink, to Houston for a civic forum. He's the Special Envoy for International Water Affairs for the Kingdom of the Netherlands. People hold up the Dutch in a lot of different ways. Sometimes they say, "Look at their big engineering projects. They built this giant wall to hold the water back with these cool gates."

The Dutch have solved the surge tide issues, and they're certainly proud of that engineering, but the thing that they're dealing with now, and the reason why they were so eager to learn from people in Houston, is that they're really worried about flooding from rain and flooding from the rivers that flow into the Netherlands. Instead of trying to use big engineering to conquer the water, they've been trying this approach that they call "making room for the river."

In a way, Houston's been pursuing that strategy, without admitting to itself that that's what it's doing, because after Allison, Houston secured a bunch of money to buy up land along the bayous and buy out houses and expand the space along the bayous. They were still in an engineering frame of mind, but a ton of federal money started pouring into the Harris County Flood Control District, which is like the local arm of the Army Corps of Engineers.

There were urban planners and parks advocates who understood the opportunity there. They proposed a park system to be overlaid on these expanded bayous, but the rhetoric of the Harris County Flood Control District is like, "We don't have anything to do with parks. That is not what we're here to do. We are just here to move water and prevent flooding. We're happy to make some space and coordinate a little with these park people over there, but we're not going to talk about it that way. The last thing we're going to talk about is working with the federal government on an urban design project to reinvent the way people move and interact in the city and connect Black and Brown and white neighborhoods with an ecological corridor. Hell no, we won't say anything like that even if that's what's happening."

But that is exactly what was happening. We see projects like Bayou Greenways 2020, which is sort of the revivification of a plan that originated in the early twentieth century with this guy, Arthur Comey, who was a nationally known landscape architect, urban planner, urban designer. They hired him to create a comprehensive park plan for the city. What he came back to them with was much more than a park plan. The document, you can Google it.[2] It's easy to read, it's beautifully written, and it's heartbreaking to read because he describes the bayou spaces as these beautiful glades covered in wildflowers. And now even though these places are covered in concrete, you can see the zombie version of what he was describing. He imagined this linear system of parks along the bayous that went through the city, and he understood that they would be central to Houston urban planning, that they would be assets for nature, for parks, for human use. They would accommodate floodwater. He also understood that they would allow for mobility. He imagined paths for people to move through the city and little parkways—not massive highways—for vehicles.

He offered an urban design, a sophisticated urban design that was responsive to the geology and morphology and the natural systems that were here. The city started making a down payment on that plan and purchased land along the bayous, and the Hogg family contributed to that, deeding Memorial Park to the city, and the city made some real progress. We still enjoy that to this day. That was the backbone, that's still the parks and green space and ecological infrastructure that we have now. It came out of that plan. Then the city experienced these catastrophic floods in the 1930s, and then the Great Depression and the World Wars. The whole park plan got sidelined. We had decades of concretizing the bayous and trying to move water and conquer the water instead of making room for it.

In the Netherlands—and this is what I learned when Henk Ovink came—the Dutch are making room for the river, but in order to do that you have to move people out of the way. A few people have to make a sacrifice to have space to prevent flooding for the other folks. The point that Henk made when he was talking to this group of several hundred people was that you have to talk about it, and you have to involve everyone in the planning, and then you make this collective plan, the bold plan.

Because you've really talked and listened to people, they are all willing to buy into it, and the ones who have to sacrifice, they're made whole to the extent that's possible. They lose their connection to the land where they lived, but the plan includes making them whole when they're displaced. They understand why their sacrifice is necessary and what the benefits are to everybody. Then, this plan is made, and it's made with the backing of the whole community as well as the government.

Once it's made, after all this talking, a frustrating drawn-out amount of talking, he basically talked about slowing down so you could speed up. You go slow, you talk to everybody, and then you make the plan and then you go as fast as you can and get the damn thing done and you save people's lives and you save your city, you save your region. He talked and talked and talked about this, and then at the end of the civic forum, we had a Q&A.

This guy from Meyerland got up and he's like, "What's the plan? I want the plan now. My house is flooded. It's going to flood again next year. What is the plan? Let's get going." Henk is like, "No, you don't understand me. Listen. The plan is to talk." The guy was like, "What are you talking about? We've been talking. You just talked. Let's get going. I thought you guys were experts." Henk wouldn't give up. He went back and forth with this guy for a very uncomfortable amount of time.

He kept insisting, "You need to understand that I'm listening to you, but we also need to listen to everybody else and then we can move forward." He spent so much time talking to the guy that eventually, I came around and understood what his point was.

It's something that we can't even conceive of doing: to listen to and engage *everybody* in this region. We can't even accept that that's in the realm of possibility, that we would gather people and listen to different perspectives. We can't be open. We can't be open about the challenge in front of us. We can't openly embrace a socialistic ecological ideal. We can only do it if the money comes from the Houston Endowment and the Kinders or if it comes from these federal dollars that get channeled through this Harris County Flood Control District in a way that nobody really understands. But that opaque planning has limits.

We can't have an open discussion about what kind of city we want, much less make a plan for it that will include everyone and coordinate all of our resources around making it happen. And because we refuse to do this, we're not up to the existential task in front of us. Which means we're not up to the task of saving ourselves.

MEMORY

AUGUST 27 12:21 AM "ROOF HATCH CODE"

AUSTIN, TX

AUGUST 27 11:27 AM "SHELTER UNITS"

AUGUST 27 9:46 AM "FLOOD"

THE STRUGGLE TO BUILD A HOME WHEN THE LAND REFUSES TO BE HABITABLE IS A REALITY OF
LIVING ON THE GULF COAST. THIS REALITY IS ESPECIALLY DISTRESSING TO THOSE WHO MOVE TO
HOUSTON RIGHT BEFORE A FLOOD, ONLY TO IMMEDIATELY BE FACED WITH THE LOSS OF EVERY
PART OF HOME THEY HAVE BROUGHT WITH THEM.

DESIGN BY LULU FLORES, CLARISSE PINTO, AND KRISTEN FERNANDES

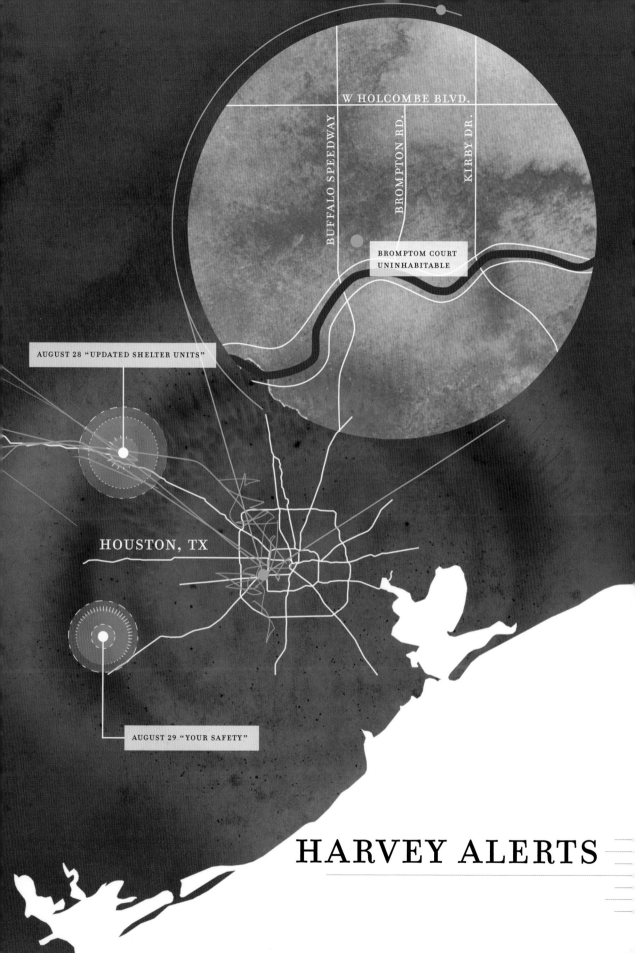

W HOLCOMBE BLVD.

BUFFALO SPEEDWAY

BROMPTON RD.

KIRBY DR.

BROMPTOM COURT
UNINHABITABLE

AUGUST 28 "UPDATED SHELTER UNITS"

HOUSTON, TX

AUGUST 29 "YOUR SAFETY"

HARVEY ALERTS

Harvey Alerts

Sonia Del Hierro

When I moved to Houston, West Texans warned me, "It rains a lot
there"

I LOOKED AROUND at the strangled, brown grass and sinewy, thorny
   mesquites
the "Pray for Rain" signs, and the depleted birdbaths
maybe rain was what I needed to grow in this Texas heat.

On August 18, 2017, my family and I drove a large U-Haul of things
to my first-floor apartment at Brompton Court
   between the Med Center and Southside Place
It was passably cozy and relatively cheap.

My dad drilled holes and locked frames into place
My mom splashed and scrubbed every surface with purple Fabuloso
   vacuumed carpets with the red Daredevil now passed down to me
She blessed my new apartment en el nombre del Padre, del Hijo y del
   Espíritu Santo.

On August 24, a day after Harvey made landfall, my father begged me
to drive to a friend's home in Austin, to outrun Harvey, so I left
   with a weekend bag of clothes: hope that nothing would happen
and a comal passed down from my mother's abuela: fear that
   everything would.

I watched from a plush, warm
Austin apartment as the radar
   Doppler blinked green, yellow, orange, and red
and then, a new color: lavender.

Emails first rapidly and then slowly came in

Aug 27	9:46 AM	**FLOOD**
		ALL 1ST FLOOR RESIDENTS:
		   WE HAVE OPENED
		UP OUR VACANT UNITS ON
		   2ND AND 3RD FLOOR
		FOR SHELTER/SAFETY

Aug 27	11:27 AM	**SHELTER UNITS** THESE UNITS HAVE BEEN OPENED TO PROVIDE SHELTER IN BUILD #1: 170, 117, 151, 137 BUILD #2: 266, 347 BUILD #4 & 5: 646
Aug 27	12:21 PM	**ROOF HATCH CODE** 0000
Aug 27	8:30 PM	**UPDATE ON SHELTER UNIT** B-2 #366

Aug 29	3:57 PM	**Your Safety**
		Our first priority is your safety and
		   we urge
		all residents to seek shelter on a temporary
		   basis with family or friends
		until such time local authorities say
		   it is safe to return.

As the floodwater slid back to the concrete bayou
those trapped at Brompton Court—some up to thirty hours
   and those returning to the soaked city
were free to float through their debris.

Management labeled all first-floor apartments: Uninhabitable
The damage was too extensive
   and our continued occupancy was a health and safety hazard
Given five days to vacate

I took only what could travel in my car along the highway
to houses, couches, and a guest room in Pearland
    later, a FEMA agent questioned
my choices: "The kitchen table seems fine."

Houston humidity fogged my head
as I joined my soon-to-be ex-neighbors
    in the intimate ritual of laying
our salvageable possessions in a twenty by thirty-foot green space.

I looked the other way
as relative strangers
    placed their belongings
beside mine to dry.

I gathered in my pile
    the Nintendo 64 console from childhood
    gray cartridges, like Banjo-Kazooie and Golden Eye
        dripped green water and rusted flecks
    the 32" TV from my sophomore year in college
        cords crusted and clogged by orange-brown sludge
    the two canvases of unfinished roses painted by my father's mother
        and handed down to me to complete
        split into one, two, three layers
        like blossoming petals
        black mold under floral hues, greens and pinks.

The sun baked the outer layers of grime
that crusted off in flakes
    but still better off than my soppy
soaked books, bleeding black ink—beyond saving.

The closet—once a walk-in selling point
felt nightmarishly lightless and long
    the carpets squished deeply under my feet
each squelch sent shivers up my spine.

Ineffable, body-deep fear sent me
elbow-deep into the slimy, molding bathtub
    clothes sunk in soapy water
as I scrubbed to release mildew moisture.

Electric had been out since the storm
but lit only by my phone's light and its rapidly depleting battery
    every room and object seemed a discolored gray
    every surface sweated a slick grime
as if the apartment was swollen with years-long neglect.

Outside, I gulped air from warm, dank breezes
the cleaning product and mold
    dizzied my vision
dots danced in the darkened corners of each room.

Choking on density and dankness
I moved between rooms that no longer felt like rooms
    but thick, strangling walls bloated with water and humidity
the paint peeled and hung paunchy along the ceiling and floor.

After, I crashed at a friend's place on Buffalo Speedway
slept in a temporary home in Pearland
    as Houston communities
welcomed me into dry, warm spaces.

Two years later, I am still breathing their fresh air
I write this from their donated chairs
    and in this swampy, subsiding land
I am growing.

DECONSTRUCTED ELEMENTS WITHIN THE MAP HEIGHTEN THE ANALYSIS OF LOSS AND OBSCURITY.
THE DAMAGE CAUSED BY HURRICANE HARVEY BECOMES THE EVIDENCE THAT, EVEN LONG AFTER THE
STORM, STILL HAS YET TO WASH AWAY. THE WATER–DAMAGED PHOTOGRAPHS TRACE WHAT REMAINS
OF OUR LIVES PRIOR TO HARVEY.

DESIGN BY MANUEL VÁZQUEZ

THE ONLY THING
YOU HAVE

Uvalde Rd

10

Maxey Rd

Buffalo Bayou

the photograph becomes the map,
there is ~~no place~~ but water

The Only Thing You Have

TRACE OF A TRACE

Lyric Evans-Hunter

> *We moved the photo albums to a higher shelf, stacked the
> furniture, moved the car from the driveway to right beside the
> house, watched the water rise toward the stop sign, moved the
> computers to a higher shelf in the house, to the next floor up.*
>
> ARNOLD HUNTER JR., my father

TO ARCHIVE I

My father has a practice. He collects and archives family photographs.[1] It is a practice of counteracting the degradation of memory.[2] It is a practice of counteracting the loss of data: names, faces, occupations, relations. So many names have been lost: to another continent, to the sea, to the rope, to white indifference.

Restore, restore, restore. At the time of his flood, my father was working as a computer repair technician. He restored data, installed RAM, wiped disk drives. *And if you wipe the photograph, then you wipe away everything.* The flood wipes away tangible memory. The flood expunges the contents of lives, leaving their unreadable evidence, these archaeological artifacts.

At the end of her introduction to the artist Leslie Hewitt's monograph, Nana Adusei-Poku's endnotes cite Saidiya Hartman: "The 'autobiographical example,' says Hartman, 'is not a personal story that folds onto itself; it's not about navel gazing, it's really about trying to look at historical and social processes and one's own formation as a window onto social and historical processes, as an example of them.'"[3]

THE PHOTOGRAPH I

In his book of reflections on photography, *Camera Lucida*, Roland Barthes interrogates photography "in relation to love and death," eschewing the divide between feeling and criticism, choosing to analyze the art of photography through the lens of his grief and his desire.[4] In so doing, he offers us a thesis of the photograph as both a visual message and a material object, both fact and affect, the echo of which comes through in the work of the photographer and sculptor Leslie Hewitt, and which shines a light on our flood-ruined photograph-artifact.

Of the photographic art and his admiration for it, Barthes says, "The loved body is immortalized by the mediation of a precious metal, silver."[5] In this age of disposable photography now available to the masses since the mid-twentieth century, we can say instead that plastic immortalizes—as it never biodegrades. But its chemicals react to a catalyst: the flood. The photographs change, their materials warp, damaged by water. The chemicals that held the image fast bleed away. The colors break down, degrade. The plastic sheet of the polaroid expands, then shrinks, and bursts into nebulaic configurations.[6]

Barthes describes the photograph as revealed, "'extracted,' 'mounted,' 'expressed,' by the action of light."[7] The flood, by the action of water, disrupts this revelation, obscuring the image. The water transforms the photograph-as-image from something legible, such as the material Leslie Hewitt often studies and works with, into the photograph-as-object. The image is illegible, even as we recognize the object.

The flood has performed a transmutation. It created an object that is at once illegible and legible: illegible in its original intention, as a photograph that can unfold a past narrative into the present; and legible as an object that tells the story of a family that met with death in a series of instants, a family that was touched by a climate-changed event and survived, and salvaged, and saved, and continued to live in a city that is overwhelmed by climate, a city that has no choice but to change with it or go under forever.

TO ARCHIVE II

When I went to see Leslie Hewitt talk at the Menil Collection, she had just finished a collaboration with the cinematographer Bradford Young; they'd been invited to view a newly acquired collection of Civil Rights–era photographs at the Menil by the curator Michelle White in 2010. Of the work that she did among the museum's photography collection, she said that the "most impactful and perhaps challenging task was to give form to the gaps, or the erasures and silences of the collection—and by extension, of our collective public imaginary of the era. . . . It led us to think of an expanding archive that includes a multitude of forms that point to the residue of lived experience often unaccounted for and rendered invisible."[8]

The residue on the pocked and warped surface of the photograph-artifact is evidence of a lived experience. When once its image might have been a witness to my father's coming-of-age in an integrating South, now it is a witness to the waters my father swam through in 2001. It is a witness to the interruptive force of his flood. Further, it is a witness to the many Houstons that have risen from the flood ruins: 45,000 homes and businesses, 70,000 vehicles, the tunnels beneath the city. Houston renewed each time, shinier than the last, at the cost of untold loss. Wiped away each time, starting anew, always built atop what had come before. Many cities under one.

The flood wipes away tangible memory. The flood expunges the contents of lives, leaving their unreadable evidence, these archaeological artifacts. It leaves behind facts. Hewitt says of playing with the readability and the unreadability of images in her work: "Even in a space without obvious legibility . . . there is something else . . . what is that thing?"[9]

THE PHOTOGRAPH II

In her introduction to Leslie Hewitt's monograph, Nana Adusei-Poku describes Hewitt's ability to tell stories in a photograph in her *Riffs on Real Time* series; by positioning a photograph in the center of a composition that layers objects, patterns, colors, images, and writing, Hewitt renders the photograph-as-object. By taking a photograph of a photograph, more than one story can be told in a single image. It is a visual thesis gesturing toward the transformation that takes place when a photograph is damaged in a flood.

Hewitt's process of stacking photographs to achieve a centered collage echoes the post-flood salvage process enacted by my father and grandmother.[10] Of the collage, Adusei-Poku writes that this act of stacking tells "relational stories that create synchronicity: they conflate histories with the contemporary, the private with the public, the spectacularized or fantasized with the documented and factual . . ."[11] What synchronicities appeared and disappeared on the lawn of the flood-ruined house on Summerwood Lane?[12]

Lisa Lee, in her essay "Opacities and Matrices," which is featured in the Hewitt monograph, describes Hewitt's work as a "meditative consideration of the photographic object. Likened to diagrams, maps, and passages of computer code, photographs are presented throughout the series as necessitating interpretation. At the same time, the difficulty—if not impossibility—of adequate interpretation is stressed by their fragmentation, or their concealment."[13] Photographs of photographs not only reveal their stories but complicate them. Hewitt seeks to transmit layered information visually and to transform the meanings of photographs through visual free association. So, too, does the flood, as a rupture or trauma, disrupt interpretation. In a roundabout way, the ruined photograph—the artifact—arrives at the sculptural.

TO ARCHIVE III

Hewitt's photo-sculptural work speaks to the trace in "Opacities and Matrices." In reference to Rosalind Krauss's writing on 1970s abstraction, Lee cites Gordon Matta-Clark's cuts, or architectural fragments, stating that they are "in line with the photograph's status as a trace or index." In other words, "Hewitt proposes that to think of the photo sculpturally is to question its status as dematerialized sign, embrace it as a material object."[14] This embrace of the materiality of the photograph is to embrace it as an object that exists, as an object that contains the passage of time. Barthes articulates this succinctly: "In Photography I can never deny that *the thing has been there*. There is a superimposition here: of reality and of the past. . . . What I intentionalize in a photograph is neither Art nor Communication, it is Reference, which is the founding order of Photography."[15]

In a lecture entitled "Archives, Documents, Traces," Paul Ricoeur interrogates the tripartite construct—the trace inherent in the notion of the document that is housed in the archive. The "document," to use Barthes's word, is evidentiary, and reveals the trace. Such a construct breaks down in the flood. What is this architecture when an archive is reconstituted from a degraded document? *We saved what we could.*[16] The architecture becomes an archaeology. The trace reinscribes itself. The archive affirms itself in the private sphere in a similar construction of document/archive/trace, but with a distinct affective turn.

I live in the afterlife of the photograph; I live in its archive. The photograph-artifact is a haunted object. It goes further than that: The photograph-artifact is a witness to the path of the storm and the destruction that followed:[17] *we watched the water rise.*[18] A photograph is a trace of an event; the photograph-artifact becomes a trace of a trace. Barthes says, "It has already disappeared: I am, I don't know why, one of its last witnesses."[19]

THE PHOTOGRAPH III

The photograph is a witness. Barthes remarks, "By making the (mortal) Photograph into the general and somehow natural witness of 'what has been' modern society has renounced the monument."[20] However, my father considers his photographs a monument to his experience. For Black people in America, to collect, record, and archive is active resistance against institutional erasure, as well as against literal death at the hands of the agents of anti-Black systems. As Adusei-Poku describes in her introduction, the primary take-away of Leslie Hewitt's work is this: By formally centering photographs or other media, Hewitt insists that we do not forget. Those objects we may take for granted: old magazines, family snapshots—they are witness to someone's presence, they are a kind of history, they are someone's history.

For the Black family, a photograph can hold identity and history that have been consistently and systemically erased again and again. The photograph is an affective object *and* a practical tool to combat systemic racism: When white supremacy tries to kill Black people, tries to erase them from history, they stay alive in oral and visual forms, in music and painting and engineering and architecture. Insurgent Black social life is stolen back and recorded in the image—this fugitivity is reversed again and again by flooding and its aftermath. When looking at photographs, Barthes says, "I then experience a micro-version of death: I am truly becoming a specter . . . I have become Total-Image, which is to say, Death in person."[21] But Black folks remember when no one else wants to remember. They (we) stay alive in both social and literal death, through image, through things that exist in the world.[22] In other words, the photograph is an act of ancestor worship. In other words, in America, the photograph is an act of Black fugitivity, of Black resistance.[23]

The importance of the face.

With whom do you walk in the world? Which ancestor do you carry with you through the world? Which ancestor was so lucky as to live again and walk again in the world, through you?[24]

THE PHOTOGRAPH IV

The series of photographs that Hewitt entitled *Riffs on Real Time* began with Hewitt's personal archive, before she built it out to cite wider cultural and historical material, with an eye toward "multiplicity, the haptic, and a kind of synesthesia." She pinpointed the moment in her childhood when photography became a way to look at the world: her grandmother had just passed away, and she was driven to visually record the objects and spaces in her house, feeling that everything was about to become very different. Her work calls back to that drive still: "My impulse is to try to give form to such absences."[25]

"Every photograph is a certificate of presence," writes Barthes, amplifying the documentness of the image again. Its trace in the archive is an inevitability. Barthes is struck by the photograph's ability to tell many times: looking at a photograph of a person who, by the time Barthes is looking at it, they have already died, he says, "the photograph tells me of death in the future."[26] Of the photograph that has met with the floodwaters, I am saying that the photograph-artifact tells of death. Or of the possibility of death that had existed for my father on June 8, 2001, when I-10 met Hunting Bayou in a terrible rush on its way to the Houston Ship Channel.

The photograph-artifact: a *memento mori*: remember that one day you will die.

TO ARCHIVE IV

In response to a question about her relationship to printed/material images, Hewitt says, "Images are both things and signs equally."[27] The photograph's image is rendered illegible by floodwater; the photograph is both an object as well as a signifier of the flood event. Out of the erased image a new meaning emerges. The photograph-artifact now falls under the discipline of archaeology, an object made legible by imagination and reconstructed in writing.

A riff on Leslie Hewitt's *Riffs in Real Time* series; a flood-ruined photograph-artifact on top of one of my family's photo albums on my kitchen floor.

Or, the object is translated and mutated, as Barthes laments, "The only way I can transform the photograph is into refuse . . . Attacked by light, by humidity, it fades, weakens, vanishes; there is nothing to do but throw it away."[28] Many of the photographs my father salvaged from his flood can be considered refuse. However, the object contains affect. It is an object of affection. Why would we keep an image that has been destroyed, that has no prospect of restoration, other than because it is filled with affect, and affection? It is love that keeps us from throwing the ruined photograph away.[29] It is love that drives us to archive: "What is it that will be done away with, along with this photograph. . . . It is the love-as-treasure which is going to disappear forever."[30]

Or, also, again, the event that rendered the image illegible, that created an archaeological object, also calls up affect: *I was pissed.*[31]

Anger can be a manifestation of post-traumatic stress. To be in the center of a trauma. The eye of the storm.[32] If memory is nonlinear, and made fragmented by trauma, the photograph is a coping mechanism. To archive is a narrative therapy. The photograph-object is a reparation.

THINGS THAT DROWN, AND WHY

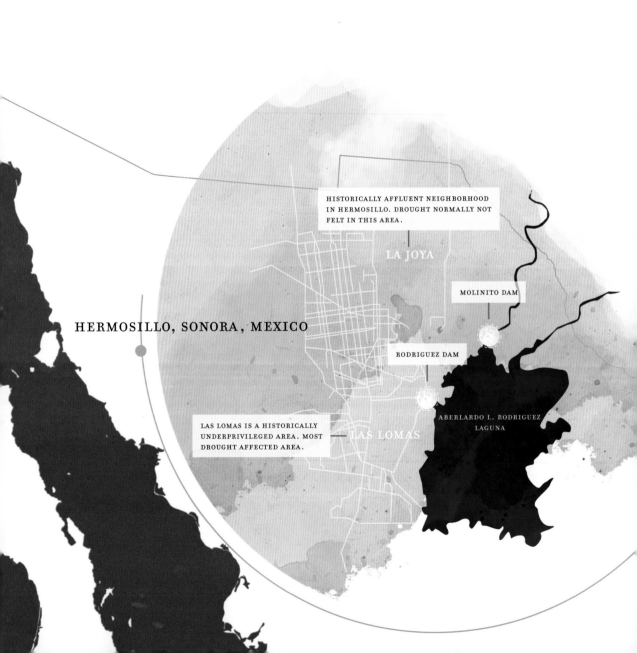

HISTORICALLY AFFLUENT NEIGHBORHOOD IN HERMOSILLO. DROUGHT NORMALLY NOT FELT IN THIS AREA.

LA JOYA

MOLINITO DAM

HERMOSILLO, SONORA, MEXICO

RODRIGUEZ DAM

ABERLARDO I. RODRIGUEZ LAGUNA

LAS LOMAS IS A HISTORICALLY UNDERPRIVILEGED AREA. MOST DROUGHT AFFECTED AREA.

LAS LOMAS

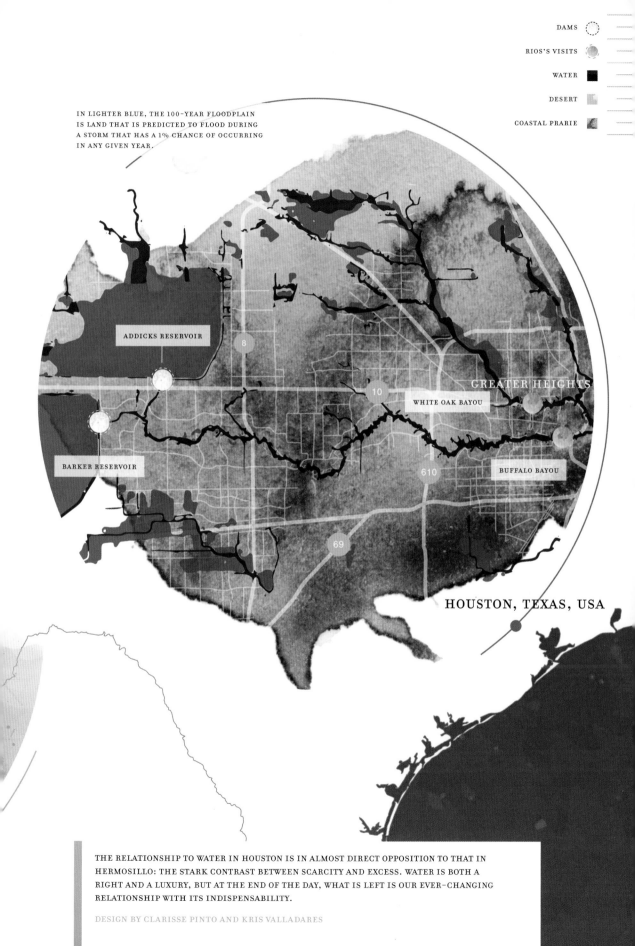

DAMS
RIOS'S VISITS
WATER
DESERT
COASTAL PRARIE

IN LIGHTER BLUE, THE 100-YEAR FLOODPLAIN
IS LAND THAT IS PREDICTED TO FLOOD DURING
A STORM THAT HAS A 1% CHANCE OF OCCURRING
IN ANY GIVEN YEAR.

ADDICKS RESERVOIR

GREATER HEIGHTS

WHITE OAK BAYOU

BARKER RESERVOIR

BUFFALO BAYOU

HOUSTON, TEXAS, USA

THE RELATIONSHIP TO WATER IN HOUSTON IS IN ALMOST DIRECT OPPOSITION TO THAT IN
HERMOSILLO: THE STARK CONTRAST BETWEEN SCARCITY AND EXCESS. WATER IS BOTH A
RIGHT AND A LUXURY, BUT AT THE END OF THE DAY, WHAT IS LEFT IS OUR EVER-CHANGING
RELATIONSHIP WITH ITS INDISPENSABILITY.

DESIGN BY CLARISSE PINTO AND KRIS VALLADARES

Things That Drown, and Why

Bruno Ríos

In my bones I hear the wailing of the waters.

CLAUDIA SANTA-ANA

I remember the water.

The spectacle was announced days before, like a premonition of the inevitable. My father took me to the edge of the dam on his shoulders, as we looked toward the gates that would open any moment. An image is vivid in my memories: the vast mirror of still water, endless, merging with the horizon, more than twenty years ago. On that December morning of 1994, the government of the desertic state of Sonora opened the gates of the dam named after Abelardo L. Rodríguez, a former Mexican president and Sonoran governor during the 1930s and '40s. After a summer of intense rains, the dam had reached maximum capacity. Hundreds of people gathered at the edge of the road to watch the waters flow through the gates, and on through the newly built concrete canals of what once was the Sonora River. My father grabbed my hand. Perched on his shoulders, I grabbed his black, soft hair and waited until something ended. I don't remember the gates closing.

That was the last time anyone saw the dam full. The only memory I have of it after that morning is of a large, dry valley where some stray cows would roam looking for sparse grass growing through the cracked soil. Less than ten years after that day, the capital and largest city of the state—Hermosillo—started rationing our water. We had it only for a few hours a day at first, then solely during certain days of the week. Those of us who could afford them grew accustomed to having water tanks on our roofs. We all grew accustomed to opening the faucet and hearing just a hiss of air come out.

But on that day in 1994, the water was a show of force, coursing through a feat of engineering, a necessary safety measure. Water was a political asset—a publicity stunt that signified the so-called progress of an otherwise oppressive government. More than twenty years later, we know water is none of those things. Water is a luxury, above anything else.

THERE IS NO SOLACE in the intimacy of things. Things become the result of their failure, their existence reduced to a moment of disastrous futility. Only when things fail do their functions become evident. One of the fathers of Continental philosophy, Martin Heidegger, thought of this as the quality of a tool that is "ready at hand," meaning that whatever thing you are using is invisible to you as you simply focus on the work to be done with it. Instead, when a tool is "*present* at hand," it means that the thing becomes visible through its failure. Only then does it become visible, necessary, indispensable. Little things like that piece of paper listing restaurants my parents might like to try when they visit; the photo of my best friend hidden in a book; the hammer that was never used to nail anything to the wall, but to tear things apart. Even the torn cardboard of our cheap bed frame, revealed when the water came. Things held everything in place, for once, when we needed to be held.

Lying in bed for a while, we tried to measure how long it took for the ants to go from the window of the bedroom to the frame of the door. It wasn't too far. It took them sixty-seven seconds. In our box-house, under our bodies, hidden below a cheap mattress, lies a digital scale with the Weight Watchers logo on it; a couple of dumbbells my wife, Linda, bought years ago; the box in which her cousin shipped the best salsa in the world to our door. A drill rested on the floor. There were empty suitcases in the restroom. A litter box next to a bookshelf. Shoes on racks, inside the closet. Nothing happened to my things for twenty-eight years. These things, our things, other things that weren't there. Things in the past drowned as well.

10,220 days was long enough.

A SENSE OF RESPECT is needed when facing the waves in Kino Bay. I would have been ten or eleven. I complained to my mother about my nipples hurting after a long day of swimming in the Gulf of California.

Mom was terrified by this, or at least that's what I remember. Be careful, she said, don't trust the water. Never trust the water when the tide comes in, goes out.

Come out, she said. It's getting late.

I remember that, but not when the house was still made of wood. It used to be that way in the '70s when my grandfather bought a plot of land across the street from the sea and built a house that is still there. It was a virgin bay then, with clean beaches and deep blue water, always in contrast with the monochromatic palette of the desert. But after a decade or so, the sea breeze became the perfect weapon against our sturdy wooden walls. Grandpa René rebuilt it in concrete about a year after I was born.

Six years later, he died after having heart surgery in Houston, the city I ended up calling home more than twenty years after he passed. I don't know if he would be proud of what I do in this city, but I'm sure he would laugh at the irony of it all: the youngest of his grandsons starting a new life where his ended.

He didn't fear the water. He respected it as a force to be reckoned with. He built our house just far enough from the beach, on elevated ground, knowing that eventually a big storm would wipe it out. We haven't had a storm like that in my lifetime. But now I know it's just a matter of time. Here, where his heart stopped, nobody really cared much about that.

IT WAS ALREADY DARK OUTSIDE. From above, the city looked like an endless web of lights. As the plane started to descend over the perfectly arranged suburbs of Houston, I thought: this is not what Texas looks like. After trying and failing to explain why it wasn't counterintuitive to come to the United States to get a PhD in Spanish to both the immigration and customs officers, and then figuring out how in the world I was going to get to my hotel without paying $60 or more for a taxi (there was no Uber back then), I exited through the doors of the terminal. Then and there, I grasped a completely different meaning of the expression "dog days of summer." In this place, it didn't have anything to do with the position of the "dog" star Sirius in the sky. Here, during the hottest days of summer, the air becomes dog breath.

Without realizing what was about to happen, I bought the cheapest thing I could find: a ticket for the "Super Shuttle," a carpool service that takes you to the city and eventually drops you off at your destination (turns out my hotel was almost at the end of the route). Even in the middle of the night I could see the vast vegetation of the city. I was stunned just looking at the roads surrounding the airport, with their forestlike trees and grass covering every inch of land. Trees—green trees! oak trees!—everywhere. Coming from the desert, this landscape only existed in photos and postcards; it was a landscape where people lived without ever worrying about thirst.

A few days later, I moved into my tiny apartment across from Buffalo Bayou. I was excited about having a river across the street. On Google Maps, it looked like a vein of blue water flowing through the city. It turned out to be a muddy and overengineered creek with paved trails alongside it for cycling and running. Since then, I've learned quite a bit about the bayous that flow through the city. The twenty-two bayou systems across the Houston region, in addition to two reservoirs, serve as drainage for our flood-prone area. The bayous have been engineered and designed over the years to withstand a large amount of rainfall. It's rarely enough.

Buffalo Bayou became a daily sight—an area where I would take long bike rides or read during the spring and fall. My wife, Linda, and I had the same experience when we moved close to White Oak Bayou a couple of years later. I loved the idea of having flowing water close by every day, even if it looked more like a canal than a river. I would sit on the trail and listen to the water while the city calmed down after rush hour.

The water in that bayou took everything from us just a few minutes before sunrise one August morning.

I KNEW WHAT DYING MEANT when the ocean dragged out Aramara. She was swimming with a friend somewhere on the Pacific Coast, maybe Los Cabos or Puerto Vallarta. One moment she was there. The next, she was gone.

The director of our school was an exceptional guy. He always joked about his baldness, pretending to "illuminate" us with the reflection of the sun on his shiny, perfect head. But on that sweltering day he came into the classroom with a face of pain and told us she was dead. My first thought was for the devastation this would cause Antonio, the author of so many stories, so many songs I liked. Aramara was his only daughter.

He taught music at my school and was one of the first people who encouraged me to write something, anything. I loved his class and the genuine dedication he put into our little artistic endeavors. With some of my friends, I formed a band to play at school after classes were done for the day. Antonio volunteered to coach us without any other remuneration but the love of teaching. He'd also written "Cachora cachorija," a children's song about a rebel desert lizard trying to run away and getting lost. I know that song by heart to this day.

A group of us went to her funeral. We wore our school uniforms, as if that would show something more than our presence. I saw her there, peacefully lying in a place where the only decent thing to do was to be silent, to cry, to not be there.

Antonio became lost after that. Many years later, I ran into him at a book fair where I was going to read from my second poetry collection. I told him one of my first poems was about Aramara. He smiled. I gave him a copy of my first book, which included that babbling poem about his daughter, and he hugged me with something more than his body. "Aramara died from water, / running through vicinities / lonely in her compassed destiny and always looked after / by our own," I wrote then. It wasn't gratitude, or compassion, or mercy. It wasn't justice either. In that moment he gave me something that doesn't have a name, in return for my words. That something, I believe, is what we are.

I knew the meaning of death. Death by water.

WATER IS NOT A THING. There is no solace in water either, but it shares the same intimacy of things. Water becomes evident not when it fails, but when it's abundant or lacking. Water cannot fail.

Unstoppable water, unintentional water, living water, fresh, oily, generally odorless, colorless, tasteless, wasteful water, gasoline water, shitty water. Water feels, fills. Water floods: an overflowing of a large amount of water beyond its normal confines.

That's what the dictionary says.

IN THE MIDDLE of the Sonoran Desert, just a few kilometers outside the city of Hermosillo, my grandfather had another idea: to plant orange trees, hundreds of hectares of orange trees. At the entrance to the orchards stood a well, pumping water out of the ground. It was always fresh and cool, even on the hottest days. Then, a giant noisy machine pumped that water toward the trees, flooding dirt canals and creating immense pools of water under the shade. On the other side of the orchards there was a small reservoir next to a secondary pump where I swam with my cousins and friends when we were kids. I gave my first kiss and got my first slap in the face there, almost simultaneously.

Eventually, that well also went dry. My uncle installed a different system years later. Our trees are now producing organic oranges sold at Costco.

Close to the orchards, a few years back, cattle died of thirst. Hundreds of them.

A few kilometers away, on the outskirts of the city, a family gets drinking water delivered twice a week to their box-house made of cardboard. They even use that water to soak the dirt roads to prevent the cloud of dust created by any car that passes through, even if that car is the same water truck that fills their two-hundred-liter tank. There are no flushing toilets in that neighborhood. There is no neighborhood in that neighborhood. There are only appropriated plots of land and some people who can barely afford to build a bedroom out of concrete blocks. And when the thermometer hits 130 degrees during the summer, and their illegal power lines overheat, there is not enough water in the city to extinguish the flames of being without a home, again.

HURRICANE HARVEY is a thing of the past. I tell myself that every time I remember Justin. He lived on the third floor of our apartment complex with his wife. I used to run into him at the gym, him looking strong with his fully tattooed arms and his old red Volvo he surely kept for its sentimental value; me still looking like I had just ingested four hundred tamales. They were newlyweds and worked from home. He came and went with a friendly attitude and his super-bright golden hair that, for some reason, still gives me the creeps.

He stored my bicycles and other stuff in his apartment for weeks while we looked for somewhere to start over. He bought tote boxes for us. That saved some of my books. When everything was over, I gave them leftover machaca my dad made that summer when my parents came to Houston, before everything happened. I gave them a few tortillas, too. It was all I wanted to save from our fridge.

Then I found out he was preparing to become a minister in Joel Osteen's church; he must be a minister by now. And that's incredibly disappointing. I remember asking him about the controversy that ensued when Osteen refused to open his megachurch to the thousands of displaced people immediately after Harvey hit. He told me a few days later: "Joel is a good guy, man. He wanted to be prepared to receive people. The church is open now that the water has gone down. You're welcome to come with us and volunteer if you can." I found it a little insulting, but at the same time I was grateful for what they did for us.

I am still grateful. I disagree with everything they do, everything they stand for, their ideology, their religion, their conservative and happy-go-lucky approach to life.

And I love them.

Harvey is a thing of the past.

THE FRENCH HISTORIAN Pierre Nora has suggested that memorial sites, or "lieux de mémoire," are monuments and places established institutionally when memory, as a shared experience, is in crisis.[1] It is as if the monument could prevent oblivion. By creating a public space, collective memory is vaccinated against the inevitable passing of time.

This is what the authorities must have thought when they established what was originally called the "Water Pavilion" in 2012. After three years of legal battles with the Yaqui tribe and the agricultural moguls from the southern region of Sonora, the first opposition government since the Mexican Revolution in the state of Sonora finished building the controversial "Independencia Aqueduct": a 145-kilometer (90-mile)-long pipeline that could transport 75 million cubic meters of water a year to Hermosillo and thus end its water rationing. To commemorate this marvel of public infrastructure, Governor Guillermo Padrés created a monument to the aqueduct on the same plaza that already memorialized the city's centennial. The monument consisted of a 16-meter (52-foot) acrylic pipe mounted under an arched roof of translucent plastic panels. Built amid rumors of corruption, the monument that was supposed to immortalize an already unpopular solution to a very old problem only lasted two months. People vandalized it every day, transforming a memorial site into a political place of dissent.

Two years later, the copper mine Buenavista del Cobre, owned by the billionaire Germán Larrea, CEO of Grupo México—the country's largest mining company and the third-largest copper producer in the world—spilled 40,000 cubic meters of copper sulphate into the Sonora River. It is still considered the largest environmental spillage in Mexico's history, affecting more than 20,000 people. Cancer rates soared in the impoverished towns along the river. Nobody has been incarcerated.

Close to one of those towns, Governor Padrés had his 3,670-hectare ranch, which has been consistently upgraded since he rose to power in 2009. The property is famous for housing the governor's purebred horses. During the spill on the Sonora River, the property came under public scrutiny. A new addition was discovered: the governor had installed a brand-new and illegal private dam, with a capacity of four million cubic meters of water. He named it "The Titanic."

People affected by the spill developed rashes and sores, started dying of cancer and other ailments due to the lack of drinking water. They lost their crops and cattle, their livelihoods.

The governors' horses were never thirsty.

NUMBERS ONLY TELL part of the story: sixty-one inches of rain; fifty-seven confirmed tornadoes; more than 300,000 structures flooded, along with more than 500,000 vehicles. Thirty thousand water rescues were conducted, and 40,000 people were evacuated from flooding.[2]

Numbers can also tell a different story. A year after the storm, a survey by the Episcopal Health Foundation shows that 27 percent of Hispanic Texans who lost their homes during Harvey report that their properties are still unsafe to live in.[3] Twenty percent of Black people and only 11 percent of whites can say the same. Half of the lower-income families surveyed said they didn't get the help they needed.

Either by thirst or by flooding, the same people always suffer the most. And even when the water has receded, and the governor's private dam has been dynamited, I think mostly about our things that drowned, and why. They drowned not because they were ours, but because we were at a place where others have lost so much more, and the very few lost almost nothing.

Michel Foucault's *Discipline and Punish* next to my wedding album next to a picture of Mikonos next to our cat's hair comb next to Paco's newly translated book next to a bill for $600 not yet paid to an out-of-network doctor next to immigration papers next to a bike saddle next to an ugly couch pillow next to a copy of my paper on poetry and violence next to a narconovela next to the sole pair of socks I hid obsessively behind the couch pillow next to the space where I cried when my mother-in-law got cancer next to where we kissed hugged laughed jumped in joy next to joy next to joy next to sadness or belief next to disbelief next to nothing like Christ or saving us.

Water is not a thing.

I remember the water.

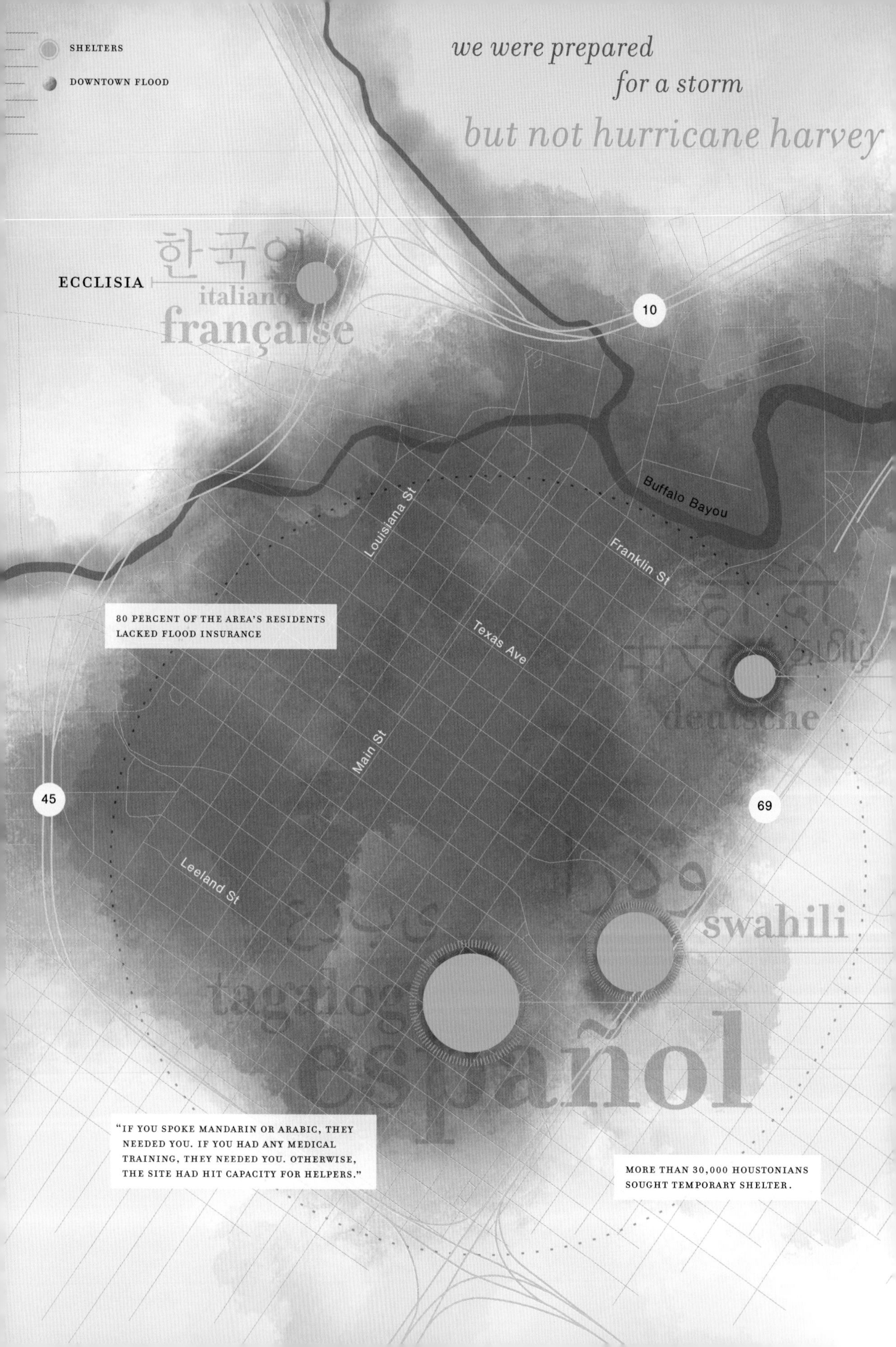

SHELTERS

DOWNTOWN FLOOD

we were prepared
for a storm
but not hurricane harvey

ECCLISIA

한국어

italiano

française

10

Louisiana St

Buffalo Bayou

Franklin St

Texas Ave

80 PERCENT OF THE AREA'S RESIDENTS
LACKED FLOOD INSURANCE

deutsche

Main St

45

69

Leeland St

swahili

tagalog

español

"IF YOU SPOKE MANDARIN OR ARABIC, THEY
NEEDED YOU. IF YOU HAD ANY MEDICAL
TRAINING, THEY NEEDED YOU. OTHERWISE,
THE SITE HAD HIT CAPACITY FOR HELPERS."

MORE THAN 30,000 HOUSTONIANS
SOUGHT TEMPORARY SHELTER.

HIGHER GROUND

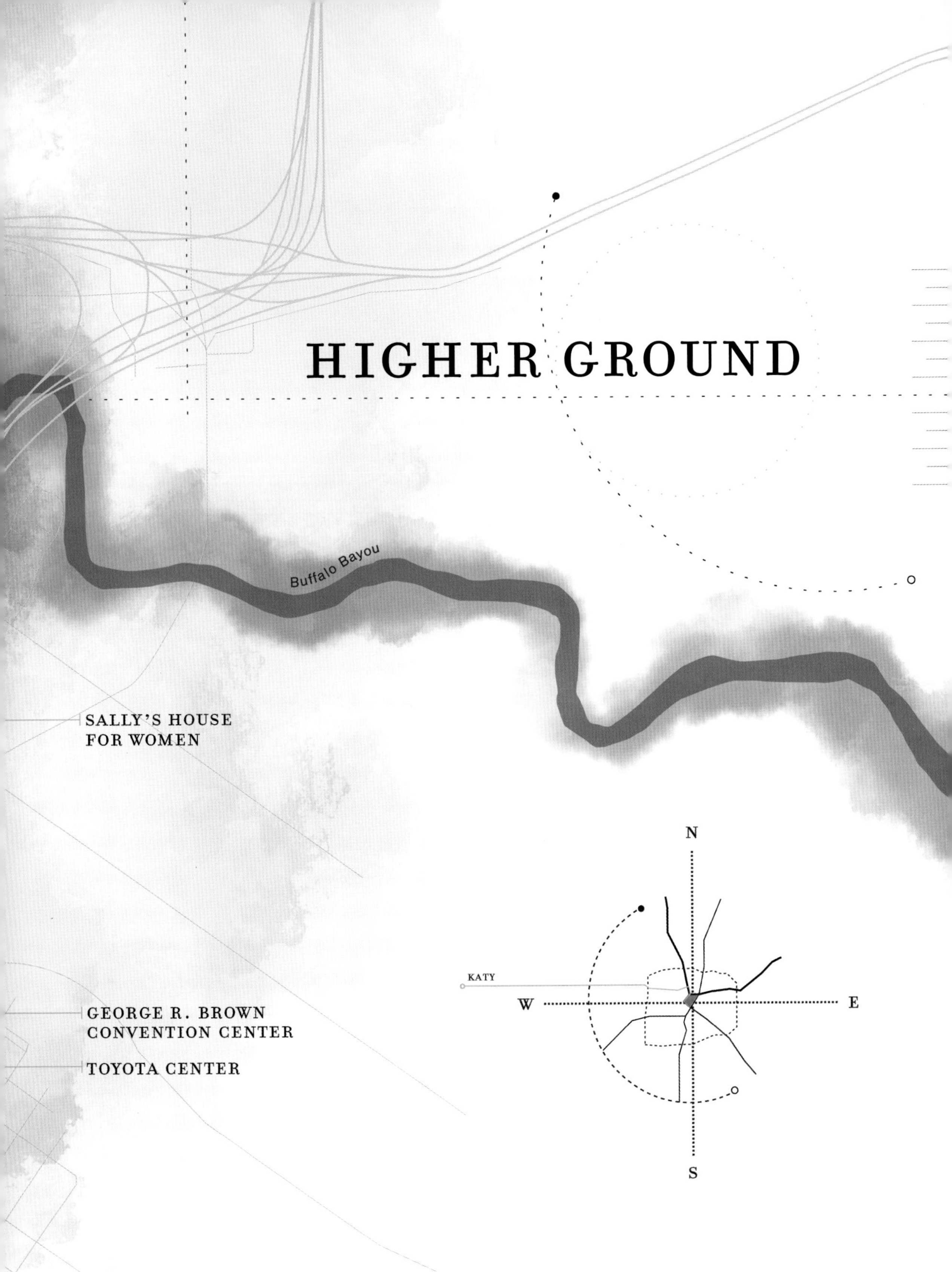

Buffalo Bayou

SALLY'S HOUSE
FOR WOMEN

GEORGE R. BROWN
CONVENTION CENTER

TOYOTA CENTER

N

KATY

W —————— E

S

IN THE DAYS FOLLOWING HARVEY, SHELTER LOCATIONS IN DOWNTOWN HOUSTON'S FLOOD AREAS
INCREASED STEADILY. WASHINGTON MADE AN ATTEMPT TO VOLUNTEER AT A SHELTER, ONLY TO
DISCOVER THE SHELTERS NEEDED ONLY BILINGUAL SPEAKERS AND THOSE WITH MEDICAL TRAINING.

DESIGN BY MIRYOUNG KIM AND MANUEL VAZQUEZ

Higher Ground

Bryan Washington

My parents stay on the west end of Houston. High ground. It's way out in the suburbs, just beyond the outer loop, and that's where I drove the night that Harvey breached Galveston's coast. I was still splitting time between Texas and Louisiana, and I'd spent that morning pacing my place by the Tremé, on the phone with my mom. She told me it probably wouldn't be that bad, and I agreed, because it probably wouldn't. Throughout their time in Fort Bend County, even at its worst, the rain hadn't been a tangible threat. So my mom told me to stay in New Orleans, or drive down, whatever was less of a hassle; and I told her I'd probably leave it alone, but I was headed west down I-10 thirty minutes later.

Harvey made landfall seconds after I hit Harris County. I know this because a guy on the radio told me. The local pop station asked everyone to pray. Our rap folks yelled the city's integral "hunker down." On NPR, our local station read from Matthew Salesses's *Hundred-Year Flood*, and when I opened our garage door, I was expecting to see my parents holding vigil over the television, or watching the sky from their back porch, but the alarm went off, waking the whole fucking block.

While I failed to disarm it, my dad shuffled over in PJs. Here was a man who prepared for everything three times over. He gave me a once-over and asked why I was there. They were sleeping. They were on high ground, he said, everything would be fine for them; and, for another half a day or so, it was.

ALTOGETHER, Harvey unloaded the highest recorded total rainfall of any storm in the history of the United States. Over a quarter of Harris County was submerged. That's around 17 trillion gallons of water. That made August 27—at 16.07 inches of rain—the wettest day ever recorded in Houston.[1] For a sense of scale, if the amount of rain that fell throughout Harvey hit New Orleans during Katrina, pending the levee failure, that city would've been covered with over twelve stories of rain.

Our sky literally fell.

A good chunk of the storm's destruction was due to its speed—or the complete lack thereof: at two miles per hour, Harvey simply sat on top of the region. And it may have been materializing for a few weeks, but plenty of Houstonians only learned about Harvey a few days beforehand: it was the end of the month. Bills were due.

September's rent was looming. And in the face of the duds and false alarms that had preceded the storm, the prospect of picking up and leaving for San Antonio or Austin or wherever simply wasn't worth it for a lot of folks. Also, who'd ever heard of flooding on high ground?

So we got what you no doubt saw on one digital screen or another: thousands of folks in the Greater Houston area were rescued from their homes. More than 30,000 sought temporary shelter. Hundreds of thousands lost electricity. More than 80 percent of the area's residents lacked flood insurance. FEMA announced that something like 450,000 people would seek federal disaster aid, and 107 people were killed in Texas as a whole.

More than a few essayists and pundits broached the question of why Houstonians didn't prepare for a storm, but the question answers itself: we did. The city rallied for *a* coming storm, not *the* storm that came. The city's recent history with flooding ranged from the pedestrian to the catastrophic, but a *Harvey* hadn't happened before. And had there actually been an evacuation, considering that some areas saw nearly ten inches of rain in under two hours, we'd have created six killing lanes across multiple highways and feeder roads. There was simply no way of "preparing" for it—unless, of course, we'd all heeded the scientists and meteorologists and journalists ruing global warming's effect on our Gulf for years.

THE FIRST MORNING, it was sunny, until all of a sudden it wasn't. The rain wasn't torrential, but it just kept going. And going. And not stopping for shit. My parents and I huddled around some lukewarm coffee, watching the situation east of our neighborhood populate across our phones: whole blocks were filling with water. The folks who could still wade through their yards carried trash bags into pickups. We did our check-ins, and my mother toyed with the idea of driving to work at the hospital, since she still could. A guy I used to fool around with texted to ask if the rain had reached us, and another friend sent a picture of her porch in Meyerland, with the garden gnomes sunk in a knee-deep puddle.

That night, my dad drove my mom to a nearby hospital in our truck, and the world responded by dumping a ton of water on top of our house. By the next morning, the surrounding roads were largely unnavigable. Most of the folks who'd tried to bounce before morning ended up stranded by the feeder road, forced to park on islands in the street, before being ferried away by emergency vehicles. The reservoir by my parents' place (Barker) started to fill, gradually, until it finally spilled over, burying the first floors of the neighborhoods surrounding it. My father and I wandered the house, watching the news, and also our porch. I texted my people and answered the texts I could. We watched newscasters debate whether a stranded car on screen was actually occupied, on a bridge, beneath rapidly rising water, or if the driver had simply left the lights on. Before the flood finally overtook it, some firemen extracted a dude from the truck's backseat.

It's mystifying to think about what you did when there was nothing you could do. I paced around the kitchen, simmering a shrimp broth I wouldn't sit down to eat. One friend reached out from the Islands. Another reached out from his townhouse in Bellaire. One reached out from the Galleria, another from downtown; another hit me up from an emergency vehicle en route to a shelter; and the ex reached out from Busan, sending footage of Houston from abroad. At one point, a friend of mine living in New Orleans told me to move all of the photos from the bottom floor. He said the thing he'd most regretted in the last flood was losing the photos his parents brought from Vietnam. Shit you couldn't replace. Family members he'd never see again. All of that was gone.

When I told my dad about that, we blinked at each other. Our dresser on the first floor was heavy. But we decided that if the water reached the porch, we'd move everything, and an hour later we were carrying the chests and the rugs and the vases right up the stairs. Carried albums full of folks in my family that I haven't spoken to in years. Carried our whole history up the stairs, laying it out on the floor. If you lined everything up, you'd see exactly how we ended up here.

THE THING ABOUT a flood narrative—or any story whose occupants are ravaged by the earth—is that there's a tangible *before* and *after*, but also an invisible one. Sometimes, a country's façades—its supposed wealth in the face of poverty, its supposed goodness in the midst of neglect—are held to the light by the images on the screen, and, in that way, there are as many Harvey stories as there are folks who endured Harvey.

Honestly, though, most everyone in Houston has one hurricane story or another. If you're here for too long, you'll end up with a litany. During Hurricane Rita, my family packed ourselves in a car and made a failed attempt to escape to San Antonio. For Ike, we took shelter in a hospital bunker for two days, watching *My Neighbor Totoro* thanks to the generator.

For the Tax Day Floods, I was on my way to see a boy when I took a turn underneath a bridge and flooded my car—the water was right in front of me; I just hadn't seen it, and then it was there. Reversing out of it was no issue, so I put my Corolla in park and sat on the concrete and watched the ripples. My brain knew the area had flooded, and it certainly *looked* like a flood, but there was still a disconnect. Like, the place was just *there*. And I was *just* there. So for a while, I leaned against my trunk and smoked and waved other cars away from the underpass, but then it got dark, and no one had come to post any warning signage, and it was late, so I got back in my seat and turned myself around.

IT RAINED FOR DAYS during Harvey, but the water westward began to recede. East of the city, the rain kept up a steady pace. The mayor imposed a curfew within the city, and Houstonians rallied when they could, and my dad and I watched the sky from the house, willing the clouds into something like complacency. Eventually, the roads cleared enough to drive to the hospital to get my mom. In her unit, one nurse had brought a tin of curry, and another had carried armfuls of Tupperware with steamed rice and nam prik. They'd spent the past few days holding down the fort, spooning up four different continents' worth of food when they could. Back at home, my mom asked why we'd moved the albums, and my dad and I shared a look.

That night, I drove downtown for no other reason than that I could: the highway headed eastward was mostly drivable, and the city was opening a second shelter. It needed volunteers. Once I made it off the highway, I had to stay on the right side of the roads, rerouting from time to time over one pool of water or another. As I drove around, the city was as silent as I'd ever heard it. Every few blocks, a bevy of pickup trucks would pass with inflatable boats and kayaks in tow. Downtown, I stopped for a trio of drift boats under a bridge. A lady all in black drove one herself, and a pair of kids handled the others.

By the time I'd reached the shelter, they'd run out of room for any new volunteers. If you spoke Mandarin or Arabic, they needed you. If you had any medical training, they needed you. Otherwise, the site had hit capacity for helpers. A white guy with a megaphone handed out bracelets to the couple hundred of us outside the stadium with our arms crossed. When he ran out of bracelets, the man told us we'd be fine without them, but a Latina standing behind me said that not everyone could afford that. The HPD was patrolling the streets in accordance with the curfew. Without exactly glancing at me, she said some of us couldn't get by on the benefit of the doubt.

But it didn't change the fact that there were no more bracelets. It was just past midnight, but I could try again in the morning. So I drove back downtown, a suddenly reasonable commute, and on a whim, I parked, and decided to take a walk. Houston's core was vacant. Who knew when that would happen again. I've spent a handful of evenings on Houston's downtown streets: One time, in the midst of a fling, I walked what felt like the entire length of the theater district, high on possibility. Another time, I'd forgotten which parking garage was mine after a show, and I walked from street to street, trying to recall their entrances. But this time, I had beer in my trunk, a remnant of living in New Orleans. Some firemen smoked by their truck, waving as I passed. Across from a glossy sushi joint, some teens skated on the curb. Occasionally other loiterers passed, pointing, brandishing cameras, and every now and again we'd make eye contact and nod.

IN THE END, Harvey's damage ranged from nonexistent to extreme. The reservoirs receded. Slowly but surely, the rain dissipated.

Today, if you drive through some parts of South Houston, or Harris County's eastern outskirts, you'll see many, many homes still in ruins. Many, many folks are still living in hotels or trailers. Many, many folks are still rebuilding in the rubble. The city has mostly moved on, because it had to, but not without leaving many of its residents behind. And the relocated, and the dislocated, and the bereft, too, have also had to move on. It makes for a strange contemporary limbo—you're home, but not home at all.

I resist the inclination to spin this into a remarkable experience—mine or anyone else's—because, if science is any indicator, these events in the Gulf will become anything *but* remarkable. Of course there will be more damage.

And then, beyond the literal devastation, there's the *feel* of what happened. It's in this city's nature, I think, to downplay catastrophe, because we are "scrappy" and we can get by with whatever's around, but as Houston continues to thrive, so will the problems it faces—and it remains to be seen how long the promise of development and capital will deem the risk required in acquiring and living around it negligible.

THE NEXT MORNING, I drove to the coffee bar I live across from now. Swaths of the city were still underwater. They'd stay that way for the next few days, and some wouldn't clear out for a couple of weeks. When I motioned to pay, the first thing the barista asked me was if I spoke Tagalog (I don't). Then he asked if I spoke Mandarin (I don't). He asked if I spoke Farsi (I don't). His wife, he said, was looking for translators. There were certain languages they just needed more of.

We were lucky, he said. So we're doing what we can.

High ground, he said, and I nodded, because this time that notion had held fast.

There will be as many different iterations of this storm, and the ones to come, as there are Houstonians. It'll be decades before we see all of them. But whenever they get here, we'll be ready to hear them, because we have to hear them. They're what will pave our map for the next one.

Not that we haven't already started. One afternoon, a few weeks later, three folks walked by this building I was volunteering at, bearing garbage sacks. I was folding clothes beside an older Latino couple, and a pair of Chinese women. We'd all seen each other around; we crossed orbits about once a week. We all spoke just enough of each other's languages to communicate, and when one of the Chinese women said that she'd also been homeless for a little while, the Latina woman joked that we all were. Her husband said, that makes us family. And eventually, he added, it always stops raining.

We all winced. Of course he was right. It always, always stops raining. But there was no way not to remember that it hadn't felt like that at the time.

This essay appeared in Catapult *on August 27, 2018, as "We Were Prepared for a Storm but Not Hurricane Harvey."*

THE GALLERY OF CRACKED PAVEMENT

○ PHOTOGRAPHIC POINTS OF INTEREST

● UNBORN CHILD WITH SURROGATE

● PATH WALKED

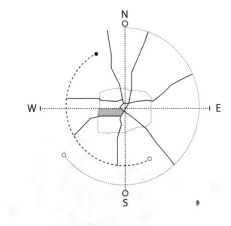

MONTROSE

Westheimer Rd

S Shepherd Dr

W Alabama St

Kirby Dr

THE MAP JUXTAPOSES COLLECTED HURRICANE AND FLOOD NARRATIVES FROM HOUSTON AND
GALVESTON AGAINST KROOS'S OWN PERSONAL EXPERIENCE DURING HARVEY THROUGH THE USE OF
ARTISTIC IMAGERY OF CRACKED PAVEMENTS IN HOUSTON.

DESIGN BY KRISTEN FERNANDES

Walking tour map. All photos in this chapter are by Dana Kroos.

The Gallery of Cracked Pavement

A WALKING TOUR

Dana Kroos

Cost: Free
Hours of Availability: Always Open

I had been tripping over the sidewalks for years—shattered as though dropped in place from twenty stories up—but I began to collect images in the summer of 2017. Houston is built on a swamp or, more specifically, an expansive clay soil that swells to absorb the generous amount of rainfall the city receives every year, then shrinks, cracking as the water is redistributed. Professionals have categorized damaged pavement based on cause. Rigid Body Uplift, for example, is when an entire slab is pushed up by the soil beneath; Tensile Shrinkage is caused by the contraction of the soils underneath and often results in a single crack that completely splits a slab. The causes are cyclical and ongoing. The results are evolving compositions: apocalyptic tales of surviving (or not surviving) earthquakes, meteor showers, or landmines.

STRUCTURAL DAMAGE

Characterized by damage that penetrates the entire slab.

Site 1. *Crater*, cracked concrete, 2' × 2', Indiana and Welch.

Site 2. *Fault Line*, cracked concrete and rebar, 5" × 3', Elmen between Vermont and Haddon.

I walk to alleviate stress (along with watching Netflix and eating chocolate), and 2017 was a stressful summer. It may be true that I was seeing more pavement damage because I was covering more miles. It may also be true that I was paying more attention to the damage to distract myself. Collecting images of my discoveries gave my wanderings purpose.

I photographed images along the five-mile loop where I walked my dog. It was a juggling act: leash, camera, poop bag; keeping my shoes, my mutt, and both of our shadows out of the shot. People frequently stopped their own walks, or leaned out of cars and apartment windows to ask if I needed help—a polite way of inquiring what I was up to—or sometimes they just got to the point, "What the hell are you doing?"

"I hope you're sending that to the city," people would say when I'd pause to set down the poop-bag and contort myself into position to get the best shot of a crumbled curb.

"I'm an artist," I'd say, which, when said resolutely, sounds authoritative, even though it requires no certification. "I'm making a gallery exhibition of cracked sidewalks."

This often led to tips about other sites. It turns out many Houstonians have been taking note of pavement damage in the city.

SURFACE CRACKING: MAP TYPE

Characterized by connected surface cracks that resemble atlases or road maps.

Site 3. *City Streets Aerial View*, cracked concrete, 4' × 6', Shepherd and Barnard.

Site 4. *Connected Continents*, cracked concrete, 5' × 8', Vermont between Elmen and Park.

SURFACE CRACKING: HIEROGLYPH TYPE
Characterized by design formations that resemble simple line drawings.

Site 5. *Sunrise*, cracked concrete, 3' × 2', Elmen and Haddon.

Site 6. *Arrow,* cracked concrete, 2' × 4', Indiana and Park.

That summer I was waiting. This gallery of cracks and crevasses helped me bide my time. One of the many things about which I had to *wait and see* was my dog. "Time bomb," the vet called the perilous way the tumor in her adrenal gland had invaded her vena cava. In July, she pointed to the ultrasound—gray bulbs around a thorny vine of backbone—the image formless, but determined, like a Rorschach, slightly resembling a face, or a flowerpot, or a winter scene. "On proper medication, she could live for years. Or the tumor could shift and kill her instantly." Nothing could be done. The dog was not in pain. We just had to go on about our lives.

Timebomb, I renamed the dog.

MOLD

Characterized by dark gray to black covering the surface in various shapes and patterns that often follow areas of water collection. Because mold is a multicelled, living organism, these thrive, continuing to grow and change in optimal conditions.

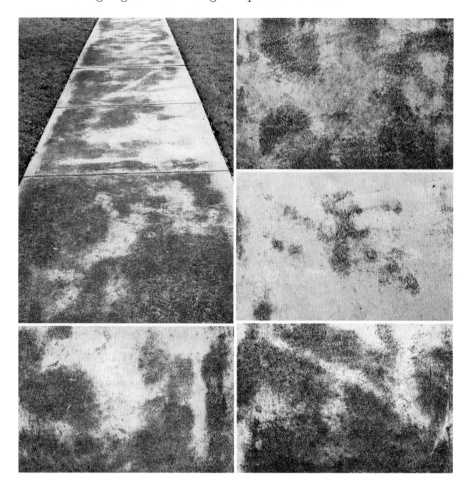

Site 7. *Ultrasound Series*, mold on concrete, 2.5' × 2.5' (each panel), Reba Dr. and Bellmeade.

Site 8. *Conjure,* mold on cracked concrete 4' × 4', Avalon between Bellmeade and River Oaks.

Timebomb and I had been together for nine years in two different states plus a year-long stint in Newfoundland, Canada, as well as countless road trips, a half dozen jobs, and just as many housing arrangements. Timebomb and I had walked miles together, through deserts and snow and swamps, working off anxieties, listening to books, thinking, and making decisions. We continued to walk that summer. Her symptoms meant she consumed a lot of water, panted constantly, and overheated easily. We adjusted our schedule to walk early in the mornings, stopping to cool off in puddles—plentiful in Houston.

By late August, we had a routine of biweekly vet visits to manage her medications. I hid her pills in chicken and hamburger. She moved from the bed to the cool bathroom tiles at night. We carried on. She didn't know that she was dying.

When Hurricane Harvey danced across the gulf, I was alone with Timebomb in the guesthouse where we lived in the swanky neighborhood of Upper Kirby. I had been living in Houston for five years and was still baffled and intrigued by the climate. The year before Harvey, I had gathered hurricane and flood narratives in Houston and Galveston for a novel that I was working on. I enrolled in a ceramics course at Galveston College that gave me access to Galveston residents. They all had disaster stories involving water. Many of them tracked personal history according to storms—"This was before Rita," "This was after Allison"—like accounts of first marriages.

Harvey's approach was visible in the satellite images on CNN, a ballerina's twirling tutu—graceful, but also ominous, dense, and massive. An interview with a couple waiting to be evacuated from an island off the coast of Texas gave a preview of what was coming, as much in their quivering voices as in their descriptions of the scene.

NATURAL INTERFERENCE
Characterized by visible natural elements that break, move, and combine with pavements to form new collaborative compositions.

Site 9. *Embrace*, concrete slabs and live oak, 15' × 8', Reba and Dickey.

Site 10. *Where Grass Grows,* concrete and grass, 6" × 4', Park between Indiana and Fairview.

I prepared for Harvey according to the public service recommendations: joining the masses who emptied nearby groceries of canned goods and bottled water, putting new batteries in flashlights, filling my tubs and sinks with water (taking into consideration Timebomb's relentless requirements). "Shelter in place," was the consistent advice.

Before Timebomb and I hunkered down to watch Harvey's approach on television, I took her for a walk. It felt like we were taking a deep breath before diving underwater.

Our neighborhood of Upper Kirby is between the offbeat neighborhood of Montrose—characterized by vintage clothing stores, gay bars, and groovy restaurants—and upscale River Oaks, where lawn maintenance companies descend daily with the roar of leaf blowers. Montrose is full of modest single-family houses, duplexes, and small apartment buildings where families, couples, students, and single people live on ungated lots. River Oaks has six-thousand-square-foot mansions giving way, as you move west, to grandiose castles set behind high walls. Everyone suffers pavement damage, but the residents of River Oaks pay for repairs, while the residents of Montrose offer safety warnings against hazards and alternative paths in the vein of wooden planks across gaping holes.

REPAIRS
Characterized by intentional interventions to restore damaged areas.

Site 11. *Grate*, metal bolted to concrete, 4' × 7', Avalon and Kirby.

Site 12. *Fillings*, concrete, 12" × 6" × 6" (each filling), Greenbriar and Kipling.

Site 13. *Patch*, concrete, 2' × 8", Shepherd and Kipling.

INFORMAL SAFETY INTERVENTIONS

Characterized by various measures taken by citizens to either warn pedestrians about potential hazards or make portions of sidewalks more passable.

Site 14 . *Yellow Step*, painted concrete slab, 3' × 4", Greenbriar and Harold.

Site 15. *Bridge*, wooden planks, 1.5' × 6', Avalon between Bellmeade and River Oaks.

That summer I was also waiting for my daughter to be born. For years, I had been making my way through an IVF process strewn with hazards. When Harvey hit Houston, my daughter's due date was two months away. Because of serious health issues, I was unable to carry her pregnancy. The gestational carrier added legal and emotional complications. In June, five months pregnant, the gestational carrier—a friend since childhood—announced that she was considering a move away from the Midwest state where we had both grown up, an act that would have terminated our contract. Regaining custodial rights in another state, if possible, could have cost tens of thousands of dollars in legal fees. When I reminded her that the contract required her to reside in the state until the birth, she threatened to move anyway and put the baby up for adoption.

She was angry that I was not more supportive, and that her life had been taken over by a baby that wasn't even hers. She refused to talk to me.

Timebomb stayed an entire day with me in my room while I sent unanswered apology after apology, cried, worried, conducted alarming online research, contemplated worst-case scenarios, then various forms of fund-raising until a friend came to talk me down. I was prone to this type of overthinking. My friend pointed out that, as with the process up until now, there was little I could do but wait and see what the gestational carrier would do. When Harvey hit, it had been two months since the gestational carrier and I had spoken. I knew through social media that she was still in the state. I felt as though I had been sheltering in place for quite some time.

DEBRIS
Characterized by complete separation from the original structure.

Site 16. *Stonehenge*, removed concrete blocks, 2.5' × 6' (each block), Fairview and Hazard.

Site 17. *Marbles*, curb debris, 6" × 10" (each piece on average), Shepherd and Kipling.

When Harvey pushed into Houston and stalled like an unwelcome party guest too drunk to take hints from the host to leave, I was thinking about Galveston and its residents' stories of wind and water.

The sky went dark. The rain was a constant waterfall down the windows. The street filled and receded with black water. Timebomb stared out the window in disbelief. When the rain would lighten, I'd open the door and encourage her to go outside to do her business.

I got a message from Timebomb's vet saying that they were closed for the duration of the storm. Everything was closed. Facebook activated a feature that allowed Houston residents to "mark themselves as safe" to assure friends and relatives in other parts of the country. Many people were not safe.

The power never went out in Upper Kirby. My house did not flood. The streets were quiet. The days were muted like dusk or dawn. It was peaceful in a way—like the last days on Earth. I sat at the kitchen table and watched CNN's constant broadcast—a mix of meteorological charts, professional footage, and video taken on cell phones by residents crying in the background as they recorded water coming through their front doors. The hurricane spiraled up the coast, drawing water in its wake. It was no longer of the sea or the sky, but a thing unto itself. I-59 became a river with cars submerged like impacted teeth. Helicopter crews rescued people from roofs of houses. People paddled canoes over what had once been streets. It no longer mattered that they had work deadlines, or that their rent was due, or that they had been fighting with their spouses about how the laundry should be done. The storm was all-consuming. It demanded our complete attention and in this act, momentarily released all other tensions.

In the house there was nothing to do but wait, listen to distant sirens call out to the thunder, hold and be held by the darkness, feel the underwater pulse. The gestational carrier was in her third trimester. I'd read that if the baby was born now, she could survive, although barely.

"Hold on," the whole city seemed to plead. "Hold on."

GARDEN

Characterized by fertile soil bound by one or more sidewalk slabs.

Site 18. *Garden Cove*, dirt and grass framed in concrete, 2.5' × 1.5'. Hazard near Westheimer.

Site 19. *Large Garden*, dirt and grass framed in concrete, 4' × 6', Vermont between Elmen and Park.

Houston had learned lessons from previous storms, and from the disaster of Hurricane Katrina. In 2001, Tropical Storm Allison knocked out power to much of Houston. My friend, who had a generator, opened her house to extended family. Afterward, more people invested in generators. Rita, which came just weeks after Katrina, was met with a mass mandatory evacuation of Galveston and suggested evacuation of Houston. Freeways turned into parking lots as a heat wave swept the city. Cars overheated and stalled. Over one hundred deaths were caused by the evacuation, including a bus full of retirement home residents that caught fire.[1]

In the ceramics studio in Galveston, the islanders recounted one incident after another of pet deaths in gridlock—dogs and cats who died on passenger seats while their owners fanned and tried to resuscitate them.

ANIMAL INTERFERENCE
Characterized by impressions in setting concrete by domestic and wild animals.

Site 20. *Signature*, dog print in setting concrete, 2.5" × 2.5", Fairview and Westgate.

Pets play a major role in rescue efforts and survival during storms. During Katrina, many residents would not leave their homes because the shelters did not accept pets. During Harvey, Houston had pet-friendly shelters that allowed people to keep their animals with them.

Because of the evacuation disaster during Rita, many Galveston residents refused to leave the island during Ike. A huge storm surge flooded much of the island. People were stranded in their water-logged homes for weeks while they awaited rescue after the storm. One woman told the story of her neighbor who had survived by standing on her kitchen counter as the water level rose, all to save her cat.

Site 21. *Meander*, cat prints in setting concrete, 1.5' × 6', Reba and Meyer Park.

DAMAGE TO CURBS AND SIDEWALK ENTRANCES
Characterized by crumbling and broken sidewalk boundaries and transitions to the street.

Site 22. *Unwelcome*, crumbling concrete, 4' × 2', Avalon and Dickey.

Site 23. *Mixed Greeting*, crumbling concrete, 8' × 6', Welch and Hazard.

Harvey made landfall on Friday, August 25, 2017, its tail of storm surge washing away the coast as it plowed inland to unleash catastrophic showers for the next five days. Many parts of Houston and Texas's southeast coast were devastated.

I was teaching an interdisciplinary course that semester at the University of Houston. Harvey came after the first day of class. We had known a storm was coming but assumed that it would be nothing special. When we returned to class a couple of weeks later, some of my students were displaced—living with relatives or friends. A couple of Iraq War vets suffered severe panic attacks from hearing their cars crashing inside their garages as they floated from one wall to the other. They did not return to class. The university set up assistance in various forms. I adjusted the syllabus both for loss of time and to accommodate the new, undeniable content. The academic year would be about Harvey, the Gulf, hurricanes, trauma, community, recovery, and the knowledge that no one could ever truly be prepared for something so vast.

On Thursday, while the storm swirled and the university closed, I emailed my students to tell them to stay safe. During the next days, a few of them checked in. That following Tuesday, as the storm subsided, the gestational carrier called to see if I was okay. She wanted to talk casually, as we had talked before—not about the baby, or the possibility of her moving and putting the child up for adoption.

I told her that I was fine but that much of Houston was underwater. I didn't push her to report on the condition of my unborn daughter or anything that had occurred during the last months of the pregnancy. She had thrown me a very fragile lifeline, not meant to pull me in, but simply to remind me that solid ground still existed in the slight tension on the other end. I understood that she needed the conversation to be about her as someone important aside from the pregnancy. My only hope of holding on to the baby was to disregard the child in that moment.

She talked to me a couple more times before declaring that she was still angry with me for controlling so much of her life.

ABSENT SLABS
Characterized by missing slabs of sidewalk varying from a single to several sections, often removed without leaving any trace, beyond an empty space, of their presence.

Site 24. *Missing*, no media, no dimensions, Hazard and Pedon.

Site 25. *Where the Sidewalk Ends*, no media, no dimensions, Vermont between Elmen and Park.

During the downpour, the Army Corps of Engineers had been reliev-
ing the Addicks and Barker Reservoirs, calling for voluntary evacua-
tions of the surrounding homes. On Tuesday, August 29, as Harvey
moved northeast to Louisiana and the Houston skies began to clear, the
reservoirs overflowed and flooded thousands of homes.

Timebomb refused to come inside. I was still watching CNN, the
mayor announcing that more water would be released from Addicks and
Barker to prevent further uncontrolled flooding. The saving grace of the
newscast was the sign language interpreter in the background—the sign
for water: three fingers pressed to the lips; the sign for flooding: hands
facing down and rising up. When the mayor said "mandatory evacuation," the interpreter bowed his eyes sympathetically and swept his hands
away from his chest—butterfly wings swimming through air.

I took Timebomb for a walk.

Usually, Timebomb and I saw nannies pushing strollers. They
walked in the streets, preferring neighborhood traffic to the perilous
obstacle course of sidewalks. I had not purchased a stroller yet. I had
stopped preparing for my daughter's arrival when it seemed like she
might not arrive. I was afraid to get my hopes up—to commit fully was
to be dangerously vulnerable. Still, I imagined that Timebomb's leash
was a child's small hand, my daughter there beside me, already three
or four, hopping from puddle to puddle.

Only a few stir-crazy explorers were out walking. There were branches
down, water-logged lawns, puddles the size of small ponds. The neighborhood had survived fairly well.

On my way back inside I saw a couple of women walking in the street.
They were the typical middle-aged, made-up women who lived in my
neighborhood, fit and wearing their workout clothes as post-storm
loungewear. One of them came toward me.

The storm had brought the city of Houston together. Volunteers were
so plentiful that they were being turned away from shelters. Neighbors
were helping each other clear flooded houses and sharing provisions.
I assumed this neighbor was approaching me in that same spirit of
camaraderie. But Harvey had not affected my neighborhood more than
to give us all a few quiet days off.

"Is that your garbage?" she asked.

CREATIVE EXPRESSION

Characterized by intentional modification that often personalizes or claims space.

Site 26. *2013*, prints and drawings in wet cement, 10″ × 2.5′, Reba and Meyer Park.

Site 27. *Gallery of Messages*, drawings in wet cement, 5′ × 30′, Shepherd and Kipling.

"Do you need to throw something away?" I asked, noticing that she was also carrying poop bags that accompanied her miniature poodle.

She disregarded my offer and launched into a diatribe about neighborhood code. My garbage bin was supposed to be concealed from the street view.

It was as though she had been asleep the past days. I was so stunned that I thought maybe I had dreamed the entire storm. I was waking to reality where people had not lost homes but were concerned about their appearances and the attached real estate values.

In response, all I said was, "I'll let the owner know."

That encounter with my neighbor stuck with me long after the city began to recover. The field trips that I'd planned for my university class had been flooded, as had the dog park, and the theater downtown, office buildings, homes. People were living with friends and relatives. Insurance companies descended on the city to file claims for vehicles. Certain streets were not passable. People were cleaning up, rebuilding, returning to work, going to school, shopping for groceries, blogging online. There was so much garbage to clean up that the city recycling was postponed for months. Cans and plastic bottles piled up in the garage. I decided not to tell the owner of my guesthouse about the neighborly complaint regarding the garbage bin.

It was still bothering me three months later when my daughter was born, safe and healthy and mine. At some point I had let my desire for her overcome my fear of losing her, and embraced the possibility of her with everything I had, going so far as to buy her a stroller, and a crib, and clothes, to take medication and pump hourly so that I could breastfeed her. All of the things she would need had crowded my life and home the last months.

Timebomb and I had found a new dog park, unaffected by Harvey. She lived into the baby's tenth day, long enough to take the baby on our scenic walk, to show her the bumps and fissures of home.

This essay was supported by a Houston Arts Alliance Make Creativity Happen! Express grant.

WALL WORTHY
Characterized by aesthetic and compositional value.

Site 28. *Water Line*, cracked wet cement, 14" × 2', Avalon and Dunlavy.

Site 29. *Torso*, mixed media, 2' × 2.5', Reba and Kirby.

HOUSTON, TX

AVALON DINER

LAWNDALE STREET
BRIDGE

FOREST PARK
CEMETERY

FLOODING CAUSED BY HURRICANE HARVEY LED WRITER ALLYN WEST TO RE-EXAMINE THE
STORIES HE WAS TOLD ABOUT FLOOD RECOVERY AS A CHILD IN FORT WAYNE, INDIANA, AND
TO RECONSIDER THE STORIES HE'S TOLD HIMSELF.

DESIGN BY CLARISSE PINTO AND KRISTEN FERNANDES

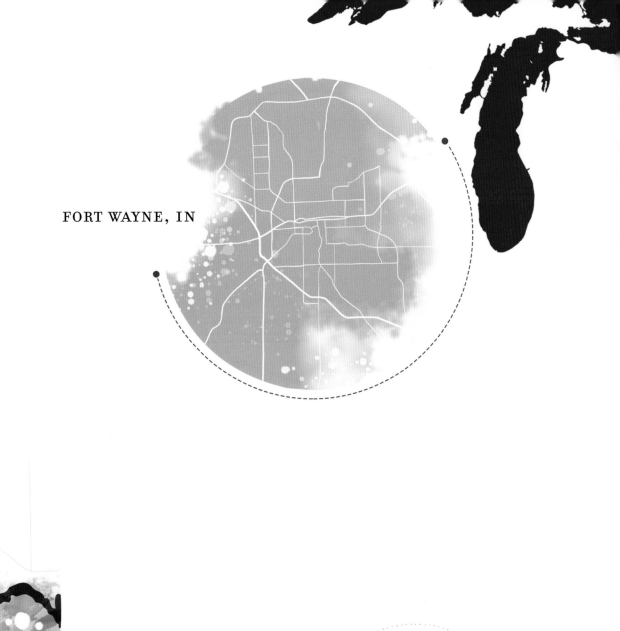

FORT WAYNE, IN

THE CITY THAT
SAVED ITSELF

The City That Saved Itself

Allyn West

The floodwater had reached the graves. It was April 2016, a Sunday in Houston, and I threw on a jacket and sloshed from a house I was renting through the last of two days of rain toward Brays Bayou.

Most days, Brays had a current that was barely discernible. Like Houston, it was in no hurry. It had a kind of lazy wisdom.

Most days, I ran on a greenway next to it, its wide banks supervised by egrets and wild with patches of evening primrose.

Today, though, Sunday, about when our taxes were due, Brays surged, and the current was creating whitecaps where the water whipped around the columns underneath the Lawndale Street bridge. I went down on the greenway until my running shoes edged up against the murk. I had never seen so much water where it didn't belong.

The last row of graves in the Forest Park Cemetery was submerged, the homemade memorials in danger of coming unstuck and floating off with the Styrofoam cups. It looked like a disaster, but I knew enough to know this is how the city had been engineered to work.

The length of Brays, as with the length of most of the bayous and creeks and gullies that ripple across the twenty-two watersheds here, had been straightened and channelized, dredged and widened, its banks paved in concrete, to do—*this*. The bayou, or what remained of it, if you could even still call it that, was intended to *convey*, to move water, engineers would tell you.

And I lived at the very end of the conveyance, as downstream as it gets, where Brays meets Buffalo Bayou and, together, they become the Houston Ship Channel, thick with tugboats and barges and cargo ships carrying gasoline products and plastic toys. All the water running off driveways and streets and down into the drainage systems in upstream neighborhoods thirty miles away was being sent here, to my neighborhood, which was now threatened.

I had been lulled into thinking *this* was how it was *supposed* to look. Someone somewhere made that decision, and we were all expected, now, to live with it.

MOST DAYS, it was easy to feel encouraged by a belief that we are able to engineer our way out of problems. Houston—which likes to think of itself as a city of innovation, a city that still brags about the historic achievements of NASA and the construction of the Astrodome, decades past the facts—reinforced this belief, but it wasn't wholly new. I think I always had some sense that the world was within my control.

I grew up in rural Indiana in a town of about five thousand people. My father packed up, got in the car, and drove away from us, and then he killed himself, and I spent most of my time alone on the farm where I lived with my grandparents. I watched the no-nonsense hardiness of my grandfather as he went around repairing whatever was broken. I would do that, too. Under the bed I kept a shoebox filled with contraptions I thought of as inventions—rubber bands stretched around a useless battery, spare buttons, just in case.

Growing up, I didn't know about disasters. In the Midwest, we worried about tornadoes, snowstorms, patches of black ice on country roads, but it was nothing we couldn't overcome. One house on the edge of town had a depressed yard that always filled up when it rained. Whoever lived there would wade out the next day to prop up a scarecrow in a rowboat. It was funny to me every time.

I would learn many years later that the nearest city, Fort Wayne, flooded the year I was born, in 1982, when exceptionally heavy spring rains combined with melting snow to cause the three rivers that converge there to rise out of their banks and drive nearly nine thousand people out of their homes. But it became part of a story of strength, not vulnerability. Volunteers—mostly high school students who were out for spring break—piled up barricades of sandbags throughout the city and went out in rescue boats. That year, Fort Wayne was called "The City That Saved Itself."

Decades later, even when I moved to Houston in 2008, I hadn't lived through anything worse than an ice storm. Houston changed that immediately. Three weeks after I packed up my little life and drove to an apartment in Montrose, a neighborhood larger than my hometown, the city braced for Hurricane Ike, swirling toward us from the Gulf of Mexico.

I didn't know what to do. I'd only seen images of hurricanes on the news, the fake bravado of weathermen pelted with sideways rain, the snapped palm trees. I asked one of the administrative assistants at the university where I was a graduate student whether she was planning to evacuate with her family. "We're staying," she said, as though she were annoyed by an inconvenience.

I would do that, too.

The hurricane crashed into Houston on a Friday night. I was asleep when it made landfall, though I lay listening to the winds whipping up into a frenzy and watched the sky turn a kind of sickly purple, light and air pollution and atmospheric pressure mixing in a dangerous way, as I nodded off.

When I woke up, the city was silent. I put on my running shoes to go have a look. The fence around my building was toppled, and broken branches lay everywhere. Entire live oaks had been uprooted and sprawled across the streets, their root systems gaping out. I wandered a few hours before trudging back to my apartment to eat the food I had before it started to spoil.

There was no power. Days passed without it. Classes at the university were cancelled. Thousands of families in neighborhoods all over the city were stuck where they were, roofs torn apart, tarps tied down, their lives threatened now by the heat and the humidity no one had the energy to air-condition away and the maladies usually ameliorated by machines that were no longer running.

Mayor Bill White pleaded with CenterPoint, the region's energy provider, to get more workers on the ground to repair lines that had been blown down and transformers that had been blown up. More than two million customers lacked power. Each day I would leave for work and hope mine would come back. Each night I would open the door, throw the switch, and rage in the dark because it hadn't.

There was nothing I could do. I could not save myself. And I realized, primally almost, how alone I was. Fundamentally. I had no way to survive like this, no way to clean or clothe my body, no way even to heat the food I was forced to buy at the grocery store because I could not grow or raise it without depending on the logistics of the supply chains of companies I couldn't understand, influence, or control. It was all *beyond* me.

The first shower I tried to take trickled out as a few drops, like a kind of baptism of helplessness.

One morning, I biked to Avalon Diner. It was one of the few restaurants able to open so soon after the hurricane. Almost everyone that morning had plugged a cell phone and a laptop to charge in the outlets. I picked at my eggs and overheard the woman next to me as she took a call.

"Finally!" she said.

She turned on her stool and announced to no one, or everyone, "We have power!"

That became the question so many of us started asking each other that first month after Ike. Do you have power? Did your power come back? How long have you been without power? These questions— or maybe my depressed answers—would come to define my life in Houston.

No, I don't.

No, it didn't.

Always, I started to think.

THEN IT WAS THAT SUNDAY in April with too much rain. The Tax Day Flood, it was called. I was living in Houston's East End then. I had stayed quiet for years, unplugged, essentially, but I was no longer alone at least.

I was married. My wife had delivered our baby. My runs on the greenway along Brays Bayou had turned into walks with a stroller. That Sunday, when my daughter was smaller than a pillow, I stood there near the water, holding her and shuddering at the strength of the current. How quickly it could whip her from my arms. How quickly the only things we love and want can disappear.

The next day, as the sun came out and the water had been conveyed out to sea, I went back to the greenway. Fish littered the path, stuck on the banks as the water receded. Most had suffocated. Some of the smaller ones flapped in the puddles that hadn't fully evaporated. I spotted a hotel ice bucket and scooped up a fish, ran it to the bayou, and dumped it. And I did that again. And then once more. But there were hundreds of fish, and the water was receding faster than I could move. There was no way I could go back for all of them. In the weeks to come, the matted wildflowers sprang back upright, stretching toward the sun.

Scavengers finished off the fish. The sediment that had caked onto the concrete was scraped away.

The Tax Day Flood, I would learn, had forced some people to evacuate their homes in canoes. In Cypress, north of Houston, a whole neighborhood was underwater. There was no going back for them, either.

HURRICANE HARVEY would come about a year and a half later. I had moved into an apartment in the middle of Houston. My daughter had moved away with her mother to another state, and I spent most of my time alone again.

I knew the city better by then. Knew much of it by heart. It had been a decade. I knew who designed what buildings. Knew where I'd have to step in the street when the sidewalks disappear.

Knew, now, that not all neighborhoods experience disasters the same way. The neighborhoods where power was slowest to be restored during Ike are the ones where Black and Hispanic people tend to live, where people with less wealth tend to live. They are the ones where the floods tend to be the worst—not because of bad luck, but because of bad design. Because of inequity. I knew now that these communities have been denied the kinds of structural investments that make it possible to survive disasters more intact: grocery stores where people can stock up on candles, gallons of water, and granola bars before the storm hits; home and flood insurance so they can receive financial assistance and rebuild after the storm leaves; trees and parks and detention basins and upgraded drainage pipes that might keep them from flooding to begin with. I knew the ways we build a city can impose vulnerabilities on some of us that are much larger than any one person could be expected to withstand.

It was almost dark when a coworker mentioned Harvey. It was forming in the Gulf. She said it looked as though it would make landfall that weekend, but the city had had so many near-misses for so many years I assumed this would be one, too. Still, I prepared. After work, I walked to the Fiesta Mart in Midtown and bought groceries and batteries, filled all the motley containers I had with tap water and went to bed as the storm swirled toward us.

I woke up to find my street underwater. The cars parked along the curb, mine included, were submerged. I sloshed to the end of my block, went the wrong way up an exit ramp to get a view of the downtown skyline. Whole freeways were underwater, and the rain was still coming down, pelting my jacket. I had never seen so much water where it didn't belong.

It kept raining for four more days.

My job, at the time, was working as an editor at a large daily newspaper, the *Houston Chronicle*. My duty was to try to see what was happening and help people with the information I thought they needed. Because it was 2017, social media was where I spent my time, and I became a witness.

I saw someone row a boat down the river of his street to rescue a neighbor. I heard the story of a teenager who stayed up all night coding a website so people could donate goods directly to emergency shelters. One person made a thousand sandwiches one day at a community kitchen. All across the city, teams of strangers were wading through floodwaters to knock on doors, deliver supplies, and help muck out other strangers' houses.

I'd spent my life alone. That shapes you. When I was a boy, I believed I had more power than I did. I believed the world was smaller than it is. I don't think I ever appreciated the fundamental precarity of having a body, the fundamental imbalance of scale between the world and me. Houston changed that. The city was too wide for me. It was too tall. I didn't understand it. I couldn't see the end of it. I couldn't comprehend it. I didn't have any power to change it. Everything about it was too much, all of it, and I was nothing, just as susceptible to any current as my daughter would be. What can one person do to fix flooding? What can one person do to fix climate change?

None of us can survive alone. That's what I witnessed after Harvey. Disasters can take away our power as individuals, and they can make us feel smaller even than we are, but they also charge us with connections to larger and larger communities. This is how we survive what we cannot control. I survived my father's suicide because my mother stayed. I survived my divorce because I had work to do. I'd spent my life alone, so I believed that was all I would ever be, that that was all there is, but I was wrong. Some of us need more help than others. Some of us have more to give, but there is power when we join with those who are near us. That is the only way this city can survive. Houston is built on decisions none of us made, imperiled by weather none of us can control. It is a city none of us can save on our own.

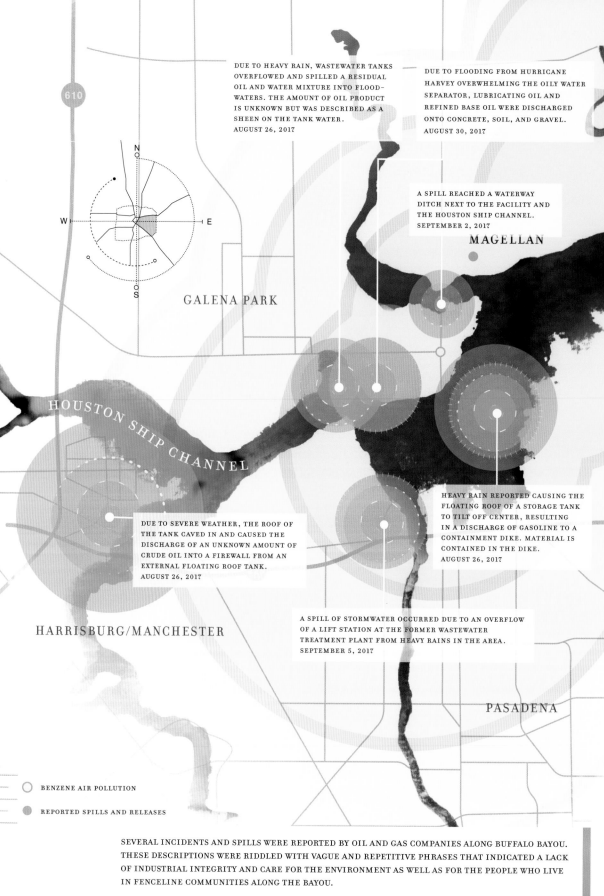

DUE TO HEAVY RAIN, WASTEWATER TANKS OVERFLOWED AND SPILLED A RESIDUAL OIL AND WATER MIXTURE INTO FLOOD-WATERS. THE AMOUNT OF OIL PRODUCT IS UNKNOWN BUT WAS DESCRIBED AS A SHEEN ON THE TANK WATER.
AUGUST 26, 2017

DUE TO FLOODING FROM HURRICANE HARVEY OVERWHELMING THE OILY WATER SEPARATOR, LUBRICATING OIL AND REFINED BASE OIL WERE DISCHARGED ONTO CONCRETE, SOIL, AND GRAVEL.
AUGUST 30, 2017

A SPILL REACHED A WATERWAY DITCH NEXT TO THE FACILITY AND THE HOUSTON SHIP CHANNEL.
SEPTEMBER 2, 2017

MAGELLAN

GALENA PARK

HOUSTON SHIP CHANNEL

HEAVY RAIN REPORTED CAUSING THE FLOATING ROOF OF A STORAGE TANK TO TILT OFF CENTER, RESULTING IN A DISCHARGE OF GASOLINE TO A CONTAINMENT DIKE. MATERIAL IS CONTAINED IN THE DIKE.
AUGUST 26, 2017

DUE TO SEVERE WEATHER, THE ROOF OF THE TANK CAVED IN AND CAUSED THE DISCHARGE OF AN UNKNOWN AMOUNT OF CRUDE OIL INTO A FIREWALL FROM AN EXTERNAL FLOATING ROOF TANK.
AUGUST 26, 2017

A SPILL OF STORMWATER OCCURRED DUE TO AN OVERFLOW OF A LIFT STATION AT THE FORMER WASTEWATER TREATMENT PLANT FROM HEAVY RAINS IN THE AREA.
SEPTEMBER 5, 2017

HARRISBURG/MANCHESTER

PASADENA

○ BENZENE AIR POLLUTION

● REPORTED SPILLS AND RELEASES

SEVERAL INCIDENTS AND SPILLS WERE REPORTED BY OIL AND GAS COMPANIES ALONG BUFFALO BAYOU. THESE DESCRIPTIONS WERE RIDDLED WITH VAGUE AND REPETITIVE PHRASES THAT INDICATED A LACK OF INDUSTRIAL INTEGRITY AND CARE FOR THE ENVIRONMENT AS WELL AS FOR THE PEOPLE WHO LIVE IN FENCELINE COMMUNITIES ALONG THE BAYOU.

DESIGN BY JULIA ONG

We All Breathe the Same Air

A CONVERSATION WITH
P. GRACE TEE LEWIS

Lacy M. Johnson

Before beginning her training as an epidemiologist, P. Grace Tee Lewis served as a Peace Corps volunteer and taught math and science in Zimbabwe. Now a health scientist with the Environmental Defense Fund (EDF), Grace studies the health impacts of air pollution, focusing specifically on environmental justice issues in the Houston region. She serves on the Regional Air Quality Planning Advisory Committee for the Houston-Galveston Area Council (H-GAC) and is a member of the executive committee, where she tries to advance education and priorities about improving our regional air quality. I spoke with Grace over Zoom at the beginning of 2021 about air quality, public health, and the links between flooding and air pollution. Our conversation has been edited for length and clarity.

LMJ: What can you tell me about air pollution in our region?

GL: I think that air pollution is one of the problems people don't give as much attention to as they should. Unfortunately, we happen to live in one part of the United States where air quality is impacted by the petrochemical industry that is replete around us. The air that we breathe, the clean water that we need, all of those things impact our health in general. Living close to a facility that produces air pollution can affect the development of lungs in children and may exacerbate or contribute to the development of chronic health conditions—such as respiratory diseases, asthma, chronic obstructive pulmonary disease for older populations, heart disease, diabetes, strokes, preterm births, babies with low birth weight, and neurological deficits in older adults. We see that air pollution has long-term implications for our health. We see differences in life expectancy, certainly, for different parts of our city, where you have sometimes up to a thirty-year difference in life expectancy for more affluent communities in comparison to lower-wealth communities of color in our region.

That's not acceptable. And it's likely a reflection of historical systemic inequities that impact communities. Obviously, the history of redlining not only defined where communities of color could live but also established what are known as "sacrifice zones"—places where developers would freely allow industry to be located right next to residential areas. These areas were home to populations of people who were disenfranchised in their ability to advocate for themselves politically and prevent this type of industry being put into their communities, whether the industry was hazardous waste sites or garbage pits and whatnot.

I think Robert Bullard's work in mapping all of those hazards in our region has been fundamental to our understanding that these overburdened African American communities were the host sites for all of the waste and other unwanted industry that fueled our city's growth and development. Really, prosperity was born on the back of these communities of color, reflecting how the city prioritized industry over community health in certain areas. The purposeful, systemic sacrifice of these communities in favor of white or more affluent communities really laid the foundation for inequities of environmental exposures in transportation, in education, in investments in the infrastructure, and in the development of these communities, and that is reflected in the health disparities of Houstonians.

I think nothing brings that more to light than the COVID pandemic, where we see that those communities that have been overburdened in the past with inequities and environmental injustice are also those same communities that are being hardest hit by the pandemic.

LMJ: And each exposure does not exist in a vacuum, right? It's generational, it's cumulative, and the effects are cumulative as well.

GL: Yes. There is a compounding overburden to these communities— layer upon layer of disenfranchisement, lack of investment in their communities, and policies that are purposely intended to try to relegate them to exposures that others do not want. It's exactly as you're saying; it's generational. If we stop and think of some of these communities—like the Fifth Ward and Sunnyside and Pleasantville—these are the areas where African American communities were first founded after slavery was abolished and people began to populate the region independently.

So when we talk about environmental injustice, we're talking about the unequal distribution of environmental hazards. We're talking about how different communities and different populations are exposed to an increased amount of pollution that's unequal in comparison to other parts of the city. You have these spatial differences in where pollution is located. Environmental injustice is born out of systemic environmental racism and the structural, historical effort to create sacrifice zones in different parts of different cities, where industry is heavily concentrated and these communities bear the greatest burden of environmental exposures in comparison to other parts of the same region.

LMJ: When we're working and advocating for environmental justice, what is the outcome that we're seeking?

GL: Obviously, equity, in my opinion, to try to ease the burden. Industry is going to go someplace, but we don't have to concentrate it all in communities of color. We need to think about how we can equitably distribute or share the burden of the industrial development and growth that is needed to maintain a strong economy. I don't think those two things are mutually exclusive. I think we need to concentrate it in areas where there's less population being exposed and there is less potential cumulative burden to a community.

We don't have to cluster every single concrete batch plant, metal recycler, and medical waste facility within a half-mile of one another. We need to think about where we can relocate these businesses so that we're not disproportionately impacting the health of Black and Brown communities, and so that we're not destroying a community by running a freeway through it and cutting it off from a neighboring community just to put up a freeway or to locate a new industrial facility or to widen the ship channel at the cost of the integrity of a community that may have been there for one hundred years.

LMJ: How do flooding events like Harvey or Imelda—or even the Tax Day or Memorial Day Floods—how do these types of flood events contribute to air pollution?

GL: These flood events, especially hurricanes and natural disasters, contribute to air pollution because if we know a hurricane is coming, most industries will shut down their production. In the process of shutting down, and then starting up again after the storm has passed, these facilities release a monumental amount of air pollution.

But also sometimes there are industrial accidents that release pollution into the air. During Harvey, the Arkema facility's storage and safety measures were overwhelmed because of the inundation. Harvey showed us that storage tanks are particularly vulnerable, and we've seen that in subsequent hurricanes as well. They have not fixed that issue completely in designing storage tanks that are able to withstand these types of natural disaster events.

In Galena Park, for instance, we have a lot of industrial facilities that are located on the road across the street from the community. During Harvey, some roads were flooded, and as a result, the residents could not get out. There are just a couple of ways in and out of the community. Residents were trapped in their homes if they didn't evacuate.

During that same time, the Magellan facility had a leak in their gas storage tanks, which released 2.5 million pounds of air pollution into the air.[1] That's an immense amount of volatile organic compounds. To give you context, the next largest release in our region was 745,000 pounds, also during Harvey. There was another facility, a pipeline facility at the Galena Park terminal, that also released 56,000 pounds of VOCs into the air. You've got several of these industrial facilities, in addition to the ones that were shutting down, having released all of their chemicals into the air, and during that time residents were not able to evacuate the area and they were out in their yards cleaning up after the hurricane. All of those chemicals—high levels of those chemicals—were in their environment, and so they were exposed to that.

LMJ: How did that release happen? Were those facilities flooded? Were they hit by the hurricane?

GL: In the case of those storage tanks for Magellan, they were damaged by the flooding. There was just too much water on the tanks. The design of those storage tanks can be better, and there hasn't been any mandate to change the design of those storage tanks. A lot of times with accidents like these the roof collapses or the pipeline is impacted. Damage to the equipment is the cause of a lot of these disasters, but the storage tanks are particularly vulnerable.

We saw that for many places in Harvey the design of the storage tank and contact with water caused it to rupture. For Magellan, it was two storage tanks, which is why Galena Park got so much exposure. It wasn't just one storage tank that failed; it was two storage tanks. And it wasn't just that facility; it was several facilities adjacent to them where that happened.

LMJ: And when these releases happen, accidentally or not, there are rarely consequences for the polluter. So it seems there's nothing preventing them from doing it.

GL: Right. There's nothing preventing them. Plus the state turned off the air monitors and didn't turn them back on for some time after the storm. The state didn't have the technical capacity to quickly deploy equipment to monitor all of the compounds that were being released. We're talking about benzene, a known carcinogen, in our environment. There's no safe level of benzene exposure, and yet we're unable to quantify how much is being released into a community where they're flooded in. They can't leave because of the flooding and they're stuck with these massive amounts of air pollution. They don't have air-conditioning; they're forced to breathe this air pollution. That's a travesty.

On top of that, the governor will often suspend reporting rules during a disaster, and the Texas Commission on Environmental Quality (TCEQ) is less concerned about enforcement. There's forgiveness for polluting, without any consequences, during these industrial events. Certainly, some of them are beyond their control, like if they've had a malfunction and they try their best to address it as quickly as possible, but even accidental releases still put people's health at risk.

I think there's a ripple effect, too. It's not just occurring in our region. You have upstream producers in the Permian Basin and other places that couldn't send their product into the Houston region for processing, so they're flaring in these communities where oil and gas are being produced. That is an added impact of flooding in our region, because these other communities will have health implications from that flaring.

LMJ: Let's go back to this question of turning off the air monitors for a moment. One of the major problems with this is that without the air monitors, these communities don't know what they're being exposed to and there's no way to hold polluters accountable for what they're releasing.

GL: Yes. When the state turns off the regulatory air monitors, it's maybe to protect their equipment to be able to withstand the storm, but they certainly could turn them on more quickly than they do. Like after Harvey, the monitors were off for quite some time in areas like Manchester, where there were high releases of benzene. That leaves the community unable to quantify what the ambient air quality is like and what exposures they're getting to potentially harmful volatile organic compounds and known carcinogens.

I think these projects in community air monitoring and low-cost air monitors that we've been working on, which are beginning to proliferate across the nation, are an important way to have an understanding of what air quality is like and not be beholden to the regulatory agencies to say, "There's no problem in your community."

In our case, what we've been doing is establishing a monitoring network that says, "Hey, we're seeing these unusual readings." While it might not be regulatory, it's sufficient to ask for investigations by city and county officials. Communities will have the air quality data to understand the patterns in their neighborhoods. For instance, are we seeing releases in the middle of the night? We have seen that periodically, spikes that are happening between 11:00 p.m. and 4:00 a.m., or releases that are happening on the weekends or at times when people are maybe unaware of what's happening.

These community air monitoring networks play a fundamental role in trying to increase accountability by industry and also to initiate investigations, so that we won't have a situation where a community member reports something and the monitoring agency can't come out until three days later and by that time the release is gone. Now, we have the measurements from these air monitoring networks. Although these are low-cost networks, and we don't have the same precision that you have in regulatory instruments, there is, at least, data to show we saw the spike here.

It's an incremental endeavor and, to be frank, why do communities have to bear this financial burden to provide evidence that the state or local government should be collecting to protect their public health to begin with? These are the same communities that have been advocating for improvements, and they shouldn't be burdened with having to collect their own information.

LMJ: What are some of the obstacles to greater transparency, to greater accountability?

GL: These networks are expensive, which is one barrier. I think community-based organizations typically work with a volunteer base. They don't typically have a large amount of money to allocate to put these things together. We've worked with Pleasantville, with Sunnyside, with Fifth Ward, and with Galena Park in our Data to Action efforts. We've had support from the Houston Endowment in the past, which has been great. But in general, community-based organizations don't have the capacity to afford to analyze and communicate this information. That's a real barrier.

Even low-cost equipment is not cheap, and to get more high-grade instruments, that's even more expensive. They may not want to spend all their money on air monitors. Then what do they do with the myriad data points they accumulate? Who helps them digest and transform those into something that can be reflected in data visualizations or communication to their residents, to the city, and to the county to show the patterns in their data? I think there's a lot that needs to happen there, and certainly, people are willing to help, but it's also a matter of finding those connections and putting people together and having willing academic partners to help them in the work, to provide the science that they need beyond the collection of the data.

LMJ: I think I'm also asking why the city and the county aren't doing what seems like their job of monitoring the air? Why don't the city and county have air monitors in these communities? The state does, but they turn them off. What obstacles are preventing the city and county from doing that work?

GL: Well, the city and the county happen to have a huge amount of land to cover, and there's a large number of permits to navigate. I think a lot of times, they spend their time having to respond to stuff and they also don't have a huge budget.

Until the county got that recent $11 million investment in pollution control services, they had been working on shoestring budgets themselves. To be fair, from my perspective, until Harris County Judge Lina Hidalgo came into office, I don't think there was a lot of dedication to enforcement beyond the requirements and there wasn't a willingness to let community groups be at the table, to engage in a community air monitoring program. Until Judge Hidalgo came into office, that didn't happen. Her willingness to have community partners at the table is a more recent evolution in transparency in government. That was not there in previous Republican administrations.

I also think there's a lot of pushback from the state to have a more conservative approach, and that has a trickle-down effect on local agencies and how they can do their work. While local agencies might want to have improvements, they can't necessarily do that without the support of the state or federal government.

We saw the Trump administration decimate the chemical disaster safety rule and other rules meant to protect public health. We saw less dedication to policing and enforcement of industry regulations and an effort to relax the rules to make it easier for businesses to pollute and to roll back some of our environmental protections that have been in place.

LMJ: Tell me about the One Breath Partnership.

GL: One Breath Partnership is an alliance of different environmental groups and nonprofits that work together in our state. A major part of our work is to amplify the narratives of communities and their advocacy efforts. Those stories, and keeping them in the forefront of people's consciousness, are a critical component of what we do. Since I first started at EDF, I have seen the importance of the role the media can play in holding government agencies accountable for what's happening. I think, personally, that the state and TCEQ, as well as the county, have been more accountable, have made more infrastructure investments because of the media spotlight and the work that these five organizations collectively have put together.

LMJ: What is one thing that you wish more people knew or thought about when it comes to air pollution or to air quality and public health?

GL: That we need stronger environmental protections. We need to take a different tack from what has been happening in previous administrations and try to right the wrongs and bring an end to environmental racism. That would ultimately help improve air quality and people's health.

But most importantly, I wish more people understood that we all breathe the same air. I have often thought that people are purposely ignorant of the fact that air quality issues affect us all. I live in the Heights, but I know other people who live north of the city, west of the city, who don't stop and think that we are all breathing the same air. I would love people to know that people who live on the east side deserve equity. They deserve to breathe the same clean air that we breathe on a regular basis.

COMMUNITY

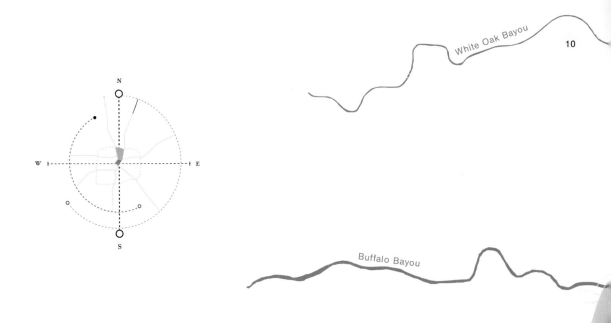

CLIMATE DIGNITY

Buffalo Bayou

AS DEVASTATING NATURAL DISASTERS BECOME THE NEW NORMAL, THE SYSTEMIC FACTORS THAT
DIVIDE THE COUNTRY'S MOST DIVERSE CITY BECOME GLARINGLY APPARENT. HOWEVER, SO DO THOSE
THAT UNITE ITS LOCAL COMMUNITIES. THIS MAP AIMS TO DEPICT HOW THE POWERS THAT BE CLASH
WITH THE POWER OF CIVIC ORGANIZATION, NOT JUST ACROSS THE HIGHWAY BUT ACROSS COUNTLESS
OBSTACLES OF FINANCE AND ACCESS.

DESIGN BY CLARISSE PINTO, MANUEL VÁZQUEZ, AND WESTON WOODFIN

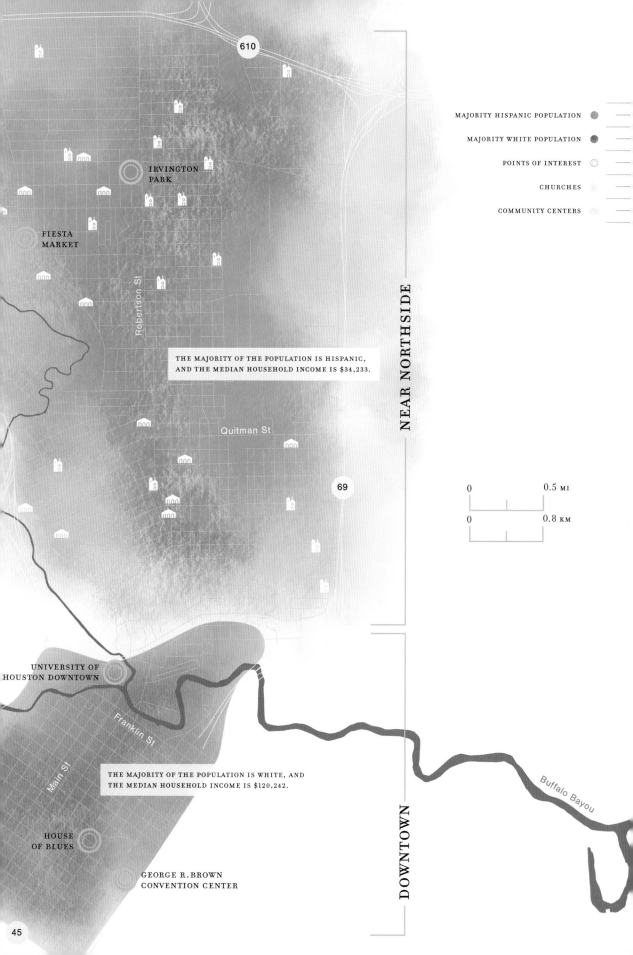

610

MAJORITY HISPANIC POPULATION
MAJORITY WHITE POPULATION
POINTS OF INTEREST
CHURCHES
COMMUNITY CENTERS

IRVINGTON
PARK

FIESTA
MARKET

Robertson St

THE MAJORITY OF THE POPULATION IS HISPANIC,
AND THE MEDIAN HOUSEHOLD INCOME IS $34,233.

Quitman St

69

0   0.5 MI

0   0.8 KM

NEAR NORTHSIDE

UNIVERSITY OF
HOUSTON DOWNTOWN

Franklin St

Main St

THE MAJORITY OF THE POPULATION IS WHITE, AND
THE MEDIAN HOUSEHOLD INCOME IS $120,242.

Buffalo Bayou

DOWNTOWN

HOUSE
OF BLUES

GEORGE R.BROWN
CONVENTION CENTER

Climate Dignity

READING BALDWIN AFTER HARVEY AND
IN THE NEAR NORTHSIDE

Daniel Peña

In the wake of Harvey, I'm reading the title essay from James Baldwin's *Notes of a Native Son* with my first-year students.[1] The first lines go, "On the 29th of July, in 1943, my father died. On the same day, a few hours later, his last child was born." Someone goes *whoooooaaaaa. What does Walter Mercado have to say about that?*

Everyone laughs—we need to laugh—or at least everyone who is vaguely familiar with Mercado, a staple in Spanish-language homes in Houston, especially in the parts of Houston where my students live: Near Northside, which is just north of downtown, which is just west of the industrial scrapyards near Fifth Ward and, a little past that, the refineries that pour benzene over Manchester, though my students have no illusions or pride over which neighborhood is safer, cleaner, less susceptible to cancer. As a student once told me, *Houston is cancer.* This, they're always careful to remind me, especially includes Near Northside.

Walter Mercado is a lot of things, but he's perhaps best known as the guy who captivates everyone's superstitious tía or 'buelito. He can foresee the cataclysmic events that might enter one's life. He can tell whether this month will be a bad month or a good month for your health, or your business. Whether your ex has or hasn't been sabotaging your love life. Whether fortune or disaster is in your future or not. He's possibly the most famous TV astrologer in Latin America. People take him seriously. And I mean *really seriously.*

First-year students always have an interesting way of connecting the dots in subconscious ways. While we take a moment to poke fun at Mercado—and by extension our superstitious aunts and 'buelitos—we unpack shades of those same generational rifts that Baldwin explores between himself and his father. But we're unpacking something deeper, too—the imagery of the 1943 Harlem riots, which, as one student points out, isn't unlike the imagery all around us in post-Harvey Houston. Talking about the riots, Baldwin writes:

> Sheets, blankets, and clothing of every description formed a kind of path, as though people had dropped them while running. I truly had not realized that Harlem *had* so many stores until I saw them all smashed open; the first time the word *wealth* ever entered my mind in relation to Harlem was when I saw it scattered in the streets.[2]

Moving through Near Northside just days after the last rain squall from Harvey has fallen—near Robertson Street, say, on the way to Irvington Park—it's easy to spot piles of debris: soggy sheetrock, splayed insulation, discarded clothes, crusting blankets, expensive waterlogged furniture baking in the humidity and sun. The debris lines the curbs, waiting to be collected. Seeing it all unpacked, I would have never guessed there was so much *stuff* in Houston. But there it is, waiting to be collected, all of that money hauled off to some dump.

SOMEHOW I KNEW Near Northside would salvage us. Us, as in me and my wife and my cousin Carlos and his girlfriend, Nancy. Carlos is my younger cousin, slightly older than my little sister, and being such, I've always felt a kind of responsibility for him, though I know well he can take care of himself—he's built like a brick shithouse and incredibly savvy with anything mechanical or electric. He unpacks and assembles too-expensive crystal chandeliers shipped over from China into the port of Houston for a living, his fingers firm but precise as jewelers. Between shifts he shoots hoops in his work uniform—the only clothes he has left when he arrives at my house.

His own apartment, near the Barker Reservoir, flooded past the roof; his car is somewhere in the wash. He admitted that he wouldn't want it anymore even if it were salvageable. "The water stunk," he told me, "something chemical. It's burning my skin."

When he arrived at my apartment downtown, on a bus carrying masses of people to the George R. Brown Convention Center, where evacuees were being temporarily resettled, he was soaked to the bone. News crews parked their satellite vans right up on the curb of the convention center, so the buses handling evacuees had to park by the House of Blues on Caroline Street, a significant walk to the convention center itself, though just two blocks from my apartment, where I had tea, a meal, and fresh clothes laid out for Carlos and Nancy.

Germaphobe that I am, I kept thinking on our walk home in the rain how the first thing I'd do was shower and then keep showering. Take off my clothes and burn them. Scrub my skin endlessly. Get into a bed and fall asleep for days. But Carlos asked for a beer. And then just a drag of tequila to celebrate their survival. And then it wasn't long before we had a feast. Pancakes and eggs and bacon and the orange juice we had left and coffee and cookies and toast and more beer and some cherry tomatoes my wife, Sophia, laid out, "to keep it healthy."

Eventually, the television went off. And then the radio. And then it was just us in our bubble, us pretending that we had enough of everything, like everything was normal for two or three days. Never mind that we hadn't planned for four people to live in six hundred square feet with only the food warming in our refrigerator. Never mind that the water reeked as it came out of the faucet. Never mind that we had only so much bottled water left. And the cars were flooding in the garage downstairs. And it kept rising and rising.

When everything was gone, I think it was Nancy—a lifelong Houstonian—who said to me, "You have to go where our people are. Those corner stores and grocery stores. They won't let us starve." Our people, as in Latinx people, as in the next neighborhood over: Near Northside. In the Fiesta Supermarkets where my students were working throughout the storm. In the panaderías where they were baking as the parking lots and culverts and homes on Fulton Street were flooding. In the taquerías owned by their parents where the first responders from all over the city were fueling up to go back out again.

Nancy knew, as her parents knew before her, that to certain grocers—and certain friends who worked in those grocery stores—those rationing signs were simply that: just signs. And if you needed it, and you had a bulletproof excuse, the eggs were yours. The bottled water, too. Even tortillas, freshly pressed, freshly packaged under a neon sign.

And when we got there, it was true. I couldn't believe it was true. The generosity of my students and their families and their neighbors. The efficiency of the operation. The eggs, the bottled water, the neon sign.

There was a middle-aged woman in a red shirt feeding masa balls into an electric prensa machine with a kind of calm efficiency verging on Zen. I remember standing in front of a stack of tortillas taller than my head and watching her. Her face was tired and red but not slack. Rheumy eyes one might mistake for sun-wearied. I remember I picked up a stack and gave her this nod, like, *thanks*. And she cut me this glance, like, *I'm busy*. And I remember thinking I'd never seen so much abundance. Especially not in a neighborhood so recently devastated. I mean, actually in the process of being devastated. And I remember that I couldn't believe she was still working as we just walked around in there, like everyone else was just walking around in there, looking at the stuff. Starving but sated by the sight of so much abundance. And calmed by the fact that you could grab it. And you could leave with it. And in knowing she, like everyone else working there that evening, was there, too, even as her home might be flooding; she was creating some sense of normalcy for all us schmucks who could actually never repay her.

OF COURSE, the circumstances between Harvey and Harlem are different, but the fault lines exposed by those events are not. Concerning Houston, we know now that while the storm largely affected everyone, the poorest (including many people of color) are still the ones left in the shelters. While FEMA assistance is available for those who had the means to own a home, those who didn't now face the bare-knuckles market that is the newfangled housing shortage. While the financial center of downtown Houston largely avoided catastrophic flooding, unscrupulous land speculators exploited poor Brown and Black Houstonians who couldn't afford not to live in floodplains, especially (like my cousin Carlos) in the vicinity of the Addicks and Barker Reservoirs. While documented people had the option of fleeing Harvey or sticking it out at home, undocumented people were either corralled as they tried to evacuate or were otherwise left to their own devices for fear of Border Patrol, who maintained a presence near area shelters.

The connective tissue I think my students were trying to articulate between Harvey and Harlem goes beyond just the surface of that image.

It goes as deep as what that image represents: a riot as a communal expression of frustration with white control over the Black body (and by extension Black dignity) through systems of oppression, financial and otherwise.

In *Notes of a Native Son*, the Harlem riots can be read as the Black body asserting its dignity over white capitalism. The catalyst for the riot is the murder of a Black soldier by a white policeman. It's no accident that in the essay, white-owned businesses are primarily targeted. That obscene amount of wealth in the face of poverty is targeted. The financial order of white landlord/white business owner leeching off the Black community is overturned.

Echoes of that frustration ring out in the classroom as we discuss it. And then we get off on another discussion with Harvey in the backs of our minds: Why were homes ever built and sold in those floodplains to begin with? Which banks, businesses, or people owned that land before? Why is flood insurance so expensive? Why was the financial center of downtown designed not to flood, but the rest of the city wasn't? Why do the reservoirs empty out into the poorest parts of town? How can that much community wealth be wiped out in a matter of days? But more importantly, who were the people who profited?

In these questions we're talking about Baldwin, but of course we're talking about ourselves, about dignity. Latinx dignity specifically. And as my students vent, it suddenly dawns on me that climate change is a social justice issue, too. Harvey alone dumped 33 trillion gallons of water over Houston, enough to cover the entire state of Arizona in one foot of water.[3] And yet there are still those invested in denying that climate change is real. But why? How?

While at once we're raging against the systems that made our communities vulnerable to the storm, we must acknowledge that climate change denial is systematic in the way it strips dignity from vulnerable communities of color not financially equipped to deal with the fallout of those superstorms. And occasionally, even among climate change believers, the rhetoric of oppression is used to place blame on communities of color for simply being (read: existing) in the path of destruction.

When a superstorm hits, news anchors, pundits, and analysts of various stripes go on the scene with their spotless LL Bean boots and cable news TV slickers to ask—in so many words—what did you do *that this happened to you?*

At first, the questions are familiar: *Why did you buy here? Why not evacuate? Are you going to hunker down?* And then they become weaponized: *Do you not bear any responsibility for your family's safety? Do you know [are you too dumb to know] that this storm will kill you? How do you think your family feels about that?*

In that way, it's easier to say, *They brought it on themselves. They deserved it.* Which comes from the same place in the heart as denying service (as Baldwin writes about) or denying someone their dignity. It's also an all-too-convenient diffusion of responsibility for climate change deniers—*this is a socioeconomic/race/class problem, not a climate change problem.* Those red herrings conveniently detract from the truth.

LINKING BACK TO WEALTH, it's obvious, but it should be said, that energy companies have the most to profit from denial. Historically, that's been the truth. But also, there are systems that have historically contributed to and sometimes benefited from the fault lines exposed in the wake of Harvey. With recovery efforts run by energy czars already under way, it seems as though there's an implied emphasis on the recovery of the energy system, which is, in effect, an emphasis on the preservation of white wealth tied up in that system. While Marvin Odum, the former Shell Oil president appointed by Mayor Turner to be Chief Recovery Officer, has boasted of the $1.17 billion brought into Houston for federal disaster relief for those affected by Harvey, we also know that that number is only a fraction of the proposed $10 billion (requested from FEMA) that Houston is considering using to build "a coastal barrier of dunes and gates to provide storm-surge protection for the region's vulnerable oil refineries and shipping channel." And as Odum and his chief of staff, Niel Golightly (also on loan from Shell Oil), phase out of their roles with the city (Odum stepped down from his role as Recovery Czar in November of 2018), there is no doubt that their visions and plans for the recovery are well in place as the city heads into the execution phase of those plans.

I THINK THE IMAGES of Harlem and Houston are more interlinked than not. Two different catalysts, but one similar struggle for dignity. And I think it's worth it to ask how Brown and Black dignities are being considered in light of climate change. It's time we start thinking, too, about climate change's systematic denial and what those who deny its existence have to gain.

Once the rain passed and the bayous fell and the Arkema chemical plant burned itself dry, it seemed (in the aftermath of the storm) as though all anyone could talk about was opening doors. People began returning home to survey the damage, to piece together what remained of their lives. And steadily, those disaster-porn-freak-show kinds of stories (news crews waiting in the wings) started pouring in to catch heartbreak in action. And I think we were supposed to feel sorry and shocked, but I felt anger before I felt any of those things—anger at the fact that those people, those victims, were being exploited twice. Once by the storm, and once by the cameras that used them as bait.

In the aftermath of Harvey, it seemed the impulse to follow someone into their flooded home—to capture their very private heartbreak on camera—came from the same place in the heart as blaming them for their misfortune. It was, I believe, where #HoustonStrong came from, too—all just ways of looking away, deflecting blame, compartmentalizing a collective trauma in order to compel an entire group of victims to survive, or not. If you are not Houston Strong, then what are you? The answer to that question is arguably a problem for a city that desperately needed to deflect blame, that desperately needed to squash any semblance of victimhood and replace it with pride. *You survived this, look at you* feels so much better than *What happened to me? And why did this happen to me? And who is responsible for this happening to me?*—questions that might unravel an entire city or its government or its government's legitimacy.

To wrap your mind around the absurdity of it all, I think it's easy to think of other major historical disasters in other major cities and see if they still ring true: #DresdenStrong #ChernobylStrong. You get the idea.

Anyway, suffice it to say that after the anger subsided, I did feel that shock, my heart breaking for other people returning to their lives, opening their doors. I'm ashamed to say my heart broke a little less for Carlos—maybe because being my first cousin, he is part me, something nearing half. And would you treat anyone nearly as bad as you might treat yourself? As for me, family is always a close second. Deep down, I'm suspicious that they'll always be able to handle it. Call it pride or whatever. The defensive, insulating kind of pride that veers away from victimhood (or reacts to it). But also a kind of pride deeper in the blood, like the suspicion that neither Carlos nor I could cry any tear our fathers and mothers haven't cried before.

How much had our families sacrificed to come to Texas from Mexico? And here we were in Texas ruin. Wrecked but alive. And even amid ruin, who is to say our 'buelito wouldn't claim even this patch of Texas as his own and be satisfied just to live in it? In the blood, I know his own hopes were deeper than just getting by, but deeper in the blood, I also know he might have bought a #HoustonStrong cap and worn it most days of the year.

I wasn't there when Carlos stood in front of his door, but in my mind he doesn't pause a moment before going in. He just walks in, Kramer-style, and surveys the damage in private. Doesn't even think about his car around the corner that's mostly flooded. Or the weird disk of kombucha bacteria that he keeps in a tank to make kombucha tea (still there in the tank on the floor but the tea long gone). In my mind, he just moves around the soggy room, the smell of mildew or mold in the air, and tries to put the furniture back where he put it before he evacuated—all of his guitars stacked high by the roof. His most valued and prized possessions worth tens of thousands of dollars.

To his amazement, the water carried them up and out into the house before laying them down gently but completely destroyed. The wood on his classical is not perforated or even warped yet, but the tension of the strings has ripped the glued-on bridge away from the body. The white powder of sheetrock dusts the black case. On the complete opposite side of his apartment, Carlos's vintage, out-of-production rosewood Ibanez Musician, an electric guitar that used to belong to his father, my uncle, rests with the case open. There are pieces missing from it, and the steel saddle is scarred with grime and patina.

The guitar is from the 1980s, but in my mind it might as well be as old as my family itself. That Ibanez had been there for every Christmas and every New Year's in San Antonio since forever, plugged into a staticky amplifier first, and then, in our teenage years, filtered through a cheap fuzz pedal to mask the crackling and pings that eventually got us relegated to the porch in the dead of winter, where the adults would drink with red eyes and someone's weird boyfriend would smoke alone and we'd play Metallica too long and our Texas heroes, too—Stevie Ray

Vaughan and Eric Johnson. Maybe a lick or two. Carlos could play the songs in their entirety. Talented in that way, even at twelve years old, he could play anything. He'd show up to contests, win more guitars. He'd bring them over. He'd let our uncle Mario play "La Bamba" on them after Uncle Mario asked if we had girlfriends and say, "Watch this." And it was always the same "La Bamba," and we had to be, like, cool. And then he'd do it again come Thanksgiving. Or my 'buelito's birthday. Or his funeral. And then the Christmas after that. New Year's after that. Mother's Day. My wedding day. That guitar just clanging away the years like it might never stop.

An earlier version of this essay appeared in Ploughshares *on September 25, 2017.*

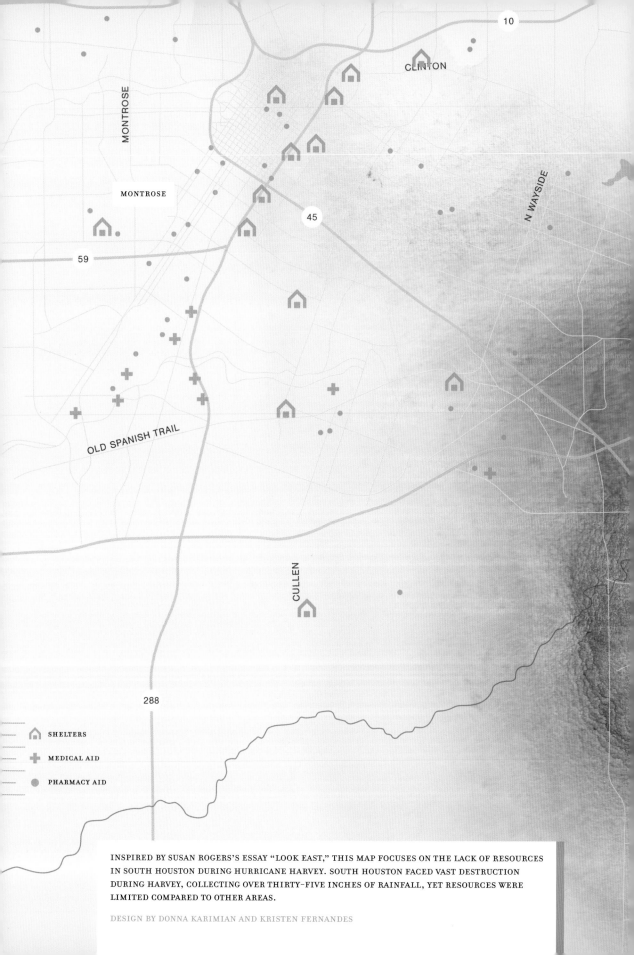

10

CLINTON

MONTROSE

MONTROSE

N WAYSIDE

45

59

OLD SPANISH TRAIL

CULLEN

288

SHELTERS

MEDICAL AID

PHARMACY AID

INSPIRED BY SUSAN ROGERS'S ESSAY "LOOK EAST," THIS MAP FOCUSES ON THE LACK OF RESOURCES IN SOUTH HOUSTON DURING HURRICANE HARVEY. SOUTH HOUSTON FACED VAST DESTRUCTION DURING HARVEY, COLLECTING OVER THIRTY-FIVE INCHES OF RAINFALL, YET RESOURCES WERE LIMITED COMPARED TO OTHER AREAS.

DESIGN BY DONNA KARIMIAN AND KRISTEN FERNANDES

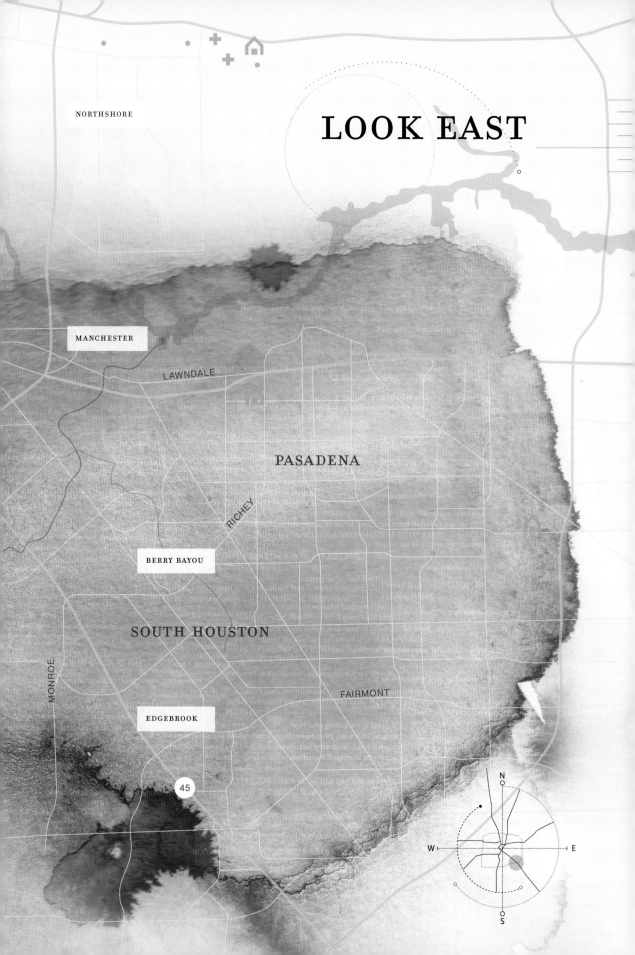

LOOK EAST

NORTHSHORE

MANCHESTER

LAWNDALE

PASADENA

RICHEY

BERRY BAYOU

SOUTH HOUSTON

MONROE

FAIRMONT

EDGEBROOK

45

N

W — E

S

Look East

Susan Rogers

It was near the end of August in 2017 when the destructive potential of Hurricane Harvey first began coming into focus. The evening news, dominated by the weather segment for days, continued to repeat the dire rainfall predictions—thirty to forty inches of rain.[1] These predictions challenged common sense, seeming more dystopian than real. Even with the precedent of Tropical Storm Allison, which dumped thirty-five inches of rain in the hardest-hit areas of Harris County over five days in 2001 and flooded 73,000 homes, the forecast was difficult to comprehend.

By Thursday evening, August 24, the reality of what we were facing settled in. I made my way to the grocery store that evening to prepare, I certainly wasn't alone, and I was late. The store was nearly empty: no water, or bread, or even a badly bruised banana remained. I shared a shrug and nervous laughter with the other delinquent shoppers. I left with a few snacks, but no water or batteries, and went back home.

By Friday, nothing had changed. The local weather forecast continued to sound the alarm, and it seemed certain the storm was going to be very, very bad. Even Space City Weather, a website run by two local weather experts to provide real information without hype or drama, could not calm the fears. I realized I needed to solve my battery and water problem. I learned something that day that I won't soon forget: that while the grocery store shelves were empty, my corner store had plenty of water, batteries, and snacks, and the auto parts stores (which we have in abundance) have plenty of flashlights. As I settled in on Friday evening, spending hours moving all of my furniture, papers, and other important memorabilia to the highest points possible in preparation for the worst-case scenario, it seemed like just maybe too much was being made of this Harvey thing. Other people were out living their lives, and the rain was holding off.

On Saturday night, the heavens opened wide and everything began to change. Around 9:00 p.m. the rain started falling, and hard. The sound of rainfall echoed throughout my house and cascaded off the roof in a continuous waterfall. I paced. I live on the east side of the city, a couple of miles south of the Houston Ship Channel in Meadowcreek Village. My house is low, sits on a slab, and is adjacent to Berry Bayou. During any rain event, my nerves shake and I open my computer and toggle between the interactive Harris County Flood Warning System site, to measure the rainfall and bayou levels, and the weather radar. This night was no different in that regard, but it was different in every other. At 1:44 a.m. I posted on my Facebook page that the rainfall gauge located across the street from me had recorded thirteen inches in just three hours. Soon after, a news crew on the Gulf Freeway, about two miles southeast, began broadcasting people wading out of the Edgebrook neighborhood in chest-high water. Around the same time, a friend in Kashmere Gardens, a northeast Houston neighborhood, was live-streaming rising water in the living room and desperately seeking help to evacuate. By 6:00 a.m. Sunday morning, less than twelve hours after the rain had started, we had received twenty inches of rain—and Berry Bayou was out of its banks for the first time ever, lapping at the end of my driveway. I knew from the rainfall map that the east side—from north to south, from Lakewood to South Houston, from Northshore to Edgebrook, had been devastated. Why was my home spared?

Around noon on Sunday, the rain temporarily subsided, the bayou receded to just inside its banks, and I headed out on foot to take a look. Debris had collected under the bridge over Berry Bayou, creating a dam and impeding the flow of water out of the neighborhood. A family of four, armed with long metal poles, were working tirelessly to free the debris and stacking what they fished out into an organized pile on the banks of the bayou. Jammed under the bayou bridge, amid fencing, coolers, lawn furniture, and all kinds of other detritus, was a sizable side-by-side stainless steel refrigerator that must have come from Edgebrook or South Houston. The family was working to save their home from the ongoing threat of rising water upstream from the dam of junk and trash; downstream, this temporary dam is likely what kept my house dry. There was a horrible stench in the air, sweet-smelling like gasoline, chemical and toxic. The odor was so powerful it seemed a stray spark might set off an explosion.

All that day I watched and calculated the amount of time it was taking the bayou to go down, to lower by a foot, two feet. My nerves eased slightly, and before it started raining again, the bayou had gone down nearly ten feet. By late Monday night and early Tuesday morning, the devastation and flooding had moved west. The release of water from the Barker and Addicks Reservoirs would create a disaster for thousands of families on the other side of town. With this shift, attention to what had occurred early Sunday morning in Edgebrook, South Houston, Lakewood, Kashmere Gardens, East Houston, Northshore, and other east side neighborhoods disappeared from the headlines.

Where you live matters. Access to the basics—healthcare, transit, fresh food, and clean air—is distributed unevenly along the dividing line that separates the west side of Houston from the east, the wealthy from the poor, the powerful from the ignored. On one side of the line is abundance; on the other, scarcity. And while floodwaters don't discriminate by income or race, access to the resources to recover from them are far less equitable. The result is that recovery unfolds in different ways in different places, reinforcing and, in many cases, exacerbating existing disparities.

On August 31—a week after I began preparing for the storm to arrive—I made my way to the closest donation site, set up in the old Dillard's department store at Pasadena Town Square, dragging along everything I had that might be useful to those who had lost so much: pillows, new towels, a cat carrier. Other volunteers and I dutifully sorted clothing donations, many of which were not suitable for distribution. It was not surprising that donation centers across the city would announce that they needed everything except clothing. The Pasadena site was overflowing with stuff, but no one was coming to get it—there was a spatial mismatch between donation sites, located in unaffected areas, and flooded areas where people needed help.

Later that day I went out to find open shelters in the South Houston and Edgebrook areas. I first stopped at the Masjid Abu-Bakr Islamic Center on Highway 3. The center had flooded. South Houston Intermediate and Pasadena High School shelters had both closed, and evacuees moved to the convention center. I stopped at the South Houston City Hall, where everything had gone underwater, and city leaders were busy with their own recovery efforts. There were no resources close to where people on the east side needed them. This is the problem, and always has been.

In those first few urgent days, neighborhoods with capable and skilled community-based organizations and leaders sprang into action, organized assistance and donations, connected flooded residents to FEMA and other recovery resources, and started the massive task of cleaning up. But the east side does not have a well-connected coalition of civic institutions, nonprofit organizations, or other infrastructure to organize around—reducing our capacity to fight for resources and assistance. Flooded South Houston residents, as reported in the *Houston Chronicle*, were still waiting for FEMA inspectors more than three weeks after their homes took on water. FEMA had the area listed as "inaccessible."

For over a week, the community tried to fill this gap. For my own part, I called every church in southeast Houston, trying to find a place to serve as a distribution center, without any luck. I emailed county commissioners and city council representatives begging them to get recovery resources and services to the east side. Finally, I started organizing donations from unaffected areas with the help of savvy friends who worked magic on social media to get food, water, diapers, cleaning supplies—the basic necessities—to the east side.

The first donation drive was coordinated with elected officials in the city of South Houston, an area devastated by flooding. When the South Houston site closed for the day, we went down the street to Edgebrook. We set up in Freeway Manor Park and started trying to spread the word. Like the rain, supplies came from everywhere, but people were hesitant to come see what was going on. We decided that what we really needed to do was to have a mobile supply chain—we loaded up the back of a pickup with diapers, water, food, cleaning supplies, and linens—and drove slowly street by street handing out anything we had to anyone who needed it. We learned a lot: cars were flooded, people weren't mobile, and they were still at home. Language barriers were impacting people's access to information and services, and for those without documentation, there was fear. The next day we went back, this time armed with more than supplies, passing out materials on what assistance was available, and how to get it, in English and Spanish.

At home that night I searched the METRO bus routes to figure out how people in the Edgebrook area might get around to centers and resources far from their neighborhood. What I found is that there is not a single bus line serving this part of Houston, even though the population density is just slightly less than the Montrose neighborhood, which is more affluent and predominately white, where there are six METRO bus routes. I reached out to my contacts at METRO, but with no result. Even today, the new redesigned METRO "Next" plan has not addressed this gap in service. METRO uses a ridership analysis to determine where to invest; in Edgebrook no one rides the bus because there is no bus, thus no ridership, and therefore no investment. It is a cycle impossible to break without power and advocacy.

In the weeks that followed Hurricane Harvey, I told the story of the east side—Edgebrook, South Houston, Northshore, East Houston— to anyone who would listen. I tried to organize a bunch of guys to do mobile relief in the Northshore neighborhood off of Maxey Road, with little success. Eventually, I organized a group of students from the university where I teach architecture and urban design to volunteer with the Cajun Army to muck out a house in Northshore for an elderly couple who had been inundated with five feet of water. The home, which had taken this couple a lifetime to build, had been destroyed in a matter of hours, first by the floodwaters and then by our hammers. The devastation in this part of Houston was so significant that the flooded local hospital, which had served the community for forty years, would shutter its doors for good. When we finished the Northshore house, we moved to a home in Edgebrook, but the elderly woman could not bear to part with her soaked belongings—the only belongings she had.

In the center of the city, largely unaffected by flooding, life quickly returned to normal. People went back to work, to school. But tens of thousands of families were struggling behind the closed doors of their homes, waging private wars against mold, FEMA, and insurance adjusters. It would take months to learn more about that terrible, flammable smell blanketing the east side of the city during the storm. Nearly a half million gallons of gasoline had been spilled at the Magellan plant in Galena Park, and at the Valero plant in Manchester, mechanical malfunctions or human malfeasance resulted in the release of hundreds of thousands of pounds of benzene, a known carcinogen. More than three years after Harvey, there are no records of a violation or of fines being levied against Magellan for the spill by local or national environmental agencies. And while Harris County filed a suit against Valero for five years of infractions, including the toxic releases during Hurricane Harvey, there has been no decision in the case.

I MET THOUSANDS of people who were struggling a year after Harvey. I have met hundreds more people who are still struggling today. Tens of thousands of families whose homes didn't get flooded suffered the consequences of a week without work, a week without pay—for many vulnerable families, on the edge, this would spiral into an economic crisis. In a number of east side neighborhoods, groups of leaders have organized and formed new entities to fill the gaps in service and advocacy—this is true in the northeast part of Houston—with new organizations such as West Street Recovery and Northeast Houston Redevelopment Council. On the southeast side of town, the vacuum remains.

IN EDGEBROOK, eight area families who tried to rebuild without a permit have had their homes red-tagged by the city's building code enforcers. The homes are deep in the floodplain, experienced significant damage, and under the new flood ordinance need to be elevated before being repaired. It is possible these families will walk away from their homes, the largest financial investment they have made in their lives. In Northshore, three hundred affordable apartments remain gutted and unoccupied. In east Houston, the risk of flooding continues to be unclear, as there has never been a commitment to remap the floodplain in an area that continues to flood. And finally, in Kashmere Gardens, where one of every five residents lives with a disability, residents anxiously await the completion of the Hunting Bayou improvements, which they hope will reduce their flood risk before the next storm.

WHILE HOUSTON has experienced historic flooding four times in less than twenty years, we are somehow never prepared. Those who were not impacted consider themselves lucky and then forget—willfully, quickly. For those who weren't so lucky, they wait—spending months or years tediously negotiating the web of bureaucracy, red tape, and denials for help. We try to turn tragedy into opportunity, and imagine that, like the flood of water, a flood of money will come along with a vision of the transformations that will save us. We are still waiting. We wait for the next hurricane season, and the next, and the next, with no new plans, no vision for the future, nothing to stop this from happening over and over. When the next flood comes, and it is sure to, we will start from scratch again.

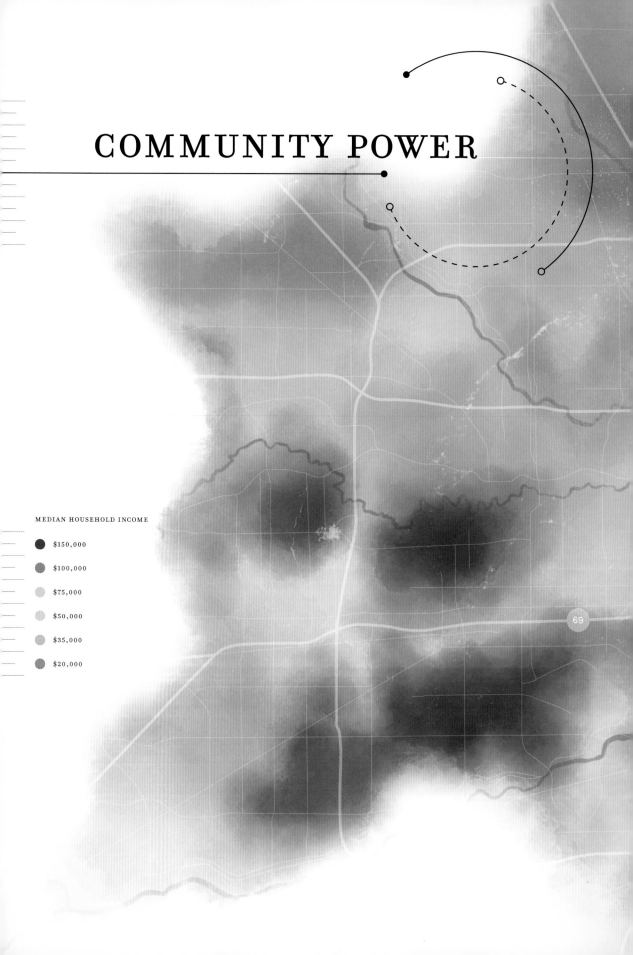

COMMUNITY POWER

MEDIAN HOUSEHOLD INCOME

- $150,000
- $100,000
- $75,000
- $50,000
- $35,000
- $20,000

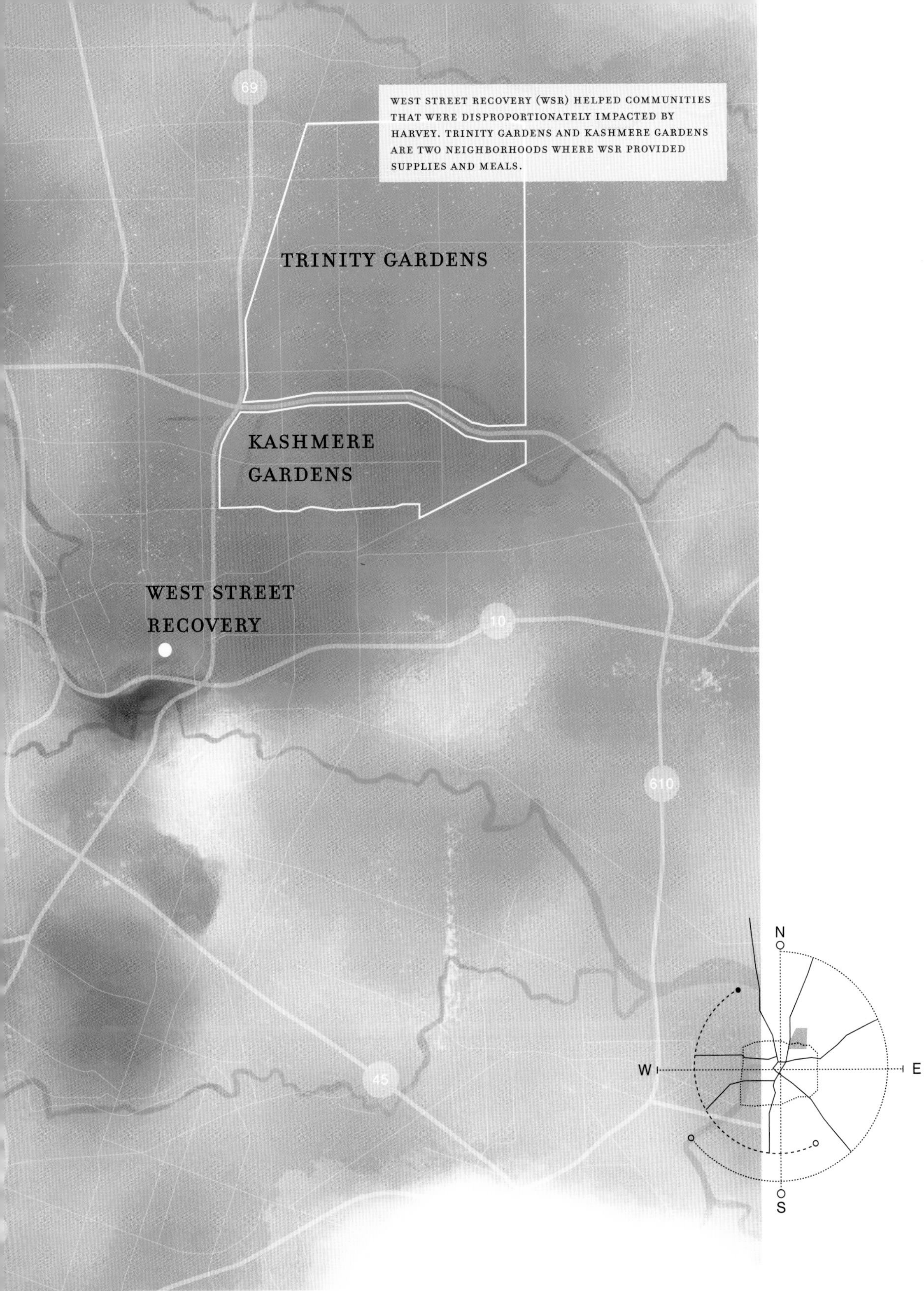

TRINITY GARDENS

KASHMERE
GARDENS

WEST STREET
RECOVERY

ALTHOUGH NATURAL DISASTERS CAN AFFECT ANYONE REGARDLESS OF SOCIOECONOMIC STATUS,
THE PATH TO RECOVERY DRASTICALLY DIFFERS. THIS MAP IDENTIFIES THE MEDIAN HOUSEHOLD
INCOME IN EACH REGION AND HIGHLIGHTS THE NEIGHBORHOODS THAT WEST STREET RECOVERY
HELPED MOST WITH VARIOUS RELIEF EFFORTS.

DESIGN BY JESSE REYES

Community Power

Ben Hirsch

Hurricane Harvey hit Houston on Friday, August 26, 2017, and the following Monday, I, along with a ragtag group of activists from Austin, Texas, got into a minivan and crept toward the city, much of which was still underwater. Late that night we arrived at a little yellow house on West Street in the Near Northside neighborhood just north of I-10 in Houston. By then, the house was one of many centers of the regional ad hoc response to flooding. The people who lived there had used social media to invite anyone willing to help with the recovery into their home; when we arrived, they welcomed us into their lives.

In the cramped kitchen, a crowd debriefed on a day of completing water rescues in partially submerged neighborhoods. The storm was moving east toward Beaumont, so plans were hatched for a small group to leave at dawn, and for another group to drive to the northeast section of the city to look for folks that still needed help getting from their neighborhoods into shelters run by the city and international charities. Over the next few days, it became clear that we couldn't reach any more people who still needed rescue from the little yellow house, and scores of volunteers began to prepare meals and serve them in areas where water had been high. As continues to be the case for the group that emerged from this first frantic weekend, the effort was coordinated through deep conversation and by empowering individuals—organizers, volunteers, and residents—to make the best decisions they could with the information they had.

At that time, my understanding of Houston's geography was limited, and over the next few weeks the Houston of my imagination became the parking lots, storefronts, and church halls where meals could be served. The cooks and drivers behind this effort were Food Not Bombs activists, urban farmers, church people, and bicycle enthusiasts all looking for a way to help, who heard about our response via Facebook, word of mouth, and over Zello. Supplies were sent from Mutual Aid Disaster Relief, a national network that supports groups like our nascent one at moments just like this. They sent mucking equipment and N-95 masks. We received supporters from the Houston Zen Center and the Quaker and B'ahai communities. This collection of outliers and alternative thinkers came together to serve thousands of meals and provide tons of cleaning and hygiene supplies while barely knowing each other, and founded West Street Recovery (WSR).

In late October 2017, as donations continued to come in, we incorporated ourselves legally with the Texas secretary of state, mostly to protect one member who had volunteered his bank account but was growing uneasy holding donations. We asked other grassroots activists that we had met through Zello—the app used to coordinate rescues during the storm—to join our group, and two of them are members of our board and staff today. In the year after the storm, WSR focused its work on case management (helping residents navigate the complex aid applications and FEMA correspondence), mucking, and eventually home repair. Most recently we have moved to community organizing, which today is at the center of our work. But before we began working, we had to formulate a vision and mission and devise ways of making decisions.

We wanted to avoid the flaws we saw in the way major aid organizations distributed assistance. In the parking lot of Catholic Charities, we saw mountains of food fenced in with armed guards standing by as hurricane survivors lined up for their rations. In apartment complex common spaces, we witnessed churches using police escorts to deliver Wonder Bread and peanut butter, and read one agency's application for assistance that included an agreement to be drug tested.

We understood that fear of the poor is a central characteristic of the aid apparatus and charitable sector at all levels. Distrust is propped up through narratives of looting, tales of welfare queens, and general racism. At WSR, we knew we didn't want to replicate this attitude of suspicion. Sitting in a cramped living room, the dozen or so organizers who had led our ad hoc response to the storm strung together a vision, a mission, and a set of common beliefs. In those early days, we, like many others in Houston, were riding a wave of adrenaline, and the urgency of the situation helped us forge a unity that is not easy to achieve in normal circumstances. More than two and a half years later, our mission still holds us accountable to the belief that unity is possible and that it is never easy.

As West Street has moved from the moment of catastrophe through the slog of long-term recovery, we have battled to maintain the utopian energy that inspired us to begin this work. Even if no one called it utopian at the time, it is my belief that many in Houston had utopia in their mind in the ways they responded to Harvey. There is no cost-benefit analysis that pushes people to get in boats and row through toxic water to save neighbors; there is no return on investment that pushes people to cook meals for strangers in their private kitchen. Disasters not only prompt a humanitarian and altruistic response; they also create ruptures in our standard way of operating that prompt us to ask "Why is the world this way?" We have tried to maintain that open and questioning spirit at WSR by experimenting with how we make decisions, changing how coworkers support and critique one another, and transforming disaster recovery so that it prioritizes the needs of the most vulnerable.

To me, and to all of us at WSR, the biggest questions are the most inspiring and open the greatest possibilities. Below I try to tell a scattering of stories that prompt those questions, because WSR believes that to have a recovery that is just, equitable, and inclusive, we must ask deep questions, try to answer them, learn why we are wrong, and try again.

INSTITUTIONAL RESPONSES AND SOLIDARITY

There is no truth in the idea that floodwaters are some divine equalizer. Harvey, like Ike and Allison before it, did more to uncover and amplify inequality than almost anything I have seen before. The experience of families in Northeast Houston validates the trends that are highlighted in nationwide analyses of natural disasters showing that they expand the wealth gap between white and nonwhite families. Despite the chorus of self-congratulations from the state and charities who proclaim an unparalleled focus on equity, access, or cultural competence, low-income households struggle to access recovery dollars, both public and private. Each home repair program skims the easiest-to-assist families from the vast pools of those still hoping to recover, and those who have faced the greatest degree of discrimination in the past do so again, this time packaged in the discourse of community and inclusion.

No, flooding doesn't level the playing field, but the massive destruction did, for a brief moment, reveal that the structures that define so much of our lives are not natural or rational. In the weeks following the flooding, the force of human kindness, altruism, and connectedness poured out. Unlike the major institutions that are tasked with directing disaster response, who retain the same social structures during crises as in day-to-day life (or, maybe worse, sharpen their hierarchies), church ladies served home-cooked meals to people they would normally fear, neighbors who had barely spoken helped muck out one another's homes, and the idea of community went from marketing mantra to a real-life practice. For a matter of days, the hegemonic logics of market competition, race, and individualism were obviously laughable. Alternative ways of thinking and doing were so clearly needed that thousands upon thousands of people got up and enacted them.

What the destruction caused by Harvey—and people's most immediate reactions—demonstrated is that another way of being is possible. But no matter the scale, natural disasters cannot reveal how we go forward enacting those values and visions that we all saw in the week after the storm. In the first weeks of September, those responding to the storm acted collectively, prioritized assisting those with the highest degree of need, insisted on humanitarianism, and emphasized community and survival over profit or order. Specifically, West Street Recovery has been an experiment in realizing that dream, of attempting to sustain the collective spirit that enables deep connections across race, class, language, and gender. Instead of "command and control," which is the standard bureaucratic and militaristic response to disaster, we tried, with youthful energy and naïve faith, another strategy: "listen and respond."

BUT HOW DOES ONE LISTEN?

How do we listen with care and patience when we need to tear out walls // deliver meals // prepare mold remediation kits // help people file FEMA appeals // replace belongings?

How do we listen to people we do not know // in languages we do not speak // with refrains that seem off-putting?

How do we listen to stories of procedural cruelty // official indifference // and widespread neglect but stay sane and focused on the material reality people face?

LISTENING

If you work long enough in Northeast Houston and demonstrate that you are open to feedback and willing to learn, you will see that there are residents who will insist that you listen, who have the courage and confidence to sit you down and teach you. At WSR we have had the luck to meet these neighborhood fixtures: the chain smokers who know the schoolchildren and can name the bad landlords; the dog owners who can list the residents who need special care or know the names of residents who are wary of seeking help; or the grandmothers who can explain how the construction of an overpass, parking lot, or house changed flooding patterns over the last fifty years. These are the storytellers who have the wisdom that can guide an equitable (and also efficient) recovery. These are the experts who can help us target our efforts and best understand the strategy we should adopt.

The perspective of flood victims has both immediate and long-term importance. On the recommendation of a heroic post-Harvey food distributor, "Mama Rosie," I drove east from Mesa Drive to Strathmore Drive to meet someone named Petra. Strathmore is in the eastern half of a low-income subdivision that residents call Lakewood; it is bordered on the north by Halls Bayou, and on the east and south by the eighth-largest landfill in the United States. Petra, with a broad smile and a sarcastic laugh, explained her ordeal—leaving her home, her dogs, and her chickens; trying to track down her children and grandchildren; and the depressing return to a home she had already rebuilt once with the help of her husband that clearly needed to be mucked out and repaired once again. Petra did not just tell me what she needed, though; instead she blew my mind by making a list of seven neighbors and what they needed also. She invited me to return and distribute supplies from her driveway "anytime." But first she insisted that I contact neighbors she was particularly worried about. In the days after our first conversation, I was able to deliver tents to five families who needed them within one block of her home. And the grooves of understanding began to appear.

Listening reveals why so many people, especially people of color, have not been able to access help from the largest agencies. One commonly excluded group are residents who live in homes owned by close relatives: elderly mothers whose sons live in houses next door, or unemployed brothers who are cared for by close family. These kinds of arrangements are a matter of survival in communities that are systematically excluded from new economic opportunities and disproportionately impacted by disinvestment. Beyond that, though, they are a real manifestation of the very sort of social fabric, reciprocity, and cohesion that conservative commentators, the same ones that demand the overbearing ethic of "fiduciary efficiency" (code for "fuck the poor"), say our societies need to be resilient and thrive.

Listening is a first step; it can help us identify, prioritize, and strategize, but it doesn't tell us how to respond.

RESPONDING

There are massive organizations and governments that will do the responding that makes the most material difference for flood victims. FEMA provided hundreds of thousands of people with critical assistance, and the biggest NGOs repaired hundreds of homes and provided many more people critical assistance of other types. From my perspective, denying this is a nonsensical starting position. And yet, there are so many who are left behind. It takes a belief in universal desert, in human rights, in justice, to even try to reach those who do not get help from the most powerful actors. To respond in this way requires a stubborn refusal to let pass the utopian moment that followed Harvey.

Early in the winter of 2018–2019 I was introduced to a Fifth Ward resident living in a home with walls that had never been repaired after the storm, a bare subfloor, and no working heat or a stove. This resident, whom I will call Sergeant, is a Vietnam War veteran who deployed as US Army Special Force and is now a neighborhood celebrity, a jokester, and a karaoke champion. I was introduced to Sergeant by Reverend Caldwell, a tireless advocate, who has time and again identified people who could not get help through the standard channels. Sergeant's home, though, was a puzzle that took relentless optimism to solve.

Most agencies would not have been able to help Sergeant because the deed to his home is held by his deceased mother. The property has become what is called "heirship property," where each child of the deceased owns equal stock in the home. Initially, Sergeant's family was hesitant to transfer the deed to one family member because they feared they would have to pay back the Medicare and Social Security Sergeant's mother had collected in her lifetime. The first part of our response was calling in trusted allies who could convincingly explain why this was not the case. The second was working with the extended family to understand why the deed needed to be transferred and initiating the process. At the convening of the Harris County Long-Term Recovery Committee, deed issues were named as a barrier to recovery. But heirship property is discussed in tones that suggest it is some sort of bad behavior, some artifact of a deficient culture, and that if only families tried, they could just resolve the situation. This attitude doesn't acknowledge the historical specificities that make heirship a common form of ownership in marginalized communities or the actual legal and social complexities of transferring property, never mind the financial barriers to doing so.

Openness to new experiences and flexibility are keys to unlearning these kinds of official narratives as we respond to disasters. When we first met Sergeant, we did not really have the funds to repair his home, but it was clear that the current conditions were unacceptable and that doing nothing would be unethical. So instead we tentatively moved forward, locating enough money to at least replace the demolished walls and make sure that the wind wasn't blowing through the house. We found another Harvey survivor we could hire to help with debris removal, and another who was a licensed electrician who could rewire the house to make it both safe and compliant with city code. As we moved forward, we were lucky to receive the additional funding that will in time allow us to finish the house. And, maybe because of our lack of funds, we took an approach that, through necessity, positioned others impacted by the storm as the key actors in helping Sergeant recover. This is key because it builds bonds between neighbors and keeps recovery dollars in the communities that were impacted by the storm. By hiring locally, WSR has also been able to provide job experience, professional references, and even storm relief to individuals we first met as laborers.

In the immediate aftermath of the storm, scores of groups sent out volunteers to knock on doors and help residents muck out their homes. The storm demanded that people connect to one another by creating obvious and critical needs. Our normal lives tend to obscure this, but critical needs caused by racism and poverty are always there. What is not there for most people is the awareness of what the needs actually are, the openness to feeling awkward by asking, by having a door slammed in your face, or just not knowing what kind of help to offer someone who needs assistance so badly. In the aftermath of the storm, our official institutions called us to action. The governor called for water rescues to act, churches mobilized members, and activists took time away from the struggles they focus on to help people recover. That moment was tightly bordered, though. Today, more than two and a half years after the flood, our institutions are no longer calling on us to help one another despite the fact that the need is still immense. Instead, we are left to motivate ourselves.

Continuing to work on the recovery is exhausting, but imagine trying to recover by yourself. For me and my colleagues, what is motivating is not just the small victories of one household recovering at a time, though those are sustaining. Instead, it is the ability to hold the energy that sustained the initial outpouring of support by understanding that it is proof that another world is possible. It is possible that we all have safe, sanitary, and secure housing. It is possible that the recovery would drive locally rooted economic growth that allows communities to be better prepared in the future. This possibility is incompatible with many ideological axioms of the current recovery. An equitable recovery and just future must be based on trust, reciprocity, and respect.

It is my belief that these feelings of mutual care and shared responsibility for one another are not unusual feelings. But they are feelings we learn to turn off to navigate the world. For me, Harvey revealed that if we do the work that affirms our values, if we allow those feelings of human connection and reciprocity to come to the surface, we can hold on to the possibility of a better world for much longer. Harvey produced unimaginable suffering, but it wasn't just the storm. The storm was so disastrous because so many of us have allowed our most human instincts to help one another be numbed. Only by denying those instincts have we been able to produce a city with such inequality and poverty, a city where people are forced to live in danger of severe and repeated flooding and in the shadows of petroleum facilities.

But for me, Harvey revealed that the numbness is a choice. And, I was lucky enough to fall into a space where people asserted the importance of a logic of feeling. You feel the suffering of others and also the immense joy of helping one another. It may be fair to say that this conclusion is delusionally optimistic, that it uses the bodily suffering of others to fuel some overly romantic project. But for me, Harvey revealed that if we do not adopt other ways of being, we are accepting both the marginalization of our neighbors and their unimaginable suffering in one of the richest cities to ever exist. If that is not what we want, we have no other choice but to be recklessly optimistic and chase that other world we *do* want and stay in that utopian moment as long as we can.

HOPE

A WHOLE CITY
ON STILTS

WE
LIVE WITH
IT

LIKE
A CONCUSSION

SLY
EEP

FLOODING IS A WAY OF LIFE FOR SOME NEIGHBORHOODS IN HOUSTON. THE PEOPLE OF THE BOYER
ESSAY HAVE TO COME TO TERMS WITH THE FACT THAT THE HURRICANES ARE ONLY GOING TO GET
WORSE. IF THEY STAY, WHAT ARE THEIR OPTIONS FOR KEEPING THEIR HOMES SAFE? IS THE FUTURE
OF HOUSTON UNDERWATER OR A CITY ON STILTS?

DESIGN BY DEVIN SCHUHMANN

A Whole City on Stilts

HYDRAULIC CITIZENSHIP IN HOUSTON

Dominic Boyer

For the past year, my colleague Mark Vardy and I have been working on a research project that aims to better understand whether the experience of multiple flooding incidents has changed how Houstonians feel about their homes, their neighborhoods, and the city itself. We're interested in how flooding might disrupt or reinforce emotional attachments, and also how the increasingly common experience of flooding in Houston could serve as the basis for new kinds of political consciousness. Our inspiration has been the work of the anthropologist Nikhil Anand, who has studied how political communities have formed around getting reliable access to drinking water in Mumbai.[1] Anand found that securing water was becoming a dominant aspect of many people's everyday lives, and he described this phenomenon as "hydraulic citizenship." We wondered whether floods could generate hydraulic citizenship, too.

The funding for our project came from the National Science Foundation, which made a special pot of money available for research related to the recovery from Hurricane Harvey. Clearly, if there is hydraulic citizenship forming in Houston, too, it's going to be about coping with an overabundance of water arriving at unpredictable times rather than about managing constant scarcity. It's well known now that Harvey was the largest tropical cyclone rainfall event in US history; less known outside Houston is that it was the third so-called "500-year flood" within three years (the other two being the Memorial Day Floods of 2015 and the Tax Day Floods of 2016).[2] Harvey was followed by the July 4 Flood of 2018, which led to the cancellation of the city's Independence Day festivities and left more than one Houstonian wondering what it is about holidays here that brings the rain. With the new intensities and frequencies of rainfall associated with climate change, flooding has become an increasingly routine aspect of life in Houston.

Our research focused initially on Meyerland and Greenspoint, which counted among the three Houston neighborhoods with the greatest number of repetitive payouts from the National Flood Insurance Program. Other than sharing floodwater, the neighborhoods represent two very different Houstons. Greenspoint is primarily Hispanic (66 percent) and African American (29 percent) and has a median household income of $26,823. Eighty-six percent of Greenspoint residents rent, and most live in apartment complexes. Meyerland, meanwhile, is majority Caucasian (56 percent), educationally privileged (54 percent have a bachelor's degree or higher), and relatively wealthy, with 35 percent of households reporting an income of over $100,000. Before the recent run of major floods, some two-thirds of Meyerlanders lived in owner-occupied single-family homes.

Virtually to a person, everyone we interviewed for this project agreed that Harvey was a devastating experience, both personally and for Houston as a whole. But no two experiences of flooding and what followed were the same. This contribution to the Houston Flood Atlas offers three portraits of what life has been like coming back from catastrophic flooding in the two bayou watersheds (Brays and Greens) that were impacted most heavily. They are the kind of personal stories that befit the individualism of American culture. But these stories, and the many others we have collected, speak to one another. They are part of the bigger story of what the arrival of all this murky floodwater is helping to reveal about living in an American coastal city today.

WE LIVE WITH IT

Greenspoint is on the northern edge of Houston, where its outer beltway meets the north-south freeway that runs from Dallas down to Galveston. Until the 1960s, the area was sparsely settled. But the opening of Houston Intercontinental Airport nearby in 1969 brought a surge of residential, retail, and office building construction that became Greenspoint. Exxon-Mobil, International Oil and Gas, Champion, and Ultramar Oil all opened major offices there. Apartment complexes catering to the new professional and service classes mushroomed, rising from only 57 units in 1970 to 7,819 units in 1980. Greenspoint Mall opened in 1976 and rapidly became the major social and commercial center for North Houston. But like much else in Houston, prosperity took a wrong turn during the oil glut of the early 1980s. Business slowed, offices emptied, crime rose, and a series of high-profile shootings earned the neighborhood the nickname "Gunspoint." Unlike other neighborhoods in Houston, though, there was little recovery for Greenspoint in the 1990s and 2000s; the white collar jobs never returned, the housing stock aged, the mall became less and less the center of anything. It did not help that the area saw major floods in 2001, 2002, and 2003 and that three-quarters of Greenspoint's apartment complexes are currently in flood zones. Without local food providers and medical services, it is even difficult for neighborhood residents to adequately prepare for storms and flooding.

Rockridge Bend Apartments is on Greens Road about five hundred yards north of Greens Bayou. Its first-floor apartments flooded severely in both 2016 and 2017. When Mark and I pull into the parking lot, we cross over a metal plate that is designed to spring vertical during flood events. The idea is to turn the road into a temporary river to evacuate bayou overflow. The complex is verdant this warm July day. Gardens and shade trees fill the spaces between the complex's buildings; birds are abundant. We can see why our host, Sandra, likes it so well there. She greets us from her balcony on the second floor and introduces us to her best friend, Betty. Despite having lost most of her possessions to Harvey (when she still lived on the first floor), Sandra's apartment feels full and comfortable. Photographs of her grown children cover the walls, and she gestures to them proudly as she recounts their achievements.

Sandra is one of the few who responded to the hundreds of door tags we left in Greenspoint apartment complexes asking if people wanted to tell their Harvey stories. She's lived in Houston for sixty-eight years and remembers when the city was still pretty much bounded by the I-610 inner loop. Then the sprawl came. "It started like a wildfire. Just like wildfire. But were you aware that in those days [State Highway] 1960 was called Jackrabbit Road? It was called that for a reason," she laughs.

For forty-two years, Sandra worked as a college registrar, and that allowed her to be a homeowner in "the white neighborhoods." She speaks with pride of the homes that used to be her own. Circumstances brought her to Greenspoint only about seven years ago.

"I guess this neighborhood could be equated to the Ninth Ward area in New Orleans. You know the people here, you've got a lot of poor and oppressed people. And downtrodden. You have a great many others.

There's a great many students, kids just trying to get someplace. You weren't always a scientist or astronaut. And you have a great number of people just passing through. My next-door neighbors are refugees from Haiti or somewhere. They're starting out, they won't stay here, they'll probably do something. But then a big percentage of people are the people that I'm telling you about. The people that are coming out of, you know, poor and oppressed situations."

Sandra sees herself as someone passing through, too, even at the other end of her life. Her children are successful, college graduates, homeowners themselves. There's talk of a big European vacation coming. Her daughter has a new home with space for her. For the moment she's content in Greenspoint.

Harvey, though, was a nightmare. She was living in the same complex but in a different apartment and, unfortunately, on the first floor. "I was asleep. And I was awakened about four o'clock in the morning because I had to go to the bathroom. My bed sits very high. You know, you have those old big mattresses like so. And I sat on the side of the bed, and the water was up to my knees. Well that cold water woke me up pretty fast." Her first thought was to get to her car. But the entire parking lot was underwater already. So everyone was stuck. It was twelve or thirteen hours until the first high-water vehicles arrived to take people down to Greenspoint Mall for evacuation. She felt for the mothers with small children. Sandra doesn't think saving the people in Greenspoint was a high priority for the city.

She lost everything. Fortunately, she had a friend who knew how the FEMA system worked, so she was able to get some financial relief. But she knew a lot of neighbors in Greenspoint who weren't so lucky. Most folks in Greenspoint rent, and most renters don't have flood insurance. A lot of her neighbors just left and never came back after Harvey; the rents might be cheap, but floods were expensive. Even if somehow your things stayed dry, you lost your car. Sandra was able to convince her apartment manager to let her move into a second-floor apartment. "God always watches over me."

It seems like the flooding is now speeding up the passing through. So I ask her: "What kind of future does Greenspoint have? If you're going to just give up on the area and forget it, that's fine. But if not, if there is an effort to try to save this community, something has to be done and pretty quickly. Because it is not an *if* it's going to flood. That's a definite. It's *when* it floods. And you don't have to sit here and wait for a hurricane. In Houston, we just have these gully washes. I mean, one minute it's not raining anywhere. Am I right, Betty? And then the next minute, you're like, 'What?!?!'" Betty nods, "Up here you can flood from just a hard rain."

Sandra was proud of how people came together after Harvey. "People crossed all lines, all barriers, all kinds, all colors to help one another. Had we not, there's not enough emergency personnel to help all of the people that were affected by Harvey. But Texans show the world who we are." Even so, she thinks Houston needs to get serious about finding solutions. The problem has been that they allowed enormous overgrowth of the city. People went on building homes in places they had no business building homes.

And there's something else, too, something else about how to compare the experience of flooding in Greenspoint with New Orleans after Katrina. Sandra stares us hard in the eyes as she says, "Let's be real, you know. Had 80 percent of those people in the Superdome been Caucasian, I'm sorry, they would never have been there that amount of time. They would have come and gotten people with their private boats and yachts, and this and that. You know, hire, whatever, the National Guard. Anybody, everybody, let's just get these people out of here. They were horrendous conditions. Until finally the world says, that's not humane. And just like you said, they got shamed. And finally you try to get those people out of there. Well why did that happen? Why should that happen? Because they were Black. That's just one of the issues we face in this country. It's still going to be a long time before there is a solution to that, and so we live with it. Yeah, we live with it."

A WHOLE CITY ON STILTS

I meet Elise at Escalante's in Meyerland Plaza. Escalante's is the kind of strip-mall restaurant that is only precariously upscale but which Houston has still managed to infuse with a certain petrobaroque style. There are what might actually be bulls' heads mounted on the walls, stuffed gallos perched in high windows, and Spanish-style mission tiles over a number of the booths. It's during the downtime between lunch and the earlybirds, so the restaurant is almost empty. We sit in the bar because

Elise says she is going to have to have a margarita to get through this. I join her.

Something about her reminds me of the actress and producer Frances McDormand; she laughs often but with a hard edge and a plowshare of gallows humor. It's been tough times since Harvey. Her husband of twenty-eight years passed away from cancer the January after Harvey, and she blames the storm for making his end come faster.

They had lived in the mid-Brays since 1997 but only flooded for the first time during Memorial Day 2015. It had only been a few inches, but it kept them out of their house for seven months. They had moved to Meyerland because her husband grew up there. They were close to family and work, and the schools were good.

Her husband was a contractor, so he rebuilt their home himself after Memorial Day. But he had already been feeling sick, so the work was hard for him. Looking back, she feels sorry that so much of their last years together was consumed by the stress of renovations. It was a sad way to end a life together. She had wanted to move to Sugarland right after the first flood, but her husband was sure the storm was a freak event and convinced her to stay.

Then they took three feet of water during Harvey. She hasn't spent a night in the home since evacuating the night before the rains began. She was able to get back into the house briefly to retrieve some things she forgot. The water was still there and it haunts her, "It was so weird hearing water lapping in your house. I can't forget that sound."

She lost nearly all of her material possessions in the storm, but those losses don't seem to weigh so heavily on her. "Just stuff," she shrugs. A year after Harvey, the repairs on her house are maybe 75 percent done. She might have considered a buyout had someone offered it, but the government only wrote to her asking if she was open to a buyout in June 2018, and by that time, she was already in it up to her knees with the contractor. "Now you write to me?! Now?!"

She knows she can't go back to that house. She wants to see the repairs through and then sell it to a young family if possible. She thinks their neighborhood can come back if younger families move in. But for her, it's only a matter of time until she leaves the city. "I can't stand the idea of it happening again. It really bothers me every time I hear about a storm forming or see the skies get dark. My coworkers notice and ask me, 'Are you ok? Are you ok?' I guess you could say it's a post-traumatic stress. I'm sure other people talk about this, too. I just can't imagine going through it again."

The light is dim in the restaurant now; the margaritas are water. She's still here for the moment, and when we talk about the future of Houston, she includes herself in its "we": "I really think we are going to end up having to build like they do on the Gulf Coast, up on stilts—wouldn't that be something? A whole city on stilts. People might not like the look of it. But this city is on the Gulf, and this is going to happen again. And we'll need to be prepared."

Mark and I have heard this more often than not in our research. The only way to truly feel safe from flooding is to elevate your home. The sentiment is especially widespread among homeowners in Meyerland. They typically see little appeal in dense high-rise living and think government buyouts and teardowns of repeatedly flooding homes make little sense because they erode the tax base and deteriorate neighborhood integrity. And don't get them started about the inadequacy and delays in the large infrastructure projects meant to widen bayous to increase flow and detention capacity. "Too little too late" is what most homeowners tell us. For those who know they are "hopelessly deep in the floodplain," as flood control experts say, the only strategy that makes sense is to elevate their mid-twentieth-century modern ranch homes. At $75 per square foot, it's an immensely expensive process, but with the help of FEMA grants and private finances, we've watched whole blocks of Meyerland elevate during our year of field research. First, a team of laborers—most of them persons of color, some undocumented—tunnel under the slab and place steel beams upon which hydraulic jacks are placed. Dozens of individual jacks are connected to a jacking system that orchestrates pressure such that the home lifts slowly and stably into the air, rising five feet in about eight hours. One resident told us proudly that the process is so incremental and steady that you could leave your good china set on the dining room table without fear.

Contradictions abound of course. It's a fine strategy if you have the resources to own good china, for example. But what about families who can only afford to rent or those who own but are already trying to manage mortgages and flood repair bills? And if there were more FEMA grants made available, how would the rest of the country feel about public funds being used to stabilize the property values of elite home-owners in risky places? But the contradiction that fascinated me the most was the new mode of camouflage that appeared in the elevated sections of Meyerland. As Elise predicted, no one wanted it to look as though their houses were on stilts. Instead, elevations were carefully hidden behind cosmetic topiary and brick façades. There is even a committee tasked with reviewing the aesthetics of elevated homes. At its core, Meyerland is still hoping to look a certain way, as though the dreams of the mid-twentieth century could extend infinitely into the soggy future.

LIKE A CONCUSSION

Raymond is a lawyer who runs a private practice in one of the many office buildings that cling to the highway spokes of the city. I often get disoriented trying to find the entrance to these buildings, and as we circle the building a second time trying to find the right access ramp, I am thinking dark thoughts about how much of Houston is devoted to the concrete knots, bows, and corridors that facilitate car travel. Some freeways serve multiple purposes and have been designed to help collect water during heavy rainfalls. But there is something paradoxical about how the concentric rings of Houston's freeway system try to overlay the natural landscape of the area—a dense arterial riverine network that slowly moves water fifty miles west to east, from the Katy prairie through to the Gulf of Mexico. Our colleague at Rice, the urban designer and theorist Albert Pope, describes the concentric design of Houston as a "malformed spatial network," one that epitomizes "Houston's presumptive dominion over the natural systems that made the city possible in the first place." Yet the increased rainfall of recent years has made that dominion ever more precarious.

Raymond is the person who first tells us that folks who've flooded in Houston call themselves "floodies." We come to know him through the Facebook page where floodies share their experiences and build community by sharing information about assistance programs and which contractors are honest, and where they debate the city's plans for reducing flood risks through new building codes and infrastructure projects. It is a lively space of hydraulic citizenship. Raymond also introduces us to the concept of "paralysis through analysis," which is how he often feels these days.

Both Raymond and his wife grew up in Southwest Houston and went to high school in Bellaire. When they were looking to buy a home, they "took the Bellaire High School zone map, middle school, elementary school and overlaid them and that's how we selected where we'll go live." Even though he had grown up nearby, his parents' home had never flooded. There was some street flooding from time to time, though; he remembers the lucky neighbor kids who had canoes that they used to paddle up and down the block.

Their mid-twentieth-century Meyerland home was in the 100-year floodplain. Raymond had no idea—he wasn't thinking about flood-plains during their home search. Now he kicks himself for that. He only realized their house might flood about an hour before it happened. The first night of Harvey, their main concern had been the sewers backing up into the dishwasher, so they washed all their dishes by hand that night. "When the water came in, our dishes were clean, but nothing was up on blocks."

The water topped out at seven inches. "I put on a pot of coffee, we fed the kids, we splish-splashed around the house. We got to some neigh-bors, and there was no sense of trauma or distress, and it was a combi-nation block party and camping trip." No one was thinking about how bad the city as a whole was at first. They concentrated on moving their neighbors in flooded homes over to the few more recently built homes that were elevated enough to stay dry.

Raymond tears up when he talks about the Peng family who took them in. Even though it was just for the one night, he's never known such generosity. The Pengs took in eight families in all and fed them and made them comfortable: "Agnostics and Buddhists and Jewish peo-ple, it was like the United Nations there. It's Houston."

The trauma for Raymond was not the flood itself but the aftermath. When I ask him about the process of recovery, he interrupts to say, "I don't know what that means." Part of the aftermath was having to learn how to remediate his house and manage the loss of possessions. But the larger part, and the source of paralysis, seems to be deciding what to do next. The family is still living in a rental place a year later while they consider the future of the Meyerland home. "You got to go somewhere, there are not many places to go, and people who haven't flooded just don't understand. Nobody who flooded can think straight, and if you haven't flooded before, you don't even know what you are supposed to think about." I ask him if he can try to explain to us what it was about the flooding experience that made it so difficult to comprehend.

"It's like a concussion. It is overwhelming that it wasn't the flood experience itself. That was fun. I remember emptying out the garage, manhandling crap that's been in there for years, taking it out to the car, and thinking to myself, 'God this is a lot more fun than being a lawyer.' But then the weeks and months that follow when the phone rings twelve times a day, and you've got seventeen things to do before you can complete one, and It. Just. Never. Ends."

His profession has colored his approach to the decision about whether or not to renovate the house. He's gathering information, assessing risks. There was bad news when he had his elevation survey redone. Subsidence had apparently lowered the height of the home two feet since it was built. Raymond didn't trust the rainfall and floodplain estimates either, since he had learned the data were fifty years out of date. He thinks it will be two or three more years before the latest NOAA precipitation data will be reconciled with topology to produce new floodplain maps. He doesn't feel like making commitments to renovation until he knows exactly "what the future risk will be." But he's also not happy not making a decision.

Raymond admits that he feels overwhelmed now. But he seems sensitive that his waiting might be interpreted as indecisiveness. Experts like him aren't indecisive; they understand risks; they sell that expertise to others. His biggest wish is to "accelerate the information" so he can make an informed decision. Yet he knows that with climate change, uncertainty about rains and floods may be impossible to dispel. Still, Raymond doesn't want to be like those neighbors who panicked and sold out at lot value. Or to be those who rebuilt too quickly without really understanding their situation. "In some sense, I feel worse for the people that are already built because they are committed and now they live in Beirut."

In the waning hours of the afternoon, we're talking about the future and whether Houston might look back at Harvey the way Galveston looks back at the 1900 hurricane that changed the city's trajectory forever. Raymond is recalling his own history in Southwest Houston and the first paycheck he earned working at a place called New York Bagels. Out of nowhere he blurts out "I'll miss Meyerland," as though something snapped into place.

AS MARK AND I have delved more deeply into the history of flood prevention and recovery measures in Houston, we've come to recognize that there has been a long history of hydraulic citizenship in the bayou city. Indeed, it would be fair to say there's never been a form of citizenship in Houston that hasn't had to take tropical storms and flooding into account. According to settler history, Houston was founded by the land-speculating Allen brothers in 1836 on 8,850 acres of prairie swamp at the confluence of the Buffalo and White Oak Bayous. The Allen brothers came to Texas from New York with the hope of founding a seat of government after the Battle of San Jacinto brought an independent Texan republic into being. The Allens depicted Houston as a hillside town, "handsome and beautifully elevated, salubrious and well watered," and convinced the new Texan government to meet there for its first two years of existence before the realities of constant heat, mosquitoes, flooding, and yellow fever convinced them to move farther inland to Austin. And this was before major storms washed out most of the bridges spanning the Buffalo Bayou in 1839, 1841, and 1843.

But Houston's hydraulic citizenship truly came into its own in the twentieth century in response to the catastrophic floods of December 1935 that inundated the entire downtown. The Harris County Flood Control District was formed two years later and worked together with the US Army Corps of Engineers to dig two massive reservoirs during the Second World War with 410,000 acre feet of detention capacity aimed at preventing a repeat of the 1935 flooding along the Houston Ship Channel and its energy and military (and, more recently, petrochemical) industrial corridor. For the most part, the reservoirs have worked (even though they came perilously close to failure during Harvey). But no similarly scaled detention capacity was ever created for the other dozen major watersheds in Harris County. And rainfall has been steadily increasing since Harris County's first floodplain maps were created in the 1980s. The most recent NOAA rainfall atlas is indicating that our current "100-year" floodplain is actually more like a "25-year" floodplain.

One might think that given this history, Houstonians would be among the most flood-attuned citizens of the United States. And yet, interestingly, 54 percent of those floodies who took part in our study reported they were "not at all" or "only somewhat" aware of the risk that their residence could flood when they first moved in. This is not just collective amnesia but also reflects how much migration impacts Houston's population across all socioeconomic levels; as Sandra said, people are always passing through, and most of those new to Houston scarcely comprehend its hydraulic challenges. Which makes one ask: How strongly will Harvey remain in Houston's memory? At first, it seemed unforgettable. But the land speculators we spoke to thought that for most people it would take two years. "Two good, dry years," one said, "and the land value will recover. People think Harvey was a once-in-a-lifetime event. We won't see that again."

For those of us who believe it will happen again, who believe that Harvey is a premonition of still greater storms and flooding to come—a new catastrophic normal—stories like Elise's and Raymond's raise the uncomfortable question of how long it will take people whose circumstances permit to leave for good. A year after Harvey, the *Texas Tribune* reported that 10 percent of those displaced still hadn't returned home. A friend who used to work for the French embassy reported to me that he had overheard the superelites of the city whispering after Harvey, speculating about how many more storms it would take for industry to relocate to safer, drier, higher country in central Texas. Whenever it rains hard now, I wonder whether Houston might eventually become the world's first ghost megacity. Unless it's Jakarta, unless it's Miami, unless it's Shanghai or Hong Kong or Osaka—hydraulic citizenship is rapidly becoming a global phenomenon. Climate change is in every respect an existential question for these cities and demands immediate and dramatic action rather than what the anthropologist Adriana Petryna calls the "diligent insanity" of continuing to rebuild according to twentieth-century norms as twenty-first-century reckonings arrive.[3]

SUBURBAN DESIGN
WITH NATURE

CROSS CREEK RANCH

BY ILLUSTRATING THE DIFFERENCE BETWEEN COMMUNITIES IN HOUSTON AND HOW THEY COEXIST WITH NATURE, AN EMPHASIS IS PLACED ON URBAN SPRAWL AND HOW MUCH HOUSTON HAS INSIDIOUSLY GROWN AS A CITY. THE MOLD-LIKE SPORES ALLUDE TO THE EFFECTS OF THE CITY'S GROWTH.

DESIGN BY JASON CARDENAS AND JULIA ONG

Suburban Design with Nature

Geneva Vest

I'm still adjusting to the big move. No, not the one from Houston to Chicago, then to, at last, New York. I'm still wallowing a bit that my parents moved two years ago from their house at the intersection of Bizarre and Delight, Hillcroft and Richmond Avenues, to . . . Katy, Texas. Specifically, they chose the golfing community of Falcon Point for its infamously technical course and close proximity to grandkids.

Look, I get the appeal! A big backyard, new appliances, and three spare bedrooms for half the mortgage sounds brilliant, especially as I write this from my Brooklyn apartment. What confounds me isn't so much about them, but just how easy and obvious it was to move to Katy even though most Houstonians, my family included, are well aware of the shitstorm that urban sprawl has wreaked on wildlife and the climate. To be precise, I look at my dad and see a birder, a conservation volunteer, and the man who instilled in me a deep appreciation for nature. Why then, didn't we talk about the waste, destruction, and displacement of habitat for master-planned communities that continue to expand the Greater Houston area and shrink habitats far more capable of flood mitigation?

It's not just my dad, the consumer, with cognitive dissonance. Many in Houston are challenged by the contradiction of sustainable ideals and suburban reality. I spoke to a landscape architect who had put aside his internal conflicts for designing suburbs. I spoke to a resident of one of his suburbs who didn't notice, let alone appreciate, the splendor of a thoughtfully designed landscape. I spoke to an engineer at the forefront of Harvey recovery who moved to the suburbs decades ago to feel a little closer to nature. Up and down the master-planned development production line, how and where we build is rarely linked with the effects this has on the local environment.

The environmental author and activist Naomi Klein warns us in her book *This Changes Everything* that "our economic system and our planetary system are now at war."[1] The privilege to ignore how our consumption habits affect the planet and its people is the crux of climate change, environmental injustice, and, as you will see, Houston's flooding problem.

THE STORY OF OUR FLOODING PROBLEM

It begins, like all environmental disasters, with natural resources perceived as commodities. Before the Allen brothers founded the city, the Gulf-Houston Region was a dynamic gradient of coastal prairie along the Gulf of Mexico that faded to savannah, post oak, and pine forest the farther inland you got. Soil is especially fertile along Houston's bayous, which drew settlers in the 1830s to convert this land to farms and ranches. Urbanization further altered soil and drainage. Bayous were dug up, then paved over. More and more highways, more and more parking lots. Ecosystems that had taken root in Houston for thousands of years were decimated in a few decades, and the floods and burns that were natural and necessary to the ecosystem became an enemy to our economy and health.

Before writing this essay, I knew that all the lakes in Texas were human-made and that all the "lakefront" properties of the suburbs were really retention pond–front properties. These fake lakes actually represent a major shift in flood management pedagogy, according to Keiji Asakura, the principal designer at the landscape and urban planning firm Asakura Robinson.

After World War II, flood infrastructure was designed to move large volumes of water away from development as fast as possible, typically through concrete channels. We've since discovered that channels are flawed for a number of reasons, primarily because channel intersections become stormwater bottlenecks that compound flooding farther downstream. This partly explains why so many of the homes that flooded during Harvey were west of Houston in the Brays and White Oak Bayou watersheds, whose channels downstream cut through dense development to the east.

More recently, since the 1980s, the goal has been to first slow the stormwater to lower peak water levels and create more time for rainwater to settle. Rather than expel rainwater as channels do immediately or detention ponds do eventually, retention ponds collect rainwater from the source and hold the water for slow evaporation into the atmosphere and percolation into the soil.

Retention ponds do one of two things that every landscape architect and environmental engineer agrees will mitigate Houston's flooding: one is "holding water where it falls," says Phil Bedient, Rice University civil engineering professor, and the other is "increas[ing] vegetation with good roots to open up soil mass," says Asakura.

The benefits of this latter method, "good roots," are numerous. Prairie grass roots have evolved to be flexitarians, adept at absorbing large volumes of water or surviving without the luxury. Moreover, typical lawn grass sequesters approximately one hundred pounds of carbon per acre; coastal prairie grasses sequester six thousand pounds of carbon per acre.

Good roots and holding water where it lands are strategies to "design with nature," a philosophy that believes that "the way we occupy and modify the earth is best when it is planned and designed with careful regard to both the ecology and the character of the landscape," according to the McHarg Center.[2] The first suburb in America to design with nature in mind was, of all places, Houston's very own Woodlands—and its boomtown origins are even more surprising in context.

DESIGN WITH NATURE

Houston of the 1970s is remembered for postmodern buildings and a desolate downtown devoid of public life, so you wouldn't think it would be a testbed for modern environmental design. But in fact, such extremes in unlivability and utilitarianism simply pushed beauty to the fringes, the ride smoothed over by highway expansion in all directions. These conditions primed George P. Mitchell, a millionaire oil tycoon, to build an experimental development method.

Half a century ago, Mitchell had a large piece of land thirty miles north of downtown in the heart of the Pineywoods ecoregion. Up to that point, the Pineywoods was unpopulated and valued mostly for its lumber. Mitchell, though, wanted to develop his plot into one of the first master-planned communities in the country, which soon became The Woodlands.

He brought on Ian McHarg, perhaps the most influential landscape designer and theorist since Fredrick Law Olmstead, to design with the flood-prone nature of the Pineywoods. McHarg tells us in his canonical manifesto, *Design with Nature*, to "abandon self-mutilation which has been our way and give expression to the potential harmony that is man-nature. . . . To do this he must design with nature."[3] This principle— design with, not against, a site's natural condition—is common knowledge in landscape architecture now, but was piloted in The Woodlands.

The site was lush with flat land and thick woods, but one-third of it sat in the 100-year floodplain. Undeterred and even inspired, McHarg planned retention ponds, golf courses, and forest preserves in the most flood-prone areas, which would double as flood infrastructure in wet conditions and recreation in normal conditions.

The Woodlands has withstood the test of real estate trends and numerous severe floods. Nearly 100,000 people live in The Woodlands Township and only five hundred houses flooded during Harvey, mostly in the south near Spring Creek (there is a lawsuit between Howard Hughes Corporation and residents of Spring Creek, who claim their homes were not built on high enough elevation). On a typical day, the presence of water is felt only in recreational settings: Lake Woodlands, golf course ponds, water canals, or Pineywood preserves.

Recent reincarnations copy the natural aesthetic of The Woodlands— tall trees and verdant greenery—and paste it onto landscapes without thinking through the differences in context. The Houston area is lovingly called a swamp, but suburban developers tend to force forests out of prairie land because that's what sells. Many of the six-million-plus people in Houston's metropolitan area live in faux-forested suburbs. Where my dad lives features rolling hills shaped from the displaced dirt of a nearby golf course lake. When the sky gifts us one of those magnificent Texas sunsets, it almost looks like Augusta. But usually it looks like The Woodlands.

CASE STUDY FOR TODAY

There are a number of master-planned communities in Houston that apply the design-with-nature approach and end up looking completely different from The Woodlands. There's Springwood Creek near The Woodlands, which has employed prairie grasses instead of pines; the Bridgelands in Cyprus that tries to be a good neighbor to the Katy Prairie; or "farm-centric" Harvest Green in Richmond. But Cross Creek Ranch is making the most of living on the prairie with the floodplain as the guiding principle to its master plan.

Houses of Cross Creek Ranch are suspiciously similar to those of The Woodlands (and all their lakes are similar to those of Minnesota), but the land upon which they stand is not. Across fifty miles of separation the piney forest of The Woodlands transitions into the coastal prairie of Cross Creek Ranch.

Johnson Development Corporation purchased the property as denuded pastures with the early intention of reviving it into something "green and sustainable," says Matthew Baumgarten, SWA Group's lead landscape architect on the project. They did so through a number of means, both familiar and novel. Just as in any other master-planned community, there's a very large basin that stores a hundred-year flood event but, on a normal day, acts as a wetland park. Cross Creek Ranch's foundation for its master plan is the same as its namesake, a three-mile-long restored creek that used to be a watering hole for cattle, but you wouldn't know it without close inspection.

Baumgarten planned for Cross Creek Ranch's flood infrastructure to blend in with the subtle landscape features typical of Texas suburbs. From my experience, subtlety verged on invisibility. While touring the area with my friend Christian, who lives at Cross Creek Ranch, finding the creek was surprisingly tricky: the band of bordering wetlands was five to ten feet wide and recessed well below street level. Once we spotted it, we parked and stepped into 100 percent humidity to walk through muddy, freshly mowed grass, which gave way to unmowed tall grasses recently soaked by rain the night prior.

At last, there was a narrow stream tucked away in a shallow valley of wet grass and native flowers. Standing in the creek's soggy bottom with no other residents around, I felt my imagination get tugged back to a time before ranching and profit trampled the creek, when perhaps the Karankawa and Akokisa nations were here. In some ways, nurturing the farmed and ranched creek with native grasses and flowers was an act of decolonizing the land. In another, more true way, Cross Creek Ranch capitalized on indigenous nature to appeal to upper-middle-class families lusting after "authenticity," who, in fact, have probably never even been to the creek.

After Harvey, Christian said no one's homes were flooded and that his family and neighbors were "really lucky." To be "lucky" during Harvey erases the design (and privilege) of living in neighborhoods that were designed to endure fifty inches of stormwater. So even though not all residents of Cross Creek Ranch are aware of the creek and its design with nature, they experience its fortuitous effects.

I am reminded of Jenny Odell's anecdote in her book *How to Do Nothing*, in which she tells us of the creek near her childhood home: "It is not there to be productive; it is not there as an amenity," rather it's a reminder that we live in an animate world.[4] Our sensitivities are expanded; our awareness of our place on this earth is grounded. So to benefit from flood infrastructure is really just one side of the relationship; in designing with nature, we are to shape *and be shaped* by nature.

FAR OUT FROM THE REFUGE

On the last day of 2019, my dad asked me if I wanted to go to the Attwater Prairie Chicken National Wildlife Refuge. So, after driving sixty miles west of downtown Houston and forty-five minutes from our house in Katy, we found ourselves in a place where all you can see is the way things are meant to be. There are no misplaced live oaks, no resuscitated creeks. What does that leave? Not much, and yet everything there needs to be. The Attwater Prairie Chicken National Wildlife Refuge in Eagle Lake is one of the last remaining large swaths of coastal prairie in this great state.

"It's quiet here," the refuge manager, John Magera, tells me. Over the phone, I can practically hear his eyes mist over as he describes the refuge. It looks quiet, too. You could just see it as a flat landscape of tall brown grass. Or, with training and curiosity, you could see layers of life. Birds, bugs, and microbes relying on one another. What you don't see at the refuge is just as important. There are no trees within, fences around, or buildings beyond the refuge center.

These are the conditions required for one of the world's most endangered bird species, the Attwater's prairie chicken, to survive. Around one hundred Attwater's roam two wild places, both in southeast Texas, bolstered by an accomplished captive breeding program from the Houston Zoo. Attwater's suffered a big blow from Harvey. The death toll is unclear, but Magera did say that there would be more than three hundred individuals in the wild, were it not for unprecedented flooding events in 2016 and 2017.[5]

With the image of drowning prairie chickens burned in our memory, we of course want to help. Unprompted, Magera pointed to the prairie as a solution. "Whenever we have a big storm, you always hear people talk about how planting prairie will be good for us, but you don't see that happening. It's infuriating," says Magera. The sprouting master-planned communities that creep farther along Grand Parkway forecast worsening conditions. The town of Eagle Lake, where the refuge is, "wants to be the next Katy," Magera says, which threatens to turn the refuge into a "postage stamp of prairie" by the time I am his age, a generation from now.

With that, my dad and I took Grand Parkway home. From the highway we could see a lot of working lands that, while not seeded with native prairie grasses, are better for wildlife conservation than looming residential developments.

MOVING FORWARD

Design with Nature was written over fifty years ago, and the world has changed. "Climate change" was coined, a demagogue was elected, and our entry into a sixth extinction event became more evident than ever. Some historians suspect McHarg wouldn't design The Woodlands today, because it is a suburb and is counter to his ideals of sustainable living. McHarg would probably also disagree with the way design with nature is used in Houston's suburbs: nature is often a selling point for suburbs, but they still lack the diversity of people that makes Houston vibrant and the density that makes way for the wild to thrive.

Examples of design with nature in urban contexts are growing: Buffalo Bayou Park reconnects millions of visitors to our history on the water; substantial pocket prairies in massive urban institutions such as Rice University and the Medical Center offer a refuge for native species and human health; more and more Houstonians can commute on the trails along Houston's two hundred miles of bayou. However, thinking of urban, suburban, and rural as separate spheres is part of the problem that has made preparing for floods so challenging. Whether it be preserving wild places an hour away or growing native prairie grasses along bayous, Houston will benefit from designing the spaces between the dense urban core and the rural outreaches as a whole ecoregion, not smatterings of developed and undeveloped land.

It's useful to return to *Design with Nature* and draw out elements that don't often make it into the built environment. McHarg's book enriched landscape design pedagogy, but it also depicted a utopia made possible when a community's built environment is rooted in natural processes. Man "must become the steward of the biosphere," McHarg tells us.[6] Unfortunately, this is lost on most suburbanites.

It's apparent that stewards aren't made through osmosis from living in a beautiful suburb. To be a steward in Houston, the design of urban and suburban places should be more explicit about the dependence we have on nature. Indeed, the landscapes we grow in should remind us that we are of nature and that it's not some far-flung destination reachable only by your Subaru. It's great to see master-planned communities experimenting with landscape design to address climate change and flooding, but taking this to a regional scale should be a coordinated effort not driven by developers.

Back at my dad's new home in Katy, goldfinches have settled in on our four bird feeders for the early months of the year. I sat on the back porch for a while and watched the birds flutter around an oak tree the feeders hung from. I counted at least twenty goldfinches and one male cardinal tolerant of their chatter. Wanting to unwind my neck, I turned my torso toward the tree, and all the birds went into hiding. I waited for them to return, and, slowly, one or two brave souls did. Then I heard from the house "-bo?" It was my dad calling for me, Genebo.

"This is as much action as we get back here," he told me contentedly, a little ironically. We sat like that with the birds and the backyard and the golf course beyond the fence for a while. I wondered if the goldfinches could tell me what this land was and could still be. For me, it was unrecognizable, ephemeral—comfortable, but not quite home.

GHOST DANCE
// NEVADA, 1890

FLOOD OF PEOPLE / BORDER
CONCENTRATION CAMPS
// ONGOING

HURRICANE HARVEY
// HOUSTON, 2017

LEAN TO THAT
FLOOD SONG

ACTS OF PROTEST, LIKE NATURAL DISASTERS, SHIFT THE GROUND BENEATH OUR FEET. THIS
ESSAY ENGAGES THE IDEA OF THE INTERCONNECTIVITY OF BOTH POLITICAL AND NATURAL
CIRCUMSTANCES THAT REMOVE THE FOUNDATIONS ON WHICH WE STAND, LITERALLY AND
METAPHORICALLY, TO CHALLENGE THE STATE OF OUR PLANET AND OURSELVES.

DESIGN BY ILSE HARRISON

FLOOD OF MY CHILDHOOD HOME
// PLAINFIELD VT, 1989

NATURAL DISASTERS

POLITICAL PROTESTS

CHEMICAL FIRE

WEATHER FLOOD

FLOOD OF PEOPLE

ITC CHEMICAL EXPLOSION
// DEER PARK TX, 2019

HURRICANE STAN
// GUATEMALA, 2015

Lean to That Flood Song

Laura August

TO BEGIN WITH

My family lived in Vermont for a few years when I was a child. We lived in a cabin that sat alongside a stream and was ill-suited to the winter. I remember the place for how its landscape invited wandering and imagining. The stream ran down from a mountain, where it had carved a winding path over hundreds of years. In the winter, the water froze solid, and my sister and I would ease ourselves onto the ice, wondering if it might crack beneath us. When the snow melted, the creek turned deluge, pouring down the mountain with unimaginable power. Water roared into thundering muscle, bringing down boulders, trees, mud, and debris in heavy crashing sounds. In one spring thaw, the water pulled free a neighbor's house, and we watched it roll down the mountain. There we stood, helpless in front of our home, as water somehow grew taller. As it surged, firemen allowed my mother to retrieve one item from our house. She disappeared for a moment before returning with her choice: a wooden dollhouse she had built for us. Threatened with losing our small, temporary home, she latched on to its even smaller symbol and held tight.

When we returned to the house, it was filled with a thick layer of silt, the soft dirt reminding us how quickly the floor—with all its associations of stability and ground—could vanish under the flood.

LEAN (ONE AND TWO)

For the past few years, I have been writing about mud, both as a material and as a metaphor for mixture, confusion, and messiness (political, personal, and communal).[1] Knowing this, the artist Devin Kenny writes to me: he has remembered that "mud" is also a term for thickly mixed lean, an addictive psychoactive beverage, also called purple drank, a mixture of codeine cough syrup, Jolly Ranchers, and soda that was, by some accounts, first mixed in Houston. It causes euphoria and slowness, a kind of thick, lethargic disassociation. It's a drink that bears a significant symbolic relationship to the character of the city itself, with its thick air, traffic congestion, and murky bayous.[2]

In art history, though, the most familiar lean comes from the Greeks. "Contrapposto" is a pose somewhere between stasis and motion, as the sculptural body leans its weight onto one foot, twisting its shoulders and arms off the main axis. It suggests that the sculptor has captured a subject just at the moment movement begins. The introduction of contrapposto into sculpture presented a world of new emotional possibilities in figural representation. Between stasis and motion, we prepare for change, trusting the floor beneath us, even as we push away from it. This twist, in art historical terms, is the sculptural embodiment of emotional experience.

ANOMALOUS PROTEST TACTICS

In 2017, dkyk, one of Kenny's musical alter egos, began producing an album he titled *los giros de la siguiente* (the turns of the next). The record draws from a year of research into Houston's chopped and screwed DJ scene mixed with cumbia, political speech, noise, punk, and indie rock. Taking *cumbia rebajada* as its subject, dkyk bridges the Caribbean musical mélange with the style of Houston's celebrated DJ Screw, known for slowing music to a soporific, lean-back tempo. *Los giros* is a recovery album, a meditation on a broken relationship, a reflection of protest tactics in a specific political moment. This is a cumbia album of a broken heart, an album about resistance as survival (or maybe it's the other way around).

In the track "Bonds," dkyk reads a text excerpted from Micah White's book *The End of Protest*, in which the author details the lessons he learned from Occupy Wall Street.[3] In particular, he considers what value a supposedly "failed" protest has. As the song begins, we hear dkyk's voice reading White's text. "Assume that human action, the form of protest, or organizational style has no significant impact on whether a movement will succeed," White writes. "Let's go further and propose that the outcome of the revolution is not up to human will." A synthe-sizer begins dkyk's melody. He continues to read: "Now what do you do to change the world? How do you act?"

One "failed" protest White describes is the Ghost Dance—or Nanissáanah in Caddo—a circle dance performed by the Nevada Northern Paiute peoples. The dance invited spirits of the deceased to return to Earth, joining the living in a battle against the encroachment of white settlers.[4] The nineteenth-century ethnologist James Mooney describes the Ghost Dance as an appeal to the landscape to rise up and defend its native peoples: "The Sioux, like other tribes, believed that at the moment of the catastrophe the earth would tremble. According to one version[,] the landslide was to be accompanied by a flood of water, which would flow into the mouths of the whites and cause them to choke with mud."[5]

White's words describe the Ghost Dance as a "ritual with political consequences," even as so many dancers would be doomed by the geno-cidal land grab of white nineteenth-century westward expansion. In a massacre that year, the US Army killed more than 150 Miniconjou and Hunkpapa from the Lakota people.[6]

"A rational voluntarist would be hard pressed to explain why danc-ing in a circle far away from cities would be a threat to a government," dkyk reads twice, as the soundscape becomes more jagged, the melody disappearing into a striking beat.

("Striking" also signifying hitting, beating, hurting. "Striking" also signifying stepping *away* from one's work, in protest. "Beat" meaning also to conquer. The melody disappears into a striking beat, I say again.)

LEAN (THREE AND FOUR)

In the United States, Sheryl Sandberg made another concept of lean widely popular among certain populations—especially women with corporate aspirations—with her 2013 book *Lean In*.[7] In the book, she encourages women to physically and metaphorically lean their bodies forward, into the work, to claim more responsibility and be more visible.

After the sudden loss of her husband, though, Sandberg admits she might have been seeing the world through certain blinders when she encouraged women to *simply lean in to leadership*. In grief, she discovers the privilege of her position, of her family, of her spouse. When he is gone, she loses one of the floors beneath her, a floor she hadn't had to notice before; she abruptly realizes that her lean forward was supported by very specific infrastructures of power. That is, perhaps centuries of gender- and race-based discrimination, violence, and lost opportunities were not only about a woman's reluctant posture in the board room.[8]

We colloquially use the phrase "drink the Kool-Aid" to describe someone's commitment to a toxic or cult-like philosophy, action, or group that puts them in danger. To drink the thickly mixed lean, though, is to drink mud is to lean *back* . . . back. To *lean* after loss is at once a contortion, a mode of survival, a search for stolen floor, a slowing down. To lean includes a gesture backward, an acceptance of the force of history's floodwaters, a physical acknowledgement of immense grief, a contorted dance of shared mourning. If contrapposto lets us find emotion in carved stone and cast metal, I imagine a lean to be laden with feelings, to be a slow and heavy twisting into one's weight.

In the face of the coming floods, to be clear, I am not at all interested in a Sandbergian forward lean of progress.[9]

ANOMALOUS PROTEST TACTICS (2) *&* SOME THOUGHTS ON HOME

In September 2018, the government of Guatemalan president Jimmy Morales declares the Cicig, the International Commission against Impunity in Guatemala, unwelcome in Guatemala.[10] He refuses to allow the president of the organization to reenter the country and he makes a public speech denouncing Cicig while surrounded by uniformed members of the military. Incongruously, in a speech describing his reasons for not allowing Cicig's investigation (notably of his own presidential campaign), he situates his argument in relation to a national idea of family.[11]

Guatemala y nuestro gobierno cree en la vida, la familia basada en matrimonio de hombre y mujer, cree y quiere elecciones libres, no intervenidas.

(Guatemala and our government believe in life, the family based on marriage between a man and a woman. We believe in and want free elections, without interference.)[12]

Writing for *Plaza Pública*, the journalist Alberto Pradilla describes Morales's strategy:

> El domingo se celebrará una manifestación bajo el lema "Guate por la vida y la familia" convocada por sectores conservadores. El martes está prevista la tercera lectura de la Iniciativa 5272, que impone mayores penas a las mujeres que abortan, prohíbe enseñar diversidad sexual y veta, aún más, el matrimonio igualitario. Con este guiño, Morales viene a decir: "Si estás a favor del modelo tradicional de familia y contra el aborto, eres de los míos y estás contra la Cicig". Los sectores afines al presidente tratan de ubicar el debate en términos ideológicos que trascienden a la lucha anticorrupción.
>
> (On Sunday, there was a demonstration under the banner "Guate pro-life and pro-family," organized by conservative parties. Tuesday, there will be the third review of Initiative 5272, which would heighten penalties for women who have abortions, would prohibit the teaching of sexual diversity, and would veto marriage equality. With this wink, what Morales is saying is: "If you believe in a traditional model of family and are against abortion, you are with us and against Cicig." The sectors affiliated with the president are trying to locate the debate in ideological terms that transcend the anticorruption fight.)[13]

The equation is uneven: Morales seems to say that investigations of (his) corruption are not welcome, because Guatemalans believe in heteronormative homemaking. In effect, his response to a threat is a gesture of tightening, again around the symbol of home.

Never mind that nearby, a memorial for forty-one girls burned to death in a state-run "safe home" is tended every day by the mothers of the girls.

A FEW WEEKS BEFORE Morales's speech, the artist Inés Verdugo installed a small house-like structure made from blocks of sugar at Concepción 41, the convent ruins in Antigua. Titled *Dulce Hogar* (*Sweet Home*), Verdugo's structure was immediately swarmed by bees, who remained eating the *panela* (and dying below and around the house)

Ines Verdugo, *Dulce Hogar*. Sugar and wood. © 2018 by Inés Hogar.
Photograph by Byron Mármol. Courtesy of the artist and Fundación Paiz.

through the month it was on view for the Paiz Biennial. As the structure deteriorated, it became more and more foreboding, the carcass of
something built to fall apart, a sweet home turned bitter, a humming
sign of impending dissolution.

From its first moments, the most startling aspect of Verdugo's sculpture was that sound. On opening weekend, it was still possible to enter
the house and stand there looking out as bees crowded around your
body, pushing their way to the sugar, their wordless droning like a physical shiver. Visitors whispered among themselves, telling each other
that the bees could sense fear. In the following weeks, rain washed away
the *panela* and dead bees piled up on the floor. The house disintegrated
in water. Home symbols are unstable.

AFTER JIMMY MORALES'S SPEECH, the streets around my home are
cordoned off by riot police as people begin marching from across the
country to the city, overwhelmingly in support of Cicig's investigations.
We await a violent altercation, or a response from the government, an
acknowledgment of the people's protest, but none of those things come.
Every September that I have been in Guatemala, there are national

protests to coincide with the day of independence, and every year my friends and colleagues make the same lament: they know even as they march and chant and dance in circles and light fires and burn effigies of politicians that very little will change for the better.

That is to say: the marching is not only about the visible *success* of a protest. It is, perhaps more significantly, a communal emotional experience, an acknowledgment that something is not right, a shared physical movement, a visible note to the future that things here are very wrong. Failed protests also make meaning for their participants, opening imaginative portals to other ways of being, specifically in collaboration. Protests work against inertia; they are gatherings that honor affinity and care, making visible the ways in which our lives are interwoven. A failed protest is still a celebration of what it means to be involved with one another in the shared struggle.

To move together, my protesting community knows, is to dance as to a shared beat, as to a shared beating, as if the floor beneath us is also shifting, as if our definition of home is necessarily, importantly unstable, and as if our feet are sinking into and pulling out of the mud left behind by the floods of change.

TO FLOOD/TO FLOOR

In a series of photos and video from 2015, Manuel Chavajay documents the abandoned structure of a house on the shore of Lake Atitlán. *Casa Hundida* (*Flooded House*) is about the larger relationship between humans and the lake, a central theme across Chavajay's practice. Together, we talk about human disregard for the rhythms of the natural world, how our species has a remarkably short memory in relation to geologic time.

In Chavajay's photograph, a *cayuco* (wooden canoe) floats in green waters within the frame of the abandoned house. The roof of the building is missing or perhaps was never there. Open squares for windows frame the foggy vista of the *volcán* behind it, of the lake, of another structure on the far bank. Mudslides happen here, too, Chavajay tells me. During Hurricane Stan in 2005, the massive rainfalls washed homes off the mountains, filling them with mud, burying people in moving earth.

Manuel Chavajay Moralez, *Casa hundida*. © 2015 by Manuel Chavajay Moralez.
Video still. Courtesy of the artist.

Over and over, we build what we imagine could be possible, and watch it wash away.

There is room in this cycle for both hope and despair.

WHEN HURRICANE HARVEY hit Houston, photographer Keliy Anderson-Staley's home flooded. As she and her family evacuated, she photographed the living room full of water, her couch piled with belongings in one last effort to keep them dry. I return often to that photograph, a representative image for what happened to many of my community members' homes. At Anderson-Staley's home, photographs hang on the robin's egg blue wall behind the sofa, and the floor is covered in green-brown floodwaters. The floor disappears, as if it has been pulled from under her.

WHEN I MOVE TO Guatemala City in June of 2016, I bring with me three suitcases of books, a few items of clothing, some records. I line the books up on the floor. They are at once a lifeline to my language, a familiar world of ideas, and my only piece of furniture. That first week, a pipe breaks in the apartment and the floor floods. The books

Keliy Anderson Staley, *Our Living Room*. © 2017 by Keliy Anderson Staley.
Courtesy of the artist.

are soaked, become heavy with water, eventually dry into wrinkled clumps of pages, stained by water and unreadable. Friends tell me I have learned my first important lesson from Guatemala: never put anything I care about on the floor.

The next year, the artist Hellen Ascoli moves from Guatemala to Madison, Wisconsin. We correspond regularly, charting each other's journeys to the new places we live, feeling the boundaries of each other's unfamiliarities. As winter starts, Ascoli walks around a nearby lake every day. The docks, their floating surfaces an unsteady but constant floor, moor her, and she sends me photographs of them. In previous installation work, Ascoli has built her own floors, even in harsh environments. She thinks of the floor as making and holding space, signifying that she has been physically present. We were here, a floor reminds us: here we stood.

In October, as Madison prepares for the coming freeze, cranes arrive to pull the docks from the lake. Ascoli writes to me that her new floor has been moved. What happens, we wonder together, when we cannot find a standing place?

After my books are flooded, my Spanish improves. That is to say, *encuentro otras palabras y construyo un base nuevo, ubicado en la gramática, en un no-lugar entre idiomas. Mi español raro no tiene piso, pues hablo siempre en círculos, como una corriente de agua. Con el no-lugar de mi lengua, descubro donde quedarme.* That is one thing that happens.

WHITE NOISE

In his project *The Ghost Variations* (ongoing since 2012), the artist Omar Barquet takes the structure of a symphony to organize six movements. Within each movement is a subproject he calls a fugue, an experimental collaboration with sound and installation to think through the phases of a hurricane:

> emulando sus intensidades y desplazamientos como un esquema de forma espiral, reflexionando principalmente sobre la percepción de tiempo y la vida, a través de los ciclos de transformación del paisaje y la naturaleza caótica del pensamiento.
>
> (Emulating [the hurricane's] intensities and displacements like a spiraling sketch, [*The Ghost Variations*] reflects on perceptions of time and human life in relation to the cycles of transformation within the landscape and the chaotic nature of thought.)[14]

For his fourth fugue, called *El naufragio* (*The shipwreck*), Barquet holds an open workspace in collaboration with the sound artist Nicolás Duarte at Asociación Tupac in Lima. He describes *El naufragio* as a visual and sonic representation of stories told by fishermen from Quintana Roo placed in dialogue with J. M. W. Turner's 1805 painting of the same title.

Record of performative action *El naufragio* (*The Wreck*) from *Ghost Variations Project*. © 2014 by Omar Barquet. Wood, cords, water, electric cables, lightbulb, and pulleys, with sound intervention. Created during a residency in TUPAC, Lima, Perú. Courtesy of the artist.

Partiendo de algunas narraciones que me fueron comparti-
das por familiares de pescadores de la zona de Punta Allen, Q.
Roo, he elaborado una propuesta de instalación escultórica que
aborde el choque, la tensión, inestabilidad y la náusea de un
naufragio. Por intuición, decidí experimentar la acción alco-
holizado, lo cuál me hizo pensar en los marineros, el azote del
oleaje, el perder del balance, generando un agotamiento al llevar
el cuerpo a un límite y finalmente, naufragar.

    (Starting with the stories shared with me by friends of fish-
ermen in the Punta Allen zone of Quintana Roo, I made a sculptural installation that touched on the shock, tension, instability,
and nausea of a shipwreck. Intuitively, I decided to make the
performance-experiment while drunk, which led me to think of
the mariners, the lash of the swell, the loss of balance, creating
an exhaustion that takes the body to a certain limit and, finally,
leads it to be wrecked.)

To understand a wreck, to hear the sound of a storm, Barquet looks to the instability of the body in an altered state. Seen alongside the percussive improvisations of the musician Santiago Pillado-Matheu, Barquet's performance included the breaking of found chairs that he had built into a ship-like abstract installation. The sensation, as he describes it, was one of enormous sound. In his notebooks kept while planning the performance, he writes, "The groans of white noise, the Flood???"

TO FILL

A flood is, at its heart, a filling. To fill abundantly, excessively, to the point of breaking. To fill with sound, with water, with people, with wreckage, with possibility, with emotion.

To ward off floods, humans build levees.

We block "floods" of other humans with walls, thinking this will stem the tide: see how we return to water metaphors to describe and dehumanize how others move across the same landscapes we ourselves have made perilous?

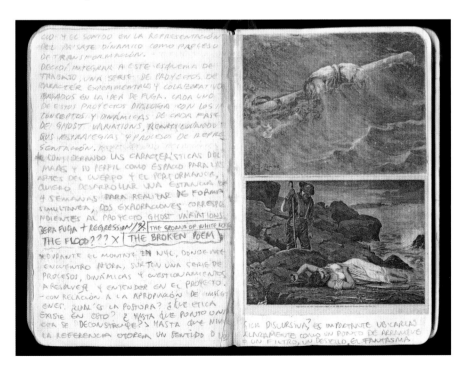

Omar Barquet, *Logbook Ghost Variations pg. 35.* © 2013 by Omar Barquet. Paper notebook, 26 × 20 cm. Courtesy of the artist.

In the news this year, specifically among conservative sources, migrant caravans are described as waves, pouring, surging, and flooding into the United States. One source suggests that a flood of immigration from Central America is orchestrated, and I wonder if that writer has ever witnessed how impossible it is to truly harness water.[15]

And yet.

UNSETTLEMENTS

In 2018, the Houston-based artist, poet, and translator JD Pluecker begins making object poems. Thinking of the objects as poems with no words, Pluecker includes things and detritus from sites around the city that are personally and local-historically significant. These sites are marked by violence around race and gender, by family legacies and losses, and by JD's own coming to terms with their particular city. They install the found things on the wall, extending onto tables or corners or the floor, petals and vines connecting to rope and feathers and stones and weirdly bodily rubber molds and bits of furniture. Even without written words to describe these individual histories, the objects remain intimate and specific. JD calls them *The Unsettlements*, and they grow to include rituals, investigations, book objects, and public activities, a reckoning with whiteness and with trauma, an engagement with the dark spaces upon which family history is built.

Unsettlement #1 is among the first object poems JD made. Six thin lines of Spanish moss are arranged in a vertical grouping, each ending with a leaf. The piece has the rhyme scheme AABBAA, JD tells me. The As are leaves from a begonia their grandmother grew, which the family still tends. The Bs are oak leaves they collected from the cemetery where their grandparents are buried. In a corresponding photograph from the cemetery, we see a small body of water, a puddle surrounded by grass, reflecting the sky. At Forest Park, the headstones keep sinking in Houston's boggy earth, JD says. They are pushed up and propped up and then sink again, small floodings pulling them downward.

It strikes me that the words for flood and floor are so close. Floods come from many directions, and we often imagine them as tsunamis—iconic giant waves—that tower above and pummel from the sides. But I am more intimately acquainted with those floods that rise from the ground up. Such floods disconnect us from a steady state, sweep us off our feet, fill our structures until we are forced to seek higher ground, to swim or paddle out, to be ungrounded. Floods take away our floors, erase our markers, loosen our grip, require a new nimbleness, a dexterity as we move together over a surface we cannot predict, cannot even see. Marching together, we also become an unruly flood.

JD Pluecker, *Unsettlement #1*. © 2018 by JD Pluecker. Courtesy of the artist.

Untitled. © 2018 by JD Pluecker. Courtesy of the artist.

IN THE END

The noise of the flood is by turns cacophonous, quiet, rhythmic, repetitive, and unbearable—music that can lead us to dance, just as the water moves the earth beneath our feet, and just as we lean in relation to all its muddy possibilities.

"To survive, we need to relearn multiple forms of curiosity," write the editors of the collection *Arts of Living on a Damaged Planet*.[16] They cite "Marrow," Ursula Le Guin's poem about listening to a rock and being unable to force a word from it: the stone speaks when it wants, but it *does* speak. Multiple kinds of listening are necessary, they argue, to face what comes next, to hear what the earth and its movements tell us. Floods are only one symptom of our violent "lean forward" to extract, crush, blow apart, and conquer this land for financial gain.

Many of the artists in my orbit in recent years have been thinking of other ways of listening, especially to the natural world. Gabriel Rodriguez Pellecer invents a machine for hearing the thoughts of the sun; a large metal bowl that he holds to his ear channels the rays of sun into *pensamiento*. Ascoli weaves a textile to the dimensions of her body and then carries it to the high plateaus of the Cuchumatanes in Guatemala, holding the weave around her and reaching it up, connecting to the sky, an antenna to talk to her slain brother. Mario Alberto López builds microphones tuned to the slight vibrations of plants and then translates these sounds into a series of drawings. There are many more.

And what if we listen to a flood as it rolls over what we imagined possible, following or fleeing its unsettling waters, shimmying and dipping to its pummeling rhythms?

This is something the ghost dancers knew: there is power in circling together, appealing to the rains and the mudslides and the living landscapes that surround us, embracing movement as a productive unmooring, a dance, and a shimmer.[17] The music of the flood might be a white noise, an epic crash, a holding, and . . . also . . . at last . . . a quiet. That flood noise lingers in devastation, in reconstruction, in social surfaces soaked through; it comes in a shudder and a smell. The music of the flood might be a way of describing our entanglements with the world around us, our inability to make sense of them, our precarious footing even as we keep moving to that beat, as to a beating.

Homes hold a special place in our shared imaginary, I think. As they did for my mother, decades ago, they symbolize certain kinds of stability, even when their symbolism fails the reality of what they hold, neglects the ways they may crumble or wash away. This disconnect between the image of home and its lived decrepitude is at the heart of many battles over national identity, xenophobia, immigration, environmental collapse, and civic values.

We gather at my home in Guatemala City after protests, for meals, to listen to records, or when visitors come to town. I certainly participate in a romance with home, as someone whose home is embodied in everything I do, as someone whose home is a *personaje*, a named character who lives with me and offers respite for others.

And yet, as I write this, a chemical cloud hangs low over Houston. A fire in Deer Park rages at a petrochemical plant, and its smoky trail hovers above our homes as poisonous runoff seeps into nearby waterways and the ship channel. A man stops in front of my apartment building and fires a shotgun into my neighbor's home nine times before speeding away. I gather with my neighbors behind the building, hugging their children to us, breathing in the toxic air, a light drizzle covering our skins with chemical rain. We choose to gather—in our homes, in our scholarship, in our visual practices, in our readings, in our politics— knowing, even as we gather, that it will not save us from the future. We know, too, that gathering holds us in the unstable present. Jorge de León paints Houston flooded, again, just weeks before Harvey hits.

We see the floods coming because they have already come.

Untitled, from the series *En los prósperos días*. © 2017 by Jorge de León. Courtesy of the artist.

IN THE END, which is likely where we are (which in this writing is exactly where we are), flood noise—which is a shared, expectant listening, an embodied dance to the water as it washes over us, a failed resistance, a movement toward other futures, a march in solidarity even as we are told to shelter in place, a yowling shriek we make at our most vulnerable moment—might be the most important thing to make, might be the only thing to be made, even (and especially) as we are washed away.

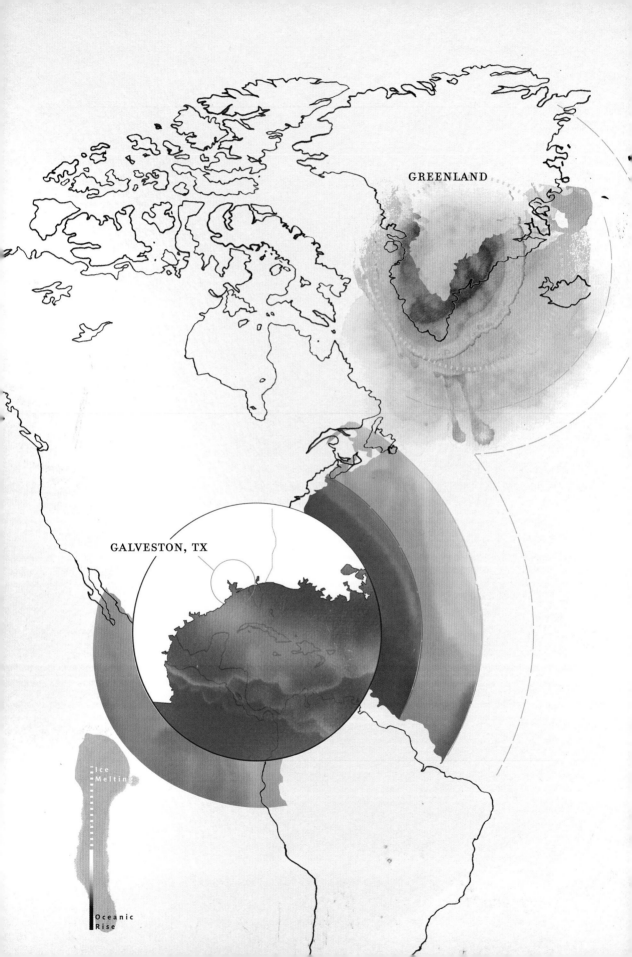

GREENLAND

GALVESTON, TX

Ice
Melting

Oceanic
Rise

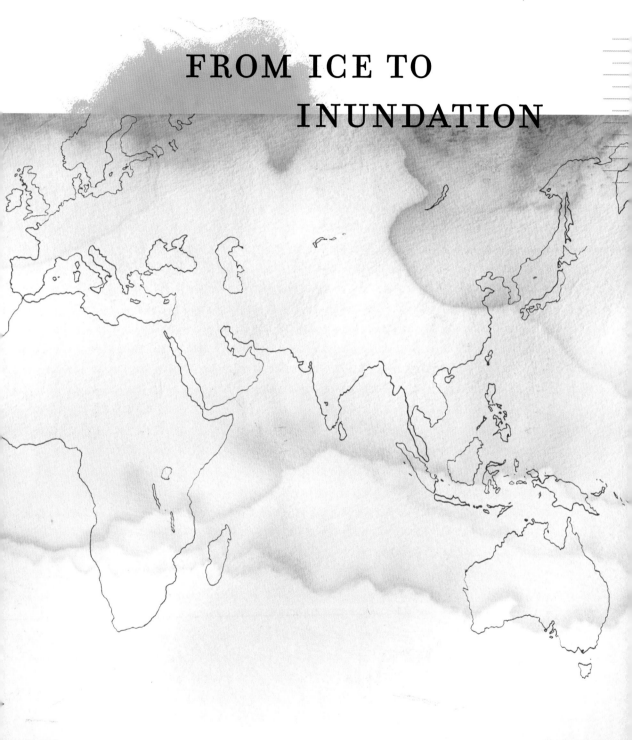

FROM ICE TO
INUNDATION

FLOOD IS WATER IN MOTION, DISPLACED FROM ONE PLACE TO ANOTHER. ICE IN THE ARCTIC THAT
IS IN THE FORM OF GLACIERS AND ICE SHEETS IS RAPIDLY CHANGING FROM SOLID TO MELTWATER.
THIS MAP ILLUSTRATES HOW, WHEN GREENLAND MELTS, GALVESTON FLOODS. IT PUTS AN
EMPHASIS ON THE CONNECTION BETWEEN SITES OF MELTING ICE AND SITES OF OCEANIC RISE.

DESIGN BY KAREN ALVARENGA AND ALEX RAMOS

From Ice to Inundation

Cymene Howe

Flood is water in motion, displaced and traveling from one place to another. Flood is inundation, saturation, contamination, a swelling hydrosphere that often rots and destroys on its way in and on its way out. Flood is biblical, but it is also banal. It leaves traces of itself in both intimate and mundane spaces, insidious markers of how water refuses containment and how porousness is a condition of living. Flood is water out of place, or, at least water that feels out of place when it moves, unwelcomed, into our homes and workplaces, gardens and garages. Of course, water out of place is a relative perspective, one dependent upon where we imagine water *ought* to be. Out-of-placeness was something that Mary Douglas, a cultural anthropologist working in the mid-twentieth century, thought quite a lot about. Douglas wrote specifically, and quite eloquently, about dirt. Dirt was an idea. But it was also materialized as a substance that might be fine over there, outside the walls of our homes, but that was never welcome inside. Indeed, some dirt—when out of place—could even rise to the level of pollution or taboo.

Douglas's meditation on dirt reveals the cultural attitudes we still hold on how the earthly, or watery, world should remain under our control. We want dirt, like water, to stay in its place. That is, in the place we want it. But that human proclivity is being increasingly challenged in times of anthropogenic climate change when there is a lot of matter, or there are many matters, out of place. Water moving outside of its usual boundaries is also much more than a philosophical question. It is a painful reality in times when extreme storms, sea level rise, and floods are increasingly flowing into, and over, our doorsteps.

Like Douglas, I am a cultural anthropologist, and I spend much of my time thinking about water out of place—in the form of melt and flood. As ice melts around the world, I am attempting, in a sense, to follow the water from one place to another. I begin where ice is melting

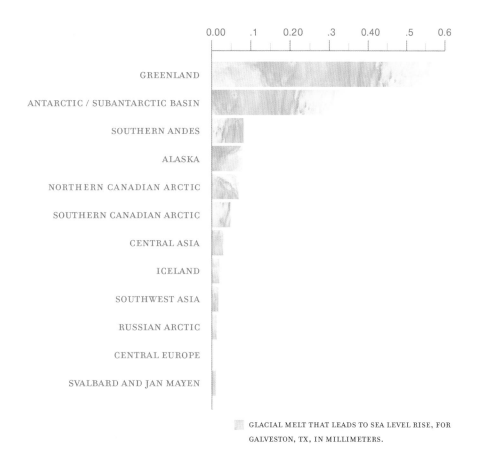

```
         0.00    .1    0.20    .3   0.40    .5    0.6
```

GREENLAND

ANTARCTIC / SUBANTARCTIC BASIN

SOUTHERN ANDES

ALASKA

NORTHERN CANADIAN ARCTIC

SOUTHERN CANADIAN ARCTIC

CENTRAL ASIA

ICELAND

SOUTHWEST ASIA

RUSSIAN ARCTIC

CENTRAL EUROPE

SVALBARD AND JAN MAYEN

GLACIAL MELT THAT LEADS TO SEA LEVEL RISE, FOR
GALVESTON, TX, IN MILLIMETERS.

and then move to places where seas are rising and flooding is immi-
nent. Part of this work involves trying to unravel how water out of place
is being charted and graphed by scientists. Another part of this work
requires asking questions about how communities, planners, and others are contending with ice loss or bracing for sea level increases.

My research has taken me to the Arctic region to see where ice—in
the form of glaciers and ice sheets—is rapidly changing from a solid
form to meltwater. Polar ice melt is widely understood as a key indicator of global temperature increase, both on land and in the seas. And
ice is melting nowhere faster, and faster than expected, than in the Arctic region, which is warming at about two to three times the rate of
anywhere else on Earth according to the Intergovernmental Panel on
Climate Change's (IPCC's) 2018 report.[1] Scientists have also concurred
that the rate of melt in polar regions—the Arctic and Antarctic—has
been considerably underestimated.

The 2018 National Climate Assessment Report, mandated by the US government to summarize the economic and social impacts of climate change on the United States, showed that global sea level rise is expected to accelerate through the end of this century, possibly rising up to 6.6 feet by 2100.[2] Because over 40 percent of the US population now lives on a coast, many Americans will be affected by changing sea levels, storm surges, and other weather events that are driven by climate change.[3] Proximity to large bodies of warming sea water that are themselves increasingly bloated is sure to spell more disasters in maritime regions. In many locations along the US coastline, according to the National Oceanic and Atmospheric Administration (NOAA), so-called nuisance flooding is between 300 and 900 percent more frequent than it was fifty years ago.[4] Melt, of course, has consequences elsewhere. In 2018, the Arctic Monitoring and Assessment Programme report—which amasses scientific data to assist Arctic policymakers—detailed that global sea levels will rise much more quickly than previously thought; new estimates are almost double the pace previously predicted by the IPCC in 2013. Melt is becoming flood, even if incrementally and unevenly.

The transformation of the world's ice into meltwater is a vivid indicator of what the critical philosopher Timothy Morton has called the "Age of Asymmetry"—a geological period in which humans have a direct effect on the substrata of earthly reality. Looking at the effects of sea level encroachment in places like Galveston and Miami, as well as places like Bangladesh and the Marshall Islands, we can see that sea level effects are also asymmetrically felt; climate crises are not distributed evenly, and in most cases, those centers of power and resource exploitation that have contributed most to climate change will not be the people and places to suffer its most egregious effects.

Not all floods are sea level rise. But sea level rise is a certain kind of flood: a slow, accretive, and, now, inevitable one.

OCEANS

In elementary school, most of us learn about world geography through maps and images. Maps neatly designate Earth's oceans: the Arctic,

Atlantic, Indian, Pacific, and Southern. Each have their proper name and place. But for oceanographers and other scientists, these are mutable waters, interconnected and moving swiftly and fluidly across lines marked on maps. This is the world ocean. One ocean. One that covers about 70 percent of Earth's surface.

Earth scientists agree that melting land ice is contributing significantly to sea level rise around the world and that continued warming will exacerbate the risks for human populations. Many climate experts now believe that an overall sea level rise of two to three feet worldwide by the end of the century is a realistic estimate. This does not mean that the ocean would come inland two or three feet, but that what we now consider "sea level" (or zero elevation) would be under two or three feet of water. This would affect different coastlines differently because there are multiple factors involved in local sea level rise. So, while these designations are valuable for estimating future potential harm and, perhaps more importantly, for alerting populations to sea level threats, these diagnoses are limited in that they speak to an average.

Many accounts of sea level rise are simplistic, such as "the median global sea level," also known as "the bathtub model." In the bathtub model, meltwater entering the world ocean appears to manifest in a uniform way, distributing evenly across the world's coasts. This is inaccurate for several reasons, including the fact that local sea levels are determined by myriad factors—fourteen in total—according to the US National Oceanic and Atmospheric Administration. These include: land composition (erosion, subsidence, sediment compaction, and bedrock porosity), weather (storms, wind, and air pressure distribution), glacial isostatic adjustment, ocean circulation (waves, tides, currents, and the global ocean conveyor), and finally, global sea level fluctuation caused by oceanic thermal expansion and melting land ice. These are complex, site-specific processes, and NOAA has, very helpfully, developed a mapping tool, the Sea Level Rise Viewer, that interactively shows a variety of local sea level rise scenarios on US coasts.[5]

In trying to follow the melted water of the Arctic to its ultimate destination as sea level rises in the lower latitudes, I have learned that unlike the lines on maps, the flow of planetary water does not conform to a simple path.

ARCTIC EVERYWHERE

The Arctic region is currently shedding its cryosphere at a rate of 447 billion tons of ice per year. From 2005 to 2015, an average of 14,000 tons of water have been pouring into the world ocean every second. From 1986 to 2005, only 5,000 tons per second were being discharged; that means that in only ten years, the amount of meltwater flowing into the world ocean has more than doubled from the previous twenty-year period.

Research from the Geological Survey of Greenland and Denmark, which was released in December 2018, overviews almost fifty years of cryospheric data from satellite readings as well as local sea level measurements. The report shows that the Arctic region is the leading contributor to overall global sea level rise. It also demonstrates that Arctic glaciers are the most significant factor affecting current sea level rise. While the Antarctic continent contains far more ice in terms of sheer quantity, its contribution to sea level rise doesn't come close to the rates of meltwater being discharged from the Arctic region. Arctic ice is causing the world ocean to swell by more than a millimeter every year.

As melted ice becomes integrated into the world ocean, the planet's gravity and its rotation are shifted, creating spatial patterns of sea level rise distribution around the world. Until very recently, the relationship between changes to Earth's cryosphere and their impact on local sea level shifts have been difficult to track, making it challenging to forecast and plan for sea level rise in coastal cities. In the hope that coastal planners and governments would benefit from a more precise understanding of future sea levels, a team of physicists at NASA created an online tool to visualize and quantify sea level impacts for nearly three hundred of the world's coastal cities. The tool is able to show, with great accuracy, where melting glaciers and ice sheets are contributing to global sea level rise among 293 coastal cities. The NASA program illustrates "gradient fingerprint mapping" (or GFM) and is, according to its creators, currently the *only* tool capable of attributing specific locations of melting ice with their effects on the world's coastal cities. In short, it illustrates the spatial patterns that are created when Earth's gravitational and rotational processes are contorted by the melting of the world's ice. Drawing on the physics of shifting ice and water, the

GFM tool allows users to see with precision where melting ice results in specific amounts of sea level rise in particular cities the world over. The tool allows us to see that in Houston, the fate of our coast is tied to that of the Greenland Ice Sheet.

FROM GREENLAND TO GALVESTON

Using an advanced mathematical property, the computational model behind the GFM creates a mesh that combines shoreline database material and "ice forcing" data measurements from 2003 to the present, gathered by satellites. The modeling tool can then render local sea level changes as they relate to local variations in ice thickness for all of the world's ice drainage systems, from Antarctica to the Alps and from the Siberian Arctic to the Andes.

The locus of inundation depends on the location of ice loss. For example, local sea level rise in London is affected about twice as much by the melting of the Alaskan basin (.13622 mm per year) than it is by Greenland, which contributes only .07191 mm annually. Far more still (.24433 mm per year) comes from the Antarctic and Subantarctic basins. The city of Melbourne, although it sits just adjacent to Antarctica, has its sea level rise far more affected by Greenlandic melt (.72110 mm per year), with only about a third as much (.25976 mm each year) attributed to the Antarctic and Subantarctic basins.

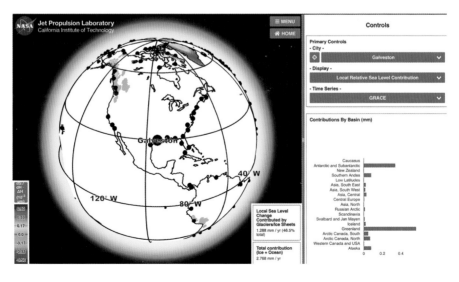

GFM map for Galveston.

For the city of Galveston, local sea level change coming from melting glaciers and ice sheets causes about 30 percent of the city's total sea level rise, meaning that Galveston is also highly affected by oceanic thermal expansion. Of that melted ice affecting Galveston, most comes from Greenland (.56689 mm/year), whereas only .33998 mm per year can be attributed to the Antarctic and Subantarctic basins. The melting of the Southern Andes also contributes a substantial amount to Galveston's coastline (.08164 mm/year), with the remainder coming (in order) from Alaska (.07942 mm/year), the Northern Canadian Arctic (.06906 mm/year), the Southern Canadian Arctic (.04805 mm/year), Central Asia (.02939 mm/year), Iceland (.02000 mm/year), Southwest Asia (.01687 mm/year), the Russian Arctic (.01259 mm/year), Central Europe (.00351 mm/year) and finally, the Svalbard and Jan Mayen basins (.01000 mm/year).

This is a lot of numbers. But what they illustrate is that when Greenland melts, Galveston floods. More importantly, perhaps, these data reveal the innate interconnectivities between sites of melting ice and sites of oceanic rise. The world ocean in this sense is not simply water in motion, infinitely intertwined; it is also ice in motion, connecting points on the globe in perhaps counterintuitive and yet meaningful ways. We might think of this as a kind of hydrological globalization: one that may not have been uniquely created by changes to the world's climate but which is sharpened by the dramatic and rapid loss of the world's ice.

SHAPE, NOT FLOW

The GFM device is a way of illustrating change and impact. It is important to note, however, that it does *not* follow water from sites of melt to sites of rise. Instead, it captures the shape of the ocean, tracking its gravitational agitations as ice becomes water, becomes ocean.

In one of our conversations together, Eric Larour, the physicist who led the development of the GFM tool, explained that the most complicated aspect of the modeling device is "sea level rotational feedback," or the change in the rotation of Earth as ice melts.

He described it like this. "It's like a spinning top. If you could modify the spinning top while it rotates, maybe touch it and remove some mass, it will start wobbling very differently. . . . As soon as you remove a bit of mass from that big giant spinning top, which is the Earth, the rotation axis of the spinning top wants to move towards the mass that was lost."

A connection between melt (here) and flood (there) exists, but not through a flow of melted water in one site to inundation in the other. In fact, the process demands understanding Earth's fluid envelope at scale and, importantly, in its distributive mass rather than its linear connectivity.

In other words, the process of melted ice becoming sea level rise and flood is not exactly about flow. It is about shape. As Eric put it in our conversation: "Melt ice anywhere on Earth and I can give you the shape that the ocean will adopt."

Sites of cryospheric loss and sea level increase are therefore linked, though not through the logic of flow, but in the gravimetric reordering of the world ocean as cryospheres continue their collapse.

TWELVE YEARS

The Intergovernmental Panel on Climate Change report released by the United Nations in October 2018 announced that fossil-fuel emissions would need to be cut in half within twelve years to avoid severe climate disruptions. I think that bears repeating: twelve years. When world leaders signed the Paris agreement in 2015, the mandate was to keep global temperature rise to well below 2 degrees Celsius, and to aim for only a 1.5 degree increase above preindustrial levels to avoid climate-related disasters like widespread food shortages and mass die-offs of coral reefs. But with global fossil-fuel emissions continuing to rise, the planet is now expected to cross that temperature threshold within thirty-five years.

There are many challenges in conveying the risks of a rapidly warming, storming, and flooding planet. Some people refuse it; perhaps the emotional load is too heavy. Others remain committed to the trajectory of burning fossil fuels for political or financial expediency. Some are baffled by the science of it all.

Sheila Jasanoff, a scholar of science and technology, reminds us that "abstraction" is the key tool by which modern science cements its validity and universality. By turning any phenomenon in the natural world into an abstraction, science can show how fragments, elements, and pieces can be meaningful independent of the whole. It is for this reason that we have abstracted entities—quite useful ones—like the periodic table, the nitrogen cycle, the metric system, biodiversity, and of course, climate change.

But if the abstraction exercised within science produces knowable fragments, taking parts from wholes and rearranging them otherwise, it is also worth remembering that we may not need more data. The ocean, after all, cannot be broken into fragments, and climate change and its effects are no longer abstract for many, maybe most, people around the world. The re-formation of the world as we knew it is already under way. And so while we do need more recognition of how science shows us a clearer picture of the changes we face, we also need more ways of feeling melt and flood and all the other socioenvironmental phenomena that we will face in the coming hundreds, indeed thousands, of years.

As the world ocean undergoes status shifts, there is an opportunity to consider the new kinds of connectivities that are created between places of melt and rise in a newly watery world. Let me end with one instance of how these kinds of connectivities may be felt.

TWO WOMEN, CONNECTED BY WATER

Kathy Jetñil-Kijiner is a poet from the Marshall Islands, situated in that part of the world ocean known as the Pacific, near the planet's equator. Aka Niviâna is also a poet, an Inuk woman from Greenland. Both of them have been following the water. But before these two Indigenous poets had ever even met in person, they had already composed a poem together. They call it "Rise."

In late 2018, Jetñil-Kijiner traveled from her island, where the water continues to encroach as the sea rises and rises, drowning the land and flooding once-human-occupied terrains. She and Niviâna wanted to compose together and then come together atop a glacier, one that is melting steadily, a pockmarked body of ice on the remote edge of Greenland's southern ice sheet. And so they did. One woman was the "sister of ice and snow" and the other, the "sister of ocean and sand." Atop the glacier, they exchanged some shells and stones and recited their words.

EXCERPT FROM THEIR POEM, "RISE"

I wait for you, here,
on the land of my ancestors

heart heavy with a thirst
for solutions
as I watch this land
change
while the World remains silent.[6]

In this kind of creation out of destruction, we may in fact have a route to follow the water toward new ways of feeling climate and melt and flood. And that may lead us toward new ways of reckoning with our collective futures.

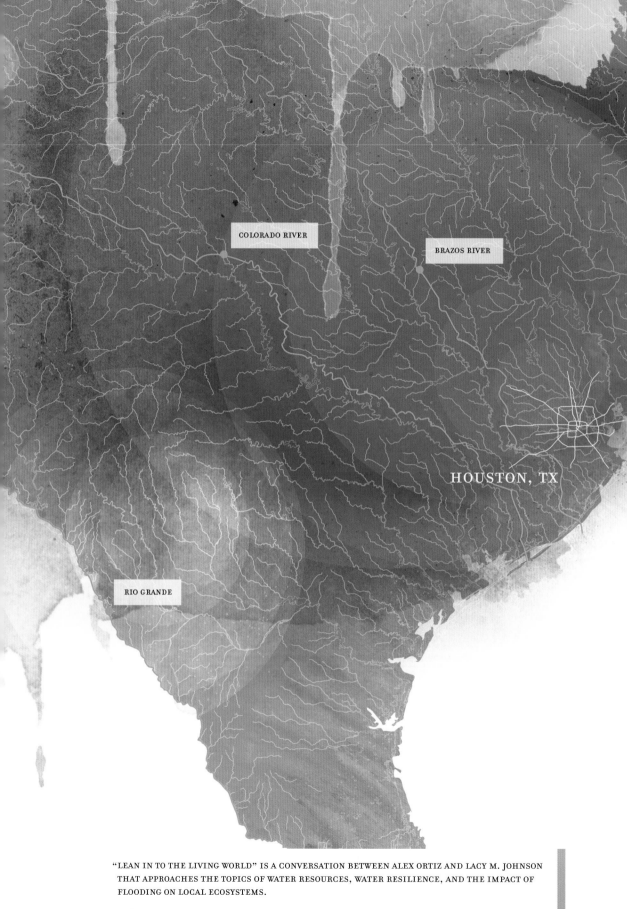

COLORADO RIVER

BRAZOS RIVER

HOUSTON, TX

RIO GRANDE

"LEAN IN TO THE LIVING WORLD" IS A CONVERSATION BETWEEN ALEX ORTIZ AND LACY M. JOHNSON
THAT APPROACHES THE TOPICS OF WATER RESOURCES, WATER RESILIENCE, AND THE IMPACT OF
FLOODING ON LOCAL ECOSYSTEMS.

DESIGN BY KRISTEN FERNANDES

Lean in to the Living World

A CONVERSATION WITH ALEX ORTIZ

Lacy M. Johnson

Alex Ortiz grew up all over South and Central Texas, and learned early on to appreciate the diversity of Texas's natural landscapes. Before joining the Sierra Club as the Lone Star Chapter's Water Resource Specialist, Alex earned a BA in linguistics from NYU and a JD from Tulane University Law School, where he also studied environmental law. At the Sierra Club, Alex coordinates with the Texas Living Waters project, which focuses on water supply and flood control, and also works on the Sustainable Management and Resilient Texas Waters project, which addresses water quality standards, discharge permits, and the impacts of oil and gas development on water supply and quality. Lacy spoke with Alex over Zoom at the end of 2020 about Texas water resources, water resilience, and the impact of flooding on local ecosystems. Their conversation has been edited for length and clarity.

LMJ: What made you want to start working on water and water issues?

AO: I grew up all over Texas, and as a kid, most of my family recreation revolved around water. I can remember being as young as five, when we lived in McAllen, going fishing with my dad and his fishing buddies. He's a big catch-and-release person. He'll keep some of what he catches, but a lot of times he just puts the fish back in the water, and the fish goes on its merry way. Or if the fish is struggling, he knows how to rehabilitate it, and I just thought that was so cool. When we lived in Corpus, we spent a lot of time at the beach, and later we lived in Lago Vista, which is right on Lake Travis, and though living near fresh water is very different compared to coastal life, water has always been right next to me in some way.

In college, I studied linguistics. I thought that's what I wanted to do—to go into academia on the linguistic side of things. Then in my senior year, I took this class in marine ecology. I had a really fascinating professor in the area, Jennifer Jacquet. I remember very vividly this conversation that we had in class about the ethics of dealing with marine life, about how society views marine life as this commercial existence compared to terrestrial life. We feel so much closer to terrestrial life, be they mammals or reptiles or birds or whatever, because we can interact with them in a very different way. We can't really interact with marine life because we can't breathe underwater, and so we don't spend a lot of time with fish or mollusks, and that lack of familiarity frames not only our discussions about marine life on an everyday level but also how we treat them in the law.

I think having that academic experience alongside my personal experience made me realize that water is really important. It's not only the habitat for all of this wildlife, but we also drink it, we recreate in it. It's important that water issues are workable for everyone and for wildlife. I think those two things fit together really easily in my head when I went to law school, and I started thinking about, "What is the work that I want to do?" Focusing on water issues seemed like a natural fit.

LMJ: I can imagine, and perhaps I'm projecting a little bit here, but I know my own thinking about water has been somewhat radicalized by living so near the Gulf Coast and becoming more familiar with the impact of industrial pollution and oil spills on the water and the coastline. I'm not a native Texan or anything, but I've lived here for quite a long time. I remember five years ago, maybe, we went to Corpus for a long weekend, and there were these tiny tar balls all over the beach. Corpus, Galveston, the whole coast has been devastated over and over again.

AO: It's hurting, and I think that makes it hard to look at the coast because it has a lot going on and there are a lot of different problems, everything from oil spills in the Gulf to the Gulf dead zone off the coast of Louisiana, which is continuing to grow, to nutrient-rich waters coming out of the Brazos River, to the huge drought that's always happening in the Rio Grande.

There are so many different problems relating to water, and then you throw in global issues with that, like sea level rise and flooding and coastal land loss, and it becomes overwhelming. I was in Corpus for most of the summer with my family. My sister and I found ourselves looking at how things have changed, how the landscape has changed from when we were kids. It's hard not to be aware of those things. I think the more educated you become, the more you get sucked into that world—it just totally takes over your brain.

LMJ: We've talked a little bit about waters along the coast. Can you tell me more broadly about the water in our region?

AO: When I think about the big inland water bodies, the first three that jump to my mind are the Colorado River, the Rio Grande, and the Brazos. Those aren't the only rivers, of course, but they're how you can split Texas into thirds, and their problems seem to be similar, at least in terms of their drainage basins.

The Rio Grande starts up in Colorado and forms the entire Texas-Mexico border, and tends to suffer from drought more than flooding. That impacts communities all along the river, most of which have a sister community across the river on the other side of the border—El Paso and Ciudad Juárez, Del Rio and Laguna, McAllen and Reynosa. In Del Rio, there's a dam to make the Amistad Reservoir, which has been good for the community and for Del Rio, but the construction of the reservoir also resulted in the extinction of a fish, the Amistad gambusia. It's not ever lost on me, I think, the way we shape our environment and how that impacts different species of wildlife.

The Texas Colorado River is one of the longest rivers to have both its source and its mouth in the same state. It starts near Lubbock, runs through Central Texas, is dammed at multiple points to create the Highland lakes, like Lady Bird Lake and Lake Travis, and it flows into Matagorda Bay. The Colorado River is sort of interesting because across most of Texas, the river's problems are drought-related, but when you get into Matagorda Bay, you find a completely different scenario. The bay area does sometimes suffer from drought, but it also sees flooding impacts that tend to devastate the area in a very different way, especially when combined with the wetland destruction, because when you destroy the wetlands, you destroy an ecosystem's capacity to manage flooding. I'll say more about that in a bit.

The next river over is the Brazos, which starts all the way up in New Mexico and flows east, near Dallas and Waco, and then through the

Houston metro area and into the Gulf. The Brazos, while not necessarily suffering as many of the drought impacts as the other two, really suffers from what we call nutrient pollution, which primarily comes from agricultural and stormwater runoff, and consists of either high fecal coliform levels or higher bacteria levels. That kind of pollution results in lower dissolved oxygen in the water, which is really bad for wildlife. And from a legal perspective, nutrient pollution is very difficult to regulate. The Clean Water Act explicitly excludes most runoff pollution from federal regulation. So unless you have a state government that's really willing to be involved in runoff water management, nutrient pollution becomes the individual's problem or nature's problem.

In Houston, you also have all of the bayous, which have a wealth of biodiversity. There are so many different animals, different wildlife that you find in marshy habitats. Wetlands and bayous really provide an invaluable ecological resource in terms of flood absorption. These are areas that can hold a lot of floodwater—whether it's storm surge or inland rain—and prevent a lot of detrimental impacts to communities that are located near and around them.

LMJ: Can you say a little bit more about what happens to waterways when there is a flood event like Harvey or Imelda, or in Houston, even just a strong rain?

AO: When a strong rain happens, when a storm event happens, flooding starts at the runoff level. You see either agricultural or industrial runoff from public water and sewage-related systems, or from farms or factories, or from refineries. You see pollutants end up in our waterways that would otherwise be in violation of the Clean Water Act because the rain is really heavy and washes things off of the surface. It washes things into the water bodies. Especially in the Houston area, you see probably a little more of the industrial stormwater, though I imagine there's plenty of fertilizer and agricultural runoff there, too.

That creates nutrient pollution, which decreases dissolved oxygen in the waterways, which threatens wildlife, and also just changes the ecosystem in general. You're introducing a totally new factor that is mostly human-made because while the rain is relatively natural and normal, everything that the rain passes through on its way into the water—be it a refinery or a yard full of fertilizer—is not something that the water-way is used to dealing with.

As you get closer to the coast, especially in all of the bays where the bayous and rivers meet the Gulf of Mexico, the problem is that you end up seeing things like saltwater intrusion, which can happen when a storm surge pushes saltwater into wetlands, and this is especially true in wetlands that have been dredged. When saltwater sits in a wetland area for any amount of time, it harms the fish and birds and everything, but it really harms the plant life. And if freshwater or brackish water plants die because they've been exposed to too much saltwater, they'll expose more land to potential erosion and to land loss, which is bad for the land and for the waters.

LMJ: It creates, I would imagine, a terrible feedback loop.

AO: Yes, the more it happens, the worse it is. The only way to really recover from that is to backfill, which needs to happen like yesterday. There've been studies done that show that the sooner you can do back-filling, the better. Any dredging that has happened, if you go and backfill it, the waterway, the wetland does heal. It might heal slower than we would like it to, but it'll heal. I think that's something that is not really touched on enough.

LMJ: That makes me think about the term "water resilience." Will you talk a little bit about that term and what it means?

AO: "Water resilience" refers to—especially when we talk about it in the Houston context—the stability to weather a storm and to have an intact water supply and a surviving, thriving water ecosystem that can respond to a flood event. That might mean wetlands that can hold floodwaters or wildlife that very quickly returns to a recently flooded area. Those things are all really good signs of water resilience. On the other side of water resilience in Texas is being prepared for drought conditions, and being willing as a society and as people to really pitch in and think about how our individual actions shape our collective access to water.

Water resilience is really such a two-headed thing, because we really do mean the drought planning and the flood planning, and in Houston

I know that a lot of that work is happening around sustainable infrastructure. How do we plan to weather the storms? How do we plan to continue to weather the storms, because it's not like hurricanes are just going to stop coming into the Gulf of Mexico. It's not like we can immediately halt coastal land loss. Water resilience is a combination of planning for the flood and recovering from it afterward.

LMJ: There is, I think, an increasing push to recognize bodies of water as living beings. How does this intersect with your thinking?

AO: It does intersect with my thinking a lot. When I was in law school at Tulane, I had this professor, Oliver Houck. He has done so much environmental legal work, but he does a lot of research and reading and even a little bit of teaching right now on the rights of nature, generally to exist, to have legal standing in court. I found this fascinating. There are countries where nature has standing to sue a government or a person for an environmental offense in court.

We don't see that in the United States, but what would it look like if we did? What would it look like if instead of a person needing to bring a suit, there was a government entity that was allowed to sue on behalf of a water body, or an endangered fish? What if we took that responsibility very seriously? What if a private citizen could bring a lawsuit on behalf of the environment without needing to assert personal standing?

Generally, when we think about a suit, whether it's an Endangered Species Act suit or Clean Water Act suit, there has to be a person involved who is feeling some sort of impact. That impact can be as minimal as aesthetic or recreational, but it needs to exist. There needs to be a harm done to the person, not just the water or the animal. I don't like it.

I really think that water bodies are living in a very real way. The ecosystem is very much alive. It is home and habitat for a lot of different wildlife. It serves such an important function for us, too. I think being mindful and respectful of this very valuable resource that we have is important. It's our responsibility to be good stewards. I definitely lean in to the living world.

LMJ: Tell me about the Living Waters project.

AO: The Texas Living Waters Project is a partnership between the National Wildlife Federation and the Galveston Bay Foundation and the

Sierra Club. The goals of the Texas Living Waters are climate resilience, looking at how good stewardship of our water allows us to be resilient in the face of climate change; conservation for the sake of wildlife is another big one; and urban water management, which revolves around green or sustainable infrastructure. Personally, this is the aspect I'm least familiar with but excited to learn about. So, The Texas Living Waters Project is a partnership between these three organizations primarily doing regulatory work. We are working with the Texas Water Development Board and, to a lesser extent, TCEQ and local governments to really implement long-term water strategies, to build resilience in whatever way we can, whether it's planning or actual infrastructure or education.

Those are, I think, the fundamental things that we mean when we talk about the concept of a living water: we mean a living water that can go on performing its ecological functions on its own. That we can continue to have access to water because access is limited when it comes to things like this. That there's still a space for wildlife at the table, that we are being mindful of the fact that there is wildlife in these habitats, and they need a certain amount of flow and a certain degree of water to themselves.

LMJ: What is at stake when it comes to the health and quality of water systems in Texas?

AO: Our waters are important in so many ways. They are important for recreation; they serve as important water supplies for our metro areas. They perform important social functions, too, and important cultural ones. Our rivers are where settlers at various times, or indigenous populations at various times, made settlements because they're important in practical ways for our survival.

And any interaction we have with water, whether it's recreation or driving down the street next to a pond, there is more than likely a wildlife existence in that water body. When water quality changes, whether it's saltwater intrusion in a storm or nutrient pollution in a flood, it changes what wildlife can survive there. And every organism, for the most part, participates in our ecosystem and performs an ecological function, whether or not we recognize it.

Our public health is tied to water health, because people not only drink that water, they recreate in it, they fish in it, they exist next to it. That water ends up getting into our food supply through irrigation. It is an important resource, and if it is not cared for or adequately regulated, there are human health consequences, public health consequences. The waters that we drink and recreate in and fish in and pollute and then treat in order to distribute to people are the same waters.

I think acknowledging that and acknowledging that we probably have an impact on it in some way, even as individuals, but especially as a collective, I think that's something that I really wish people thought about more.

I've said it over and over again, but I really find there is an insufficient focus on wildlife when it comes to the way we regulate and protect our waterbodies. It's so important to be centered in this mindset of stewardship, I think, not just to one another and our communities, but to the wildlife—both plant and animal—that we exist with. So many of the regulatory or legal successes in preventing harm to our waters in the United States have been earned by wielding the Endangered Species Act. Extending concrete rights of nature beyond only those species that society has pushed to extinction, whether extending them to wildlife as a whole or waterbodies themselves, is one of the best ways to protect our waters.

Acknowledgments

THIS BOOK WAS MADE POSSIBLE through the generous support of the Houston Endowment and the Humanities Research Center at Rice University; Rice University provided additional support for this project through a grant jointly funded by the Office of Research and the School of Humanities.

The editors offer our thanks and congratulations to the University of Houston graphic design graduating class of 2019, who, under the supervision of Professor Cheryl Beckett, spent the spring of their senior year artfully, poetically, and bravely reimagining this city; special thanks to the designers who continued working on this project after their graduation: Manuel Vázquez, Kristen Fernandes, Ilse Harrison, Jesse Reyes, Julia Ong, and Clarisse Pinto. We offer a deep bow of gratitude in particular to Julia Ong and Kristen Fernandes for their vision, ambition, and tireless commitment to this project.

We are indebted to Georgie Devereux, who provided research support in the early stages of this project, and to Chaney Hill, who provided editorial support. Thanks also to Linda Evans and Adriana Chiaramonti for their administrative talents; this project would have been impossible without them. Thank you to Long Chu, our program officer at Houston Endowment, for his support and the encouragement to begin this work.

We are grateful to the editors of *Catapult*, *Ploughshares*, the *New York Times*, and *Mustarinda* for permission to reprint several of the essays included here.

Thank you also to Ethan Bassoff, literary agent extraordinaire, and to Casey Kittrell, our editor at the University of Texas Press, for sharing our vision for this book. Finally, we offer our gratitude to the entire team at the University of Texas Press for your dedication to bringing this book into the world.

This book is a project of the Houston Flood Museum, which seeks to exhibit the connections between human activities and catastrophic flooding—as linked to wealth inequality and racial disparities—and to act as a catalyst for reimagining the ways in which Houston, the Gulf Coast, and the wider world evolve in a context of persistent natural disasters.

Learn more at www.houstonfloodmuseum.org.

Notes

INTRODUCTION. MORE CITY THAN WATER

1. Eric S. Blake and David A. Zelinsky, "National Hurricane Center Tropical Cyclone Report: Hurricane Harvey," August 17–September 1, 2017, https://www.nhc.noaa.gov/data/tcr/AL092017_Harvey.pdf?source=your_stories_page.

2. Toni Morrison, "The Site of Memory," in *What Moves at the Margin: Selected Nonfiction*, edited and with an introduction by Carolyn C. Denard, 77 (Jackson: University Press of Mississippi, 2008).

GUSHER

1. Crafting any narrative necessitates a blend of fact and useful simplification, and I am forced to admit that this essay is no exception. That does not mean, however, that I think facts should be subjugated to story; on the contrary, facts are enormously important to me—perhaps even more so because "fact," as it has been normatively defined in certain times and places, has been used as a tool for oppression. I've done my best to base this essay on fact, but the epistemological limits of that designation must also be acknowledged, if not applied or reckoned with. This particular quote comes from the January 16, 1917, edition of the *Houston Post*, which I accessed through an online archive devoted to Texas history. The historical documentation for how exactly the discovery of oil at Goose Creek occurred is, admittedly, wanting—as discussed by Jack E. Davis in *The Gulf: The Making of an American Sea* (New York: Liveright, W. W. Norton, 2017). My version of Gaillard's discovery is semifictionalized for effect and draws its basis both

from articles in the same paper and an account found in the book *Baytown Vignettes: One Hundred and Fifty Years in the History of a Texas Gulf Coast Community* (Baytown, TX: Lee College, 1992), by John C. Britt and Muriel H. Tyssen, as well as a master's thesis by Olga Haenel, "A Social History of Baytown, Texas, 1912–1956" (University of Texas, 1958).

2. On a similar note, much of my information on the business and environmental history of Houston comes from an article by Joseph A. Pratt, "A Mixed Blessing: Energy, Economic Growth, and Houston's Environment," found in the volume *Energy Metropolis: An Environmental History of Houston and the Gulf Coast* (Pittsburgh: University of Pittsburgh Press, 2007), edited by Martin V. Melosi and Joseph A. Pratt. I also consulted Henrietta M. Larson and Kenneth Wiggins Porter's *History of Humble Oil and Refining Company* (New York: Harper, 1959) and Tommy Thompson's *Great Oil Fields of the Gulf Coast* (Houston: Houston Chronicle, 1967).

3. Meanwhile, the facts of these various inequalities have been investigated in stories from various media outlets, including the *Houston Chronicle*'s *Silent Spills* (https://www.houstonchronicle.com/news/houston-texas/houston/article/In-Houston-and-beyond-Harvey-s-spills-leave-a-12771237.php) and NPR's *Code Switch* (https://www.npr.org/sections/codeswitch/).

4. That's not to say there aren't degrees of culpability, or that most people are not, in one way or another, implicated in the inequalities of the current system. If you participate, likely you are contributing to someone else's suffering. When you are a part of an economic, social, and political system that operates locally, regionally, and globally, complicity is inescapable. But neither is that inescapable entanglement an excuse for apathy. The perfect, after all, is the enemy of the good.

5. Though I am focusing on local interconnectedness for the purpose of this essay, the same patterns hold on regional and global scales as well. As the authors of the UN's famous 2018 report note, the effects of climate change will be most drastically felt by the regions of the globe that consume the least. Likewise, the same organization's 2019 report on climate change in the Arctic region is pointedly titled *Global Linkages*. While greenhouse gas (GHG) emissions and pollution from global activities mainly originate outside the region, the authors of the report state, they are causing wide-ranging changes and impacts on the Arctic environment. These changes will, in turn, affect the health of the planet as a whole. Glacial melt impacts both sea level and the circulation of global currents, two issues near and dear to Houston's heart. Climate models predict, for example, that the freshening and warming of the Arctic Ocean will contribute to the weakening of deep, cold-water currents like the Gulf Stream. Weakened cold water circulation combined with warming temperatures caused by both human emissions

and large releases of carbon compounds from melting Arctic permafrost will likewise lead to stronger and more intense hurricanes.

6. The course of the waterway is fairly circuitous, although in places various generations of human engineers have straightened, paved, and otherwise altered its course. The straight lines and concrete banks of Buffalo, Brays, and White Oak Bayous are in large part the legacy of the mid-twentieth-century's philosophy of flood control: if we can shape the water's course, then during heavy rains we can direct the rising tide. The irony is that in the present day, with Houston's floodplains increasingly covered in concrete and more water being diverted to the bayous, these early flood control measures actually *worsen* flash flooding by eliminating natural bulwarks against heavy rainfall.

7. From Bill Gilmer, "Proximity Counts: How Houston Dominates the Oil Industry," *Forbes*, August 22, 2018, https://www.forbes.com/sites/uhen ergy/2018/08/22/proximity-counts-how-houston-dominates-the-oil-in dustry/?sh=f3b0fe861078.

8. This figure comes from the Texas Economic Development Corporation.

9. Quote from University of Minnesota, "US Black and Hispanic Minorities Bear Disproportionate Burden from Air Pollution," *ScienceDaily*, March 11, 2019, www.sciencedaily.com/releases/2019/03/190311152735.htm; Christopher W. Tessum et al., "Inequality in Consumption of Goods and Services Adds to Racial-Ethnic Disparities in Air Pollution Exposure," *PNAS* 116, no. 13 (2019): 6001–6006.

10. That's just to say that in a system that offers greater support and opportunity to people with lighter skin and whiter names, class mobility becomes easier for poor whites than for their counterparts of color. I don't intend to undermine the accomplishments and hard work of all individuals who are both white and working class—money makes our world go round; having or not having it can have a huge impact on one's life. I'm not even saying that whiteness in some way guarantees success—merely that in a system of white supremacy, the dominant conception of "whiteness" *promises* success. For many, that promise is a broken one, much along the lines of (or perhaps indistinguishable from) the much-vaunted American Dream. That being said, the origins of the promise (as well as the identity of those who must bear the anger of its unfulfillment) are worth questioning. Class and racial inequality are *entangled* systems. Pitting them against one another might prove convenient for those benefiting from both structures, but that opposition is not, strictly speaking, true.

11. And not just individuals; each community I've mentioned had its own distinctive, vibrant life that flourished in the face of hardship. *Houston Bound: Culture and Color in a Jim Crow City* (Oakland: University of California Press, 2015) by Tyina L. Steptoe provides much of the history I can't include

271

here. Projects like the Emancipation Economic Development Council's revived Houston Red Book, Marc Newsome's *I Love 3W* art installation at Project Row Houses, and Tracy Hicks's *Third Ward Archive* also document the people and places that make up those stories, both on the east side and elsewhere in the city. I don't include much here partially because I don't believe those stories are mine to tell, and partially because I don't want to risk using the things people built despite overwhelming odds as an excuse to gloss over the forces they were working against.

12. Quote and figures are from a 2006 report by a mayoral task force, "A Closer Look at Air Pollution in Houston: Identifying Priority Health Risks," https://www3.epa.gov/ttn/chief/conference/ei16/session6/bethel.pdf.

13. Census data, it should be noted, are not the best sources for measuring the demographic makeup of a given area. This is partially because a government-administered head count does not tend to yield an accurate count of individuals who, for various reasons, have little trust in federal officials, and partially because, at this point in time, the 2010 census is nearly ten years out of date. And in one of the nation's fastest-growing metropolitan areas, ten years is a long time.

14. Another fact of our local history found in Pratt's *Energy Metropolis* piece, "A Mixed Blessing."

15. Despite the Marxist framework I employ in this essay, I'm also a big (and possibly naïve) believer in both personal and group agency. We make choices every day; all we can do is try to ensure that some of those choices make our world a marginally better place. Many groups are working to combat climate change and environmental inequality in the Houston area, among them t.e.j.a.s., Environment Texas, Houston Air Alliance, One Breath Partnership, the Environmental Defense Fund, and more. All of them need community support.

16. Part of what I'm advocating here, though I don't say it outright, is a different sort of thinking when it comes to how we decide what is and isn't worth doing. Thinking beyond the self includes considering the well-being of others in the present, of course. But it also means considering the well-being of those in the *future*. Thinking on the scale of generations might not come naturally to us (it certainly doesn't to me, but that could just be my youth), but it does provide hope and possibility where it might otherwise be easy to surrender to apathetic nihilism.

17. According to EPA recommended guidelines, "The maximum time-weighted average exposure limit is 1 part of benzene vapor per million parts of air (1 ppm) for an eight-hour workday, and the maximum short-term exposure limit is 5 ppm for any fifteen-minute period." From "Substance Safety Data Sheet, Benzene," *1910.1028 App A—Substance Safety Data Sheet, Benzene | Occupational Safety and Health Administration*, United States

Department of Labor, www.osha.gov/laws-regs/regulations/standard number/1910/1910.1028AppA.

There is little independently reported information on these events; during the storm, the Texas Commission on Environmental Quality (TCEQ) left environmental monitoring to a handful of federal regulators and the industries themselves. What data are available have not been forthcoming for public access. And when it comes to enforcement, another responsibility of the TCEQ, response is lackluster as well. According to self-published industry data, of the 4,069 emission events across Texas in 2017, only 58—1.43 percent—received penalties from the TCEQ. The most decisive local action on toxic releases, it is important to note, has not come from government agencies, but rather from the legal victories of various NGOs. ExxonMobil, for example, only received an EPA mandate to reduce emissions in Texas and Louisiana after a judge ruled in favor of a joint suit brought against the company by Environment Texas and the Sierra Club.

18. This reality inflects virtually every legal, social, and economic system in this country—to the point that wealthier, whiter parts of Houston received the majority of post-Harvey federal funding. Government aid after the storm actually *exacerbated* existing inequality. Those with means, helped along by plentiful emergency assistance, recovered, but elsewhere people continue to wrestle with the wake of the storm.

19. According to Theron Garcia, Douglas Ming, and Lisa Tuck of the Clay Minerals Society, this subsidence is likely related to the withdrawal of oil from the Goose Creek Oil Field. The memory of the gusher writes itself upon the land.

HISTORY DISPLACED: FLOODING THE FIRST BLACK MUNICIPALITY IN TEXAS

1. As the historian Bernadette Pruitt has shown,

> thousands of migrants . . . came to Houston in the first half of the twentieth century. Some 44,000 Black women, children, and men moved to Houston between the years 1914 and 1945, principally from eastern Texas and southern Louisiana. Migration boomed from 1914 through 1930 before slowing in the 1930s because of the Great Depression and then expanding rapidly after the United States entered World War II in late 1941. Like their contemporaries who left the rural, small-town, and urban South for industrialized centers in the Midwest, Northeast, and West, migrants to Houston helped define the Great Migration and Second Great Migration of the twentieth century.

"In Search of Freedom: Black Migration to Houston, 1914–1945," *Houston Review of History and Culture* 3, no. 1 (Fall 2005): 49.

2. *The Free Man's Press* (Austin, TX) 1, no. 3, ed. 1, Saturday, August 1, 1868, p. 1; accessed July 16, 2021, https://texashistory.unt.edu/ark:/67531/meta pth596274/m1/1/, University of North Texas Libraries, The Portal to Texas History, https://texashistory.unt.edu.

3. Steven Fenberg and Eric Stange, *Brother, Can You Spare a Billion? The Story of Jesse H. Jones*, documentary, PBS, 2000, https://www.pbs.org/jessejones /jesse_bio2.htm.

4. Robert D. Bullard, *Dumping in Dixie: Race, Class, and Environmental Quality*, 3rd ed. (New York: Westview Press, 2008); Richard Rothstein, *The Color of Law: A Forgotten History of How Our Government Segregated America* (New York: Liveright Publishing, W. W. Norton, 2017); Ta-Nehisi Coates, "The Case for Reparations," *The Atlantic*, June 2014, accessed May 28, 2020, https://www.theatlantic.com/magazine/archive/2014/06/the-case-for -reparations/361631/; Keeanga-Yamahtta Taylor, *Race for Profit: How Banks and the Real Estate Industry Undermined Black Homeownership* (Chapel Hill: UNC Press, 2019); and scores of other studies on this topic.

IF YOU DIDN'T KNOW YOUR HOUSE WAS SINKING

1. Phyllis Trible, *God and the Rhetoric of Sexuality* (Philadelphia: Fortress Press, 1978).

2. Simone Weil, *The Notebooks of Simone Weil*, translated from the French by Arthur Wills (London: Routledge and Kegan Paul, 1956), 552.

MEANDER BELT: A NATIVE HOUSTONIAN REFLECTS ON WATER

1. Glenn S. Johnson et al., "Air Quality and Health Issues along Houston's Ship Channel: An Exploratory Environmental Justice Analysis of a Vulnerable Community (Pleasantville)," *Race, Gender & Class* 21, no. 3–4 (2014): 273–303.

2. Elizabeth Trovall, "Along Ship Channel, Houston's Manchester Neighborhood Grapples with Poor Air Quality," *Houston Public Media*, June 22, 2018, https://www.houstonpublicmedia.org/articles/news/politics/immigra-tion/2018/06/22/292344/along-ship-channel-houstons-manchester-neigh-borhood-grapples-with-poor-air-quality/.

3. "HI-A-389-A Platform," *Flower Garden Banks National Marine Sanctuary*, November 13, 2020, https://flowergarden.noaa.gov/about/hi389platform. html.

4. Melissa Gaskill, "In Its First Life, an Oil Platform; in Its Next, a Reef?" *New York Times*, June 17, 2012, https://www.nytimes.com/2012/06/18/us/a-fight -to-convert-high-island-a-platform-into-a-reef.html.

5. Benjamin Jones, "White Oak Bayou: History of a Houston Waterway," *History Section*, July 2016, http://whiteoakbayou.org/uploads/3/4/9/1/34911613/historysection.pdf.

6. Teresa Tomkins-Walsh, "Houston's Environmental Legacy: Terry Hershey, Community, and Action," *Houston History* 10, no. 2 (2013): 2–7.

7. Johnson et al., "Air Quality and Health Issues."

8. Jen Weaver, "Houston Water Considers Options for Post-Harvey Resilience," *Texas Architect*, May/June 2018, https://magazine.texasarchitects.org/2018/05/08/houston-water-considers-options-for-post-harvey-resilience/.

9. Pingfeng Yu et al., "Elevated Levels of Pathogenic Indicator Bacteria and Antibiotic Resistance Genes after Hurricane Harvey's Flooding in Houston," *Environmental Science & Technology Letters* 5, no. 8 (2018): 481–486.

10. Alex Stuckey, "Port Arthur Plant Had Largest Wastewater Spill in Texas after Harvey," *Houston Chronicle*, December 17, 2017, https://www.houstonchronicle.com/news/houston-texas/houston/article/Port-Arthur-plant-had-largest-wastewater-spill-in-12375679.php.

11. Amanda Shore et al., "Corrigendum: On a Reef Far, Far Away: Anthropogenic Impacts Following Extreme Storms Affect Sponge Health and Bacterial Communities," *Frontiers in Marine Science*, July 8, 2021.

OMBROPHOBIA (FEAR OF RAIN)

1. "Remembering the Great Hurricane, September 8, 1900," *Galveston County Daily News* (Galveston Newspapers Inc., 2014), https://www.1900storm.com/facts.html.

2. Aaron Barker, "Remembering Hurricane Alicia," *Click2Houston*, August 15, 2018, https://www.click2houston.com/weather/2018/08/15/remembering-hurricane-alicia/.

3. Jim Blackburn, "Living with Houston Flooding" (Houston: James A. Baker III Institute for Public Policy of Rice University, 2017), 13, https://www.bakerinstitute.org/media/files/files/68acbe10/bi-pub-livingfloodinghouston-120617_kF7klri.pdf.

4. "Turn Around, Don't Drown: A Public Awareness Campaign," FEMA, last updated February 2021, https://www.fema.gov/case-study/turn-around-dont-drown-public-awareness-campaign.

5. "Katrina Impacts," *Hurricanes: Science and Society* (Narrangansett, RI: University of Rhode Island Graduate School of Oceanography, 2020), HurricaneScience.org, http://www.hurricanescience.org/history/studies/katrinacase/impacts/.

6. Sarah Pruitt, "How Levee Failure Made Hurricane Katrina a Bigger Disaster:

Breaches in the System of Levees and Floodwalls Left 80 Percent of the City Underwater," History.com, August 27, 2020, https://www.history.com/news/hurricane-katrina-levee-failures.

7. Matt Levin, "How Hurricane Rita Anxiety Led to the Worst Gridlock in Houston History," *Chron*, September 22, 2015, https://www.chron.com/news/houston-texas/houston/article/Hurricane-Rita-anxiety-leads-to-hellish-fatal-6521994.php.

8. "Hurricane Ike 2008," Harris County Flood Control District, https://www.hcfcd.org/About/Harris-Countys-Flooding-History/Hurricane-Ike-2008.

9. Blackburn, "Living with Houston Flooding," 13.

10. Blackburn, "Living with Houston Flooding," 13.

11. "Hurricane Ike 2008," Harris County Flood Control District.

12. Mihir Zaveri, "Despite Massive Projects to Upgrade Houston Bayous, Thousands Remain in Floodplains," *Houston Chronicle*, March 3, 2018; updated March 6, 2018, https://www.houstonchronicle.com/politics/houston/article/Despite-massive-projects-to-upgrade-Houston-12725685.php.

13. "Tropical Storm Imelda," National Weather Service, NOAA, https://www.weather.gov/lch/2019Imelda.

14. "Tropical Cyclone Naming History and Retired Names," National Hurricane Center and Central Pacific Hurricane Center, NOAA, https://www.nhc.noaa.gov/aboutnames_history.shtml.

THE TASK IN FRONT OF US: A CONVERSATION WITH RAJ MANKAD

1. There are two main ways this works: FEMA gives more money for repair of higher-valued houses, and the Army Corps of Engineers uses cost-benefit analysis to evaluate infrastructure. See Rebecca Hersher and Robert Benincasa, "How Federal Disaster Money Favors the Rich," NPR, March 5, 2019, heard on *All Things Considered*, https://www.npr.org/2019/03/05/688786177/how-federal-disaster-money-favors-the-rich. See also Chrishelle Palay, "Opinion: Four Ways Biden Can Address Racial Inequity in Disaster Recovery," *Houston Chronicle*, February 26, 2021, https://www.houstonchronicle.com/opinion/outlook/article/Opinion-4-ways-Biden-can-address-racial-inequity-15982052.php.

2. Arthur C. Comey, "Houston Tentative Plans for Its Development: Report to the Houston Park Commission," 1913, Rice University, https://scholarship.rice.edu/handle/1911/77141.

THE ONLY THING YOU HAVE: TRACE OF A TRACE

1. Of all the plastic containers, cardboard boxes, filing cabinets, shoeboxes, and envelopes full of photographs, newspaper clippings, documents, and photocopies, he keeps several photo albums close at hand: black-and-white, sepia, and color photographs, 35mm and polaroid—photographs of family members dating through the decades back to the 1930s.

2. My father is afraid of forgetting. He watched his grandfather forget who his wife was. He watched his grandfather forget how to use his hands.

3. Leslie Hewitt, *Leslie Hewitt*, edited by Cay Sophie Rabinowitz, with contributions by Nana Adusei-Poku, Lisa Lee, and Eva Respini (New York: OSMOS Books, 2019), 26n10.

4. Roland Barthes, *Camera Lucida: Reflections on Photography*, translated by Richard Howard (New York: Hill and Wang, 2010), 73.

5. Barthes, *Camera Lucida*, 81.

6. *And we just tried to save what we could. And we would take the books, open them, lay them out in the sun, try to pull some of the photos out of the books so they could dry without wiping them. There is some photo development paper that, as soon as water hits it, it starts to react. And if you wipe it, then you wipe away everything. If you leave it in the book, it dries in the book, and the plastic cover in the book sticks to it. We realized that if you take the photos out and stack them on top of each other, they're going to stick together. That's what happened to a lot of photos. Over time, after two years or so, you could pull them apart very delicately. That was because there was some type of greasy substance in the water that got in between some of the photos. You could peel them apart because the greasy substance kept them from really sticking together.* Interview with the author's father, Arnold Hunter Jr., February 15, 2019.

7. Barthes, *Camera Lucida*, 81.

8. Hewitt, *Leslie Hewitt*, 122.

9. Hewitt, *Leslie Hewitt*, 125.

10. *We pulled everything out of the house, onto the lawn, into the sun.* Interview with the author's father, Arnold Hunter Jr., February 15, 2019.

11. Hewitt, *Leslie Hewitt*, 20.

12. Summerwood Lane is just south of Herman Brown Park and just east of Hunting Bayou, which wends through the park. The street is now only half houses: every other lot is empty but for a flat plane of short grass.

13. Hewitt, *Leslie Hewitt*, 104.

14. Hewitt, *Leslie Hewitt*, 106.

15. Barthes, *Camera Lucida*, 76.

16. Interview with the author's father, Arnold Hunter Jr., February 15, 2019.

17. Tropical Storm Allison made landfall twice, first at Galveston on June 5, 2001, and then again over southeast Texas and western Louisiana on June 8–9, 2001. It moved on over Louisiana, Mississippi, Alabama, Florida, and South Carolina before drifting off the New England coast. Twenty-two people died in Houston, and the flood was the most expensive at that time, since surpassed by Katrina and Harvey. The heat and the moisture perfected conditions for the heavy rains that fell on Houston on June 8 and 9.

18. *When we looked back, we saw the water had reached up to the roof. In the Denny's, the water was at our knees. There was water in the seats, so we sat on top of the back of the seat; now the water was at the window. The water was in the food, in the cakes and the fridges. The lights went out. We waded to the La Quinta, where travelers offered their rooms. With nothing dry to change into, we lay down to sleep in our wet clothes. At Kroger's, the shelves were empty. At the La Quinta, the vending machines were unlocked and opened. On the third day the waters receded.* Interview with the author's father, Arnold Hunter Jr., February 15, 2019.

19. Barthes, *Camera Lucida*, 94.

20. Barthes, *Camera Lucida*, 93.

21. Barthes, *Camera Lucida*, 14.

22. Fragments from a quilt-covered photo album: Alan's shoulder in Santo Domingo; *a place I recognized from my dream*; a cousin with an unremembered name; big grass skirts; the house on Mississippi, my great-grandfather's truck. My father dates photographs by the hairstyles he and his brothers wore.

23. *We wanted to save as many photos as we could because photos are memories. Sometimes it's the only thing you have.* Interview with the author's father, Arnold Hunter Jr., February 15, 2019.

24. *If you want to see what your great-grandmother looked like, you have to go to those photo albums.* Interview with the author's father, Arnold Hunter, Jr., February 15, 2019. And I can see my great-grandmother's face because my father salvaged that photograph. I can see her, and she looks like me. Her name was Vera, like Veronica, my middle name. Barthes writes of this holy true image, "... to attest that what I see has indeed existed.... Photography has something to do with resurrection: might we not say of it what the Byzantines said of the image of Christ which marked St. Veronica's cloth: that it was not made by the hand of man?" Barthes, *Camera Lucida*, 82.

25. Hewitt, *Leslie Hewitt*, 115.

26. Barthes, *Camera Lucida*, 96.

27. Hewitt, *Leslie Hewitt*, 116.

28. Barthes, *Camera Lucida*, 93.

29. My father is an amateur archivist. Amateur in its original definitory form: *amare*, from Latin: to love. And in love, he remembers and tells what he lost to the waters.

30. Barthes, *Camera Lucida*, 94.

31. *The water was up to my chest, and I lost everything I owned, and we salvaged what we could, but I was pissed.* Interview with the author's father, Arnold Hunter Jr., February 15, 2019.

32. *The pressure of the water pushed the front door open. The water was ankle deep, then knee deep. I could see that the bayou was overflowing, the water was coming very rapidly. I thought, "Something big is open, this isn't normal." The lights went out, the phone was dead, and we got whatever we could get. I grabbed clothes and a camera and put them in a bag.* Interview with the author's father, Arnold Hunter Jr., February 15, 2019.

THINGS THAT DROWN, AND WHY

1. Pierre Nora, *Les Lieux de Mémoire* (Centre National des Lettres, n.d.), 2.

2. See https://www.click2houston.com/weather/2019/09/20/8-of-the-most-destructive-storms-in-houstons-history/; https://www.pennlive.com/nation-world/2019/08/hurricane-harvey-hammered-the-gulf-coast-two-years-ago.html#:~:text=Hurricane%20Harvey%20was%20a%20category-ry,25%2C%202017.&text=%E2%80%9CThe%20damage%20caused%20by%20Harvey's,cars%20reported%20flooded%20as%20well.

3. Liz Hamel et al., "An Early Assessment of Hurricane Harvey's Impact on Vulnerable Texans in the Gulf Coast Region," Episcopal Health Foundation, December 5, 2017, http://files.kff.org/attachment/Report-An-Early-Assessment-of-Hurricane-Harveys-Impact-on-Vulnerable-Texans-in-the-Gulf.

HIGHER GROUND

1. Daniela Sternitzky-Di Napoli et al., "Houston Area Records Record Rainfall after Hurricane Harvey Hits," *Chron*, August 25, 2017, https://www.chron.com/news/houston-weather/hurricaneharvey/article/Hurricane-Harvey-rainfall-amount-Houston-area-11959445.php.

THE GALLERY OF CRACKED PAVEMENT: A WALKING TOUR

1. Matt Levin, "How Hurricane Rita Anxiety Led to the Worst Gridlock in Houston History," *Chron*, September 22, 2015, https://www.chron.com/news/houston-texas/houston/article/Hurricane-Rita-anxiety-leads-to-hellish-fatal-6521994.php.

WE ALL BREATHE THE SAME AIR: A CONVERSATION WITH P. GRACE TEE LEWIS

1. Taylor Goldenstein, Austin Bureau, "After Harvey, Bill to Regulate Storage Tanks Idles," *Houston Chronicle*, April 29, 2019, https://www.houstonchronicle .com/politics/texas/article/After-Harvey-bill-to-regulate-storage-tanks -idles-13805686.php.

CLIMATE DIGNITY: READING BALDWIN AFTER HARVEY AND IN THE NEAR NORTHSIDE

1. James Baldwin, *Notes of a Native Son* (Boston: Beacon Press, 2012), 132.
2. Baldwin, *Notes*, 166.
3. Angela Fritz and Jason Samenow, "Harvey Has Unloaded 24.5 Trillion Gallons of Water on Texas and Louisiana," *Washington Post*, August 30, 2017, https://www.washingtonpost.com/news/capital-weather-gang/ wp/2017/08/30/harvey-has-unloaded-24-5-trillion-gallons-of-water-on- texas-and-louisiana/.

LOOK EAST

1. James Rainey, "How Forecasters Nailed Harvey's Massive Rain Dump," NBC News, https://www.nbcnews.com/news/us-news/how-forecasters -nailed-harvey-s-massive-rain-dump-n797506.

A WHOLE CITY ON STILTS: HYDRAULIC CITIZENSHIP IN HOUSTON

1. Nikhil Anand, *Hydraulic City: Water and the Infrastructures of Citizenship in Mumbai* (Durham, NC: Duke University Press, 2017).
2. *Peter Ingraham*, "Houston Is Experiencing Its Third '500-year' Flood in 3 Years. How Is That Possible?" *Washington Post*, August 29, 2017.
3. Adriana Petryna, "Wildfires at the Edges of Science: Horizoning Work amid Runaway Change," *Cultural Anthropology* 33, no. 4 (2018): 570–595.

SUBURBAN DESIGN WITH NATURE

1. Naomi Klein, *This Changes Everything: Capitalism vs. the Climate* (Toronto: Vintage Canada, 2015), 24.
2. The McHarg Center, "What Does It Mean to Design with Nature Now?," https:// mcharg.upenn.edu/conversations/what-does-it-mean-design-nature-now.
3. Ian McHarg, *Design with Nature* (John Wiley and Sons, 1992), 5.
4. Jenny Odell, *How to Do Nothing: Resisting the Attention Economy* (Brooklyn, NY: Melville House, 2019), 126.

5. On a brighter note, since writing this essay in 2019, the Attwater's is at its highest wild population in the past twenty-eight years, despite devastation wrought by Harvey. This is due to the love and care of some very passionate Texan researchers and land conservationists, and a couple of years of respite from extreme flooding, but I like to think that the bird deserves some credit, too.

LEAN TO THAT FLOOD SONG

1. Laura August, "Mud Canción," *Gulf Coast* 30, no. 2 (Summer/Fall 2018): 262–284; *Mud & Blue* [exhibition], sites across Houston, (2018–2019); Laura August, "25 Notes on Mud," in *Core Yearbook* (Houston: Museum of Fine Arts, 2018), 50–59.

2. Jia Tolentino writes about Houston's relationship to religious and chemical ecstasies, sharing my association of lean with a Houston feeling. She writes, "Chopped and screwed mimics the feeling you get from lean—a heady and dissociative security, as if you're moving very slowly toward a conclusion you don't need to understand. It's perfect for Houston, where you can pass a full day without ever getting off the highway, where the caustic gleam of daytime melts into a long, swampy night." Jia Tolentino, "Losing Religion and Finding Ecstasy in Houston," *New Yorker*, May 20, 2019, https://www.newyorker.com/magazine/2019/05/27/losing-religion-and-finding-ecstasy-in-houston.

3. Micah White, *The End of Protest: A New Playbook for Revolution* (Toronto: Alfred A. Knopf Canada, 2016).

4. In a report to the War Department in 1890, J. M. Lee offers one of the few written accounts of the dance, ostensibly as told to him by a Paiute man he interviewed, notably told from a settler language and interpretive framework: "All Indians must dance, everywhere, keep on dancing . . . [When the Great Spirit] comes this way, then all the Indians go to the mountains, high away from whites. . . . Then . . . big flood comes like water and all white people die, get drowned." Lee's report is cited in James Mooney, *The Ghost-Dance Religion and the Sioux Outbreak of 1890* (Washington, DC: Smithsonian Institution, 1896), 784. Please note that this is a report written by a white military captain, given to the War Department; these are settler sources, not to be trusted on their surface.

5. Mooney, *Ghost-Dance Religion*, 788.

6. Many sources document the 1890 massacre at Wounded Knee. See, among others, Susan Forsyth, *Representing the Massacre of American Indians at Wounded Knee, 1890-2000* (Lewiston, NY: Edwin Mellen Press, 2003).

7. Sheryl Sandberg, *Lean In: Women, Work, and the Will to Lead* (New York: Alfred A. Knopf, 2013).

8. Sheryl Sandberg and Adam Grant, *Option B: Facing Adversity, Building Resilience, and Finding Joy* (New York: Alfred A. Knopf, 2017).

9. Built on an inhospitable bayou landscape, Houston's economy is bound to a single industry: energy. The effects of that industry on climate change can be seen directly as the city regularly weathers major hurricanes and 500-year storms.

10. The Associated Press, "Guatemala's President Shuts Down Anti-Corruption Commission Backed by U.N.," *New York Times*, August 31, 2018, https://www.nytimes.com/2018/08/31/world/americas/guatemala-corruption-commission-morales.html.

11. For excerpts from Morales's speech, see Alberto Pradilla, "Morales cierra la puerta a la Cicig y amaga con autogolpe de Estado, con música de mariachis al fondo," *Plaza Pública*, September 1, 2018, https://www.plazapublica.com.gt/content/morales-cierra-la-puerta-la-cicig-y-amaga-con-autogolpe-de-estado-con-musica-de-mariachis-de.

12. Ibid.

13. Ibid.

14. Omar Barquet, personal correspondence with the author, 2018; translation by the author.

15. The association of refugees attempting to cross into the United States with flooding is nothing new. See, among too many others, Bob Unruh, "Ex-Border Agents: Immigrant Flood 'Orchestrated,'" *WND*, June 11, 2014, https://www.wnd.com/2014/06/ex-border-agents-immigrant-flood-orchestrated/.

16. Anna Lowenhaupt Tsing et al., eds., *Arts of Living on a Damaged Planet: Ghosts and Monsters of the Anthropocene* (Minneapolis: University of Minnesota Press, 2017).

17. Deborah Bird Rose, "Shimmer: When All You Love Is Being Trashed" (lecture, Center for Research on Social Inclusion, Macquarie University, Sydney, Australia, May 9, 2014), https://vimeo.com/97758080.

FROM ICE TO INUNDATION

1. See V. Masson-Delmotte et al., eds., Intergovernmental Panel on Climate Change (IPCC), 2018: Summary for Policy Makers, "Global Warming of 1.5°C: An IPCC Special Report on the Impacts of Global Warming of 1.5°C above Pre-industrial Levels and Related Global Greenhouse Gas Emission Pathways, in the Context of Strengthening the Global Response to the Threat of Climate Change, Sustainable Development, and Efforts to Eradicate Poverty" (Geneva, Switzerland: World Meteorological Organization, 2018), 6, https://www.ipcc.ch/sr15/.

2. Elizabeth Fleming et al., "Coastal Effects," in *Impacts, Risks, and Adaptation in the United States: Fourth National Climate Assessment*, vol. 2, edited by David R. Reidmiller et al. (Washington, DC: U.S. Global Change Research Program, 2018), 322–352, https://nca2018.globalchange.gov/; Rebecca Lindsey, "Climate Change: Global Sea Level," National Oceanic and Atmospheric Administration, January 25, 2021, https://www.climate.gov/news-features/understanding-climate/climate-change-global-sea-level.

3. Fleming et al., "Coastal Effects," section "State of the Coasts," https://nca2018.globalchange.gov/.

4. Lindsey, "Climate Change."

5. "Sea Level Rise Viewer," NOAA, n.d., https://coast.noaa.gov/slr/.

6. Kathy Jetñil-Kijiner and Aka Niviâna, "Rise: From One Island to Another," 350, 2018, https://350.org/rise-from-one-island-to-another/#poem.

Contributors

Laura August, PhD, is a writer and independent curator working between the United States and Central America.

Cheryl Beckett is an associate professor and area coordinator at the Kathrine G. McGovern College of the Arts, University of Houston School of Art, Graphic Design Program. Beckett's interest in public space issues is reflected in spearheading notable award-winning experiential graphic installations within classroom curriculums. Beckett has served as the creative director at Minor Design in Houston since 1987. Committed to the community, the graphic design firm has a client base that includes a wide array of corporate, cultural, educational, and environmental institutions, such as museums, theater and arts organizations, parks, gardens, schools and libraries, the architectural community, and public space environments.

Dominic Boyer is an anthropologist and writer who has lived in Houston for twelve years (and through five "500-year" flood events). Together with Cymene Howe, he has researched wind power in Mexico and memorialized the first Icelandic glacier (Okjökull) to have fallen victim to climate change. They are currently writing a screenplay about Houston called *Petropolis*.

Tanya Debose is an activist, organizer, and advocate for preserving African American history and culture. Debose is best known for her work in Independence Heights, where she has deep roots. Her great-grandfather was among the first to purchase land in what would become the first African American municipality in Texas.

Sonia Marie Del Hierro is a Chicana poet and scholar of American literature. Interested in the intersections of history, culture, and narratives, she studies literature from Chicanx and Latinx communities who deploy fashion and aesthetics to perform political and radical praxis.

Lyric Evans-Hunter's poetry and prose can be found online at *Tagvverk*, Counter, *Cordella Magazine*, and Organism for Poetic Research. She is the author of two chapbooks, *Motherwort* (Guillotine, 2017) and *Swallower* (Ugly Duckling Presse, 2014). She earned her MFA in creative writing from the Pratt Institute in 2017. She lives in New York.

Sonia Hamer is an MFA candidate in fiction at the University of Houston. She also serves as online nonfiction editor at *Gulf Coast* and as a UH Creative Writing Program fellow at Brazos Bookstore. In addition to receiving the Inprint Donald Barthelme Prize in Nonfiction, her work has appeared or is forthcoming in *Creative Nonfiction*'s *True Story*, *Archipelago*, *Prometheus Dreaming*, *Not Very Quiet*, *The Dollhouse*, *plain china*, and elsewhere.

Ben Hirsch is an activist, community organizer, musician, and writer who cofounded West Street Recovery. He is a graduate of the University of Texas LBJ School of Public Affairs, where he focused on the intersection of poverty and the environment, alternative organizational structures, and participatory democracy.

Cymene Howe is a professor of anthropology at Rice University and the author of *Intimate Activism* (Duke University Press, 2013) and *Ecologics: Wind and Power in the Anthropocene* (Duke University Press, 2019) and coeditor of *The Johns Hopkins Guide to Critical and Cultural Theory* (Johns Hopkins University Press, 2021; formerly called *The Johns*

Hopkins Guide to Literary Theory and Criticism) and *The Anthropocene Unseen: A Lexicon* (Punctum, 2020). She currently researches the dynamics between human communities and bodies of ice in the Arctic and the effects of sea level rise in coastal cities around the world.

Lacy M. Johnson is a Houston-based professor, curator, and activist, and is the author of the essay collection *The Reckonings* (Scribner, 2018), the memoir *The Other Side* (Tin House, 2014)—both National Book Critics Circle Award finalists—and the memoir *Trespasses* (University of Iowa Press, 2012). Her writing has appeared in the *New Yorker*, the *New York Times*, the *Los Angeles Times*, *The Best American Essays*, *The Best American Travel Writing*, the *Paris Review*, *Virginia Quarterly Review*, *Tin House*, *Guernica*, and elsewhere. She teaches creative nonfiction at Rice University and is the founding director of the Houston Flood Museum. In 2020, she was awarded a Guggenheim Fellowship in General Nonfiction.

Dana Kroos received a PhD in creative writing and literature from the University of Houston and an MFA in ceramics from the Rhode Island School of Design. Her short stories and poems have appeared in *Glimmer Train*, *Florida Review*, *Superstition Review*, *Minnesota Monthly*, and other literary publications.

P. Grace Tee Lewis is an environmental epidemiologist focusing on health impacts of hazardous air pollutants, particularly among environmental justice communities. Her work includes mapping and development of a data-driven tool to identify, prioritize, and visualize risk factors contributing to neighborhood vulnerability from inequities in environment, health, climate, and social stressors.

Raj Mankad has served as the op-ed editor for the *Houston Chronicle* since 2019. He was the editor of *Cite: The Architecture and Design Review of Houston* for eleven years and a managing editor at the journal *Feminist Economics*. Mankad holds a PhD in creative writing from the University of Houston.

Alex Ortiz is an environmental advocate with a background in water quality and endangered species protection. Currently, he is the Water Resources Specialist for the Lone Star Chapter of the Sierra Club. In his free time he can be found walking Texas beaches and hiking in the Hill Country.

Alexandria Parson is an aspiring journalist with a weakness for arch-top guitars and 1950s sapphic romance novels.

Daniel Peña is an associate professor, Pushcart Prize–winning writer, and the author of *Bang: A Novel* (Arte Público Press, 2018). A former Fulbright-García Robles Scholar and a graduate of Cornell University, he has taught creative writing as a Picador Guest Professor at the Universität Leipzig and in various capacities in Houston. He splits his time between Austin, Houston, and Berlin.

Bruno Ríos is a translator, multigenre writer, and academic from Sonora, Mexico. He holds a PhD in Latin American literature from the University of Houston. He is the author of three poetry books, most recently *Cueva de leones/Lion's Den* (2015), partially translated into English by Roberto Tejada, and a novel, *La voz de las abejas* (Sediento Ediciones, 2016).

Susan Rogers is an associate professor at the Gerald D. Hines College of Architecture and Design at the University of Houston and the director of the Community Design Resource Center. A designer, educator, and activist, her work focuses on justice and equity within the disciplinary foundations of architecture and city planning.

Roy Scranton is the author of *We're Doomed. Now What? Essays on War and Climate Change* (Soho Press, 2018) and *Learning to Die in the Anthropocene: Reflections on the End of a Civilization* (City Lights, 2015), among other books. He is an associate professor of English at the University of Notre Dame, where he directs the Environmental Humanities Initiative.

Martha Serpas is a poet whose collections include *Double Effect* (Louisiana State University Press, 2020), *The Diener* (Louisiana State University Press, 2015), *The Dirty Side of the Storm* (W. W. Norton, 2007), and *Côte Blanche* (New Issues Poetry & Prose, 2002). She coproduced *Veins in the Gulf*, a documentary about southern Louisiana's coastal erosion crisis. She teaches creative writing at the University of Houston and serves as a hospital trauma chaplain.

Elaine Shen is a PhD student studying marine ecology at the University of Rhode Island. She was born and raised in Houston, where she graduated from Rice University in 2018. Elaine is interested in the socio-ecological dynamics of seafood and currently works on understanding the biodiversity in coral reef fisheries.

Geneva Vest is the program manager of Community Strategies at the Trust for Public Land. She received her BA in sociology from Rice University (2017). She lives in Brooklyn but will always be from Houston.

Aimee VonBokel holds a doctorate degree in American culture from the University of Michigan. She works with neighborhood leaders and museums to develop community-driven narratives, assemble archival evidence, and promote economic justice—particularly in historic Black towns and settlements where public policies have unfairly eroded family real-estate wealth.

Bryan Washington is the author of *Lot: Stories* (Riverhead Books, 2019) and *Memorial: A Novel* (Riverhead Books, 2020). He lives in Houston.

Allyn West is a writer, editor, and teacher in Houston. Previously, they worked for the *Houston Chronicle* and served on the editorial board. Now, they are a communications manager for an international environmental nonprofit.

SENIOR DESIGN TEAM

Kristen Fernandes is a recent graduate of the University of Houston with a BFA in graphic design. As an illustrator and designer, her work is heavily influenced by her love for pop culture, sci-fi, and fantasy.

Julia Ong is a recent graduate of the University of Houston with a BFA in graphic design. Her approach to design and its effects on culture and community comes from a place of empathy and collaborative solutions.

Clarisse Pinto is a graphic designer currently based in Houston, with an interest in how design exists and interfaces in public space. Her personal experience as an immigrant and avid student drives her passion for design as a tool for social justice and solving problems for all types of people.

CORE DESIGN TEAM

Ilse Harrison is an enthusiastic reader of many books at once, a really great off-topic conversationalist, and deeply passionate about helping others. As a graphic designer, she hopes to find a sustainable way of helping people and to maintain open dialogues that benefit humanity at large.

Jesse Reyes is a designer graduating from the University of Houston with a BFA in graphic design. He has always enjoyed drawing and utilizes his skills to sketch out ideas before refining his work digitally. He believes that form follows function because design is much more than just aesthetic.

Manuel Vázquez is a first-generation college graduate from Mexico based in Houston. He is a multidisciplinary graphic designer with curated experiences that have all encompassed understanding the needs and details of intentional design. He has an eye for typography and enjoys being able to communicate through visual content in more than one way. He believes design is an engaging and never-ending process.

MAP DESIGNERS

Alexa Abad is a graphic designer based in Houston. A graduate of the University of Houston with a BFA in graphic design, she is proficient in concept development, identity systems, motion graphics, and environmental and print design. A California native, she indulges in the diversity of any environment she is in.

Karen Alvarenga is a designer based in Houston. She graduated with a BFA in graphic design from the University of Houston. She believes that design is driven by communication and is inspired by culture and conversation. It is a way to learn and acknowledge others and create meaningful connections between people and a wide audience. It encourages empathy, responsibility, and intention.

Tamila Amanzholova is a graphic designer with a graphic design BFA from the University of Houston. She enjoys developing identities, working with type, and exploring new things within the graphic design field.

Jason Cardenas is a graphic designer and illustrator based in Houston. As a graduate with a BFA in graphic design, he is proficient in multiple aspects of design, whether it be video or print. His designs are influenced by his passion for illustration. He believes that good design starts with pencil and paper, the original computer.

Maham Choudry is a designer who graduated from the University of Houston with a BFA in graphic design. She follows her intuition and curiosity to explore and refine her design skills within the limits of grid structures and necessary rules. Her strengths lie in hand-made illustrative work, writing, and working on multidynamic projects.

As a first-generation college graduate, **Jessica Flores** is currently following her passion by pursuing a graphic design career. After being accepted into the Graphic Design Block program at the University of Houston, she got to build up a diverse portfolio full of projects that have brought her fulfilment and excitement. She finds inspiration through all the different types of typography and layout found in media, branding, and even book layouts.

Lulu Flores is a graphic designer based in Houston and a graduate of the University of Houston with a BFA in graphic design. She is proficient in design in both web and print media. She believes design is a powerful tool that can bring us together. It inspires thoughts, spreads knowledge, and pushes us to create outside the comfort zone.

Grant Flowers is a Houston-based designer whose practice is rooted in efforts toward personal growth, gratitude, and balance. Growth can be gained by examining multiple perspectives through the colorful and dynamic lens of a designer. Gratitude is felt when our surroundings are absorbed and small details can be enjoyed from several angles through art, culture, and commerce. He believes in a life in which work and play are equal.

Donna Karimian is a passionate graphic designer from Houston. On projects, she enjoys collaborating with others and finding creative solutions. When she is not glued to her computer screen, she enjoys traveling and getting to know other people. Some of her other hobbies include cooking, dancing, and mastering the art of coffee.

Miryoung Kim is a graphic designer who graduated with a BFA from the University of Houston. She has come to understand graphic design as a powerful force of expression. She also thinks that through visual communication, design allows anyone to express ideas across cultural divides.

Parichat Kittikornmeta is a graphic designer who was born and grew up in Thailand. She traveled to study and graduated from the University of Houston. She believes that design is a visual way to communicate to other people without knowing other languages.

Milan Mathew designs to connect with people and create a lasting impression. While she appreciates the subtle details of design, she's never afraid to embrace design in a bold and outspoken way. She enjoys collaborating with individuals of creative abilities. With design, every moment is an opportunity to learn.

Camilo Monroy is a graphic designer based in Houston. Camilo believes that design has the power to make people see things in a different light. This can help them explore different avenues of communication that can lend fresh perspectives to situations that may not have been considered previously. Telling stories, solving problems, and developing strong concepts are what he values most as a designer.

Ruled by an unwieldy imagination, **Jaalon Pratt** has always gone through life weaving together stories of a cinematic scope. This perspective has informed his approach to every creative endeavor, from graphic design to illustration. Both disciplines are fulfilling, but design is the perfect intersection of sound, image, color, and type.

Alex Ramos is the youngest of five children and is the only one in his family who enjoys horror films. He gravitates toward movies, music, and any kind of art. You can find him watching, wandering, and taking pictures. He hopes to use graphic design as a vehicle to explore and investigate what others see through their creative lens and compare it to what he sees through his.

Devin Schuhmann is graduating from the University of Houston with a BFA in graphic design. She thinks of design as a way to make ordinary things beautiful. She is passionate about design because she can always explore and grow by finding new ways to create things.

As the world becomes increasingly automated, **Kris Valladares** finds herself interested in initiatives that allow her to deepen her connection to people and places. Design allows her to not only be investigative but craft stories that honor the past while looking toward the future. There are two things she is certain of: always design with empathy, and the devil's in the details.

Annette Wong loves collecting anything relating to particular instances. In addition, she seeks to mold tangible experiences and promote deeper questioning about the world both in our heads and around us. Her day-to-day practice revolves around being sustainable, which is a huge driving force in her process.

Weston Woodfin designs to find greater meaning in the things he creates. He is passionate about people and the experiences around him. With a BA in graphic design, Weston is hoping to make lasting impacts through the people he meets and the work he designs.